MY LIFE IS MY WORD

Malcolm Le-Hair and Bettina Croft

AN M-Y BOOKS PAPERBACK

© Copyright 2019
Malcolm Le-Hair and Bettina Croft

The right of **Malcolm Le-Hair and Bettina Croft** to be
identified as the author of
This work has been asserted by him in accordance with the
Copyright, Designs and Patents Act 1988

All Rights Reserved
No reproduction, copy or transmission of this publication
may be made without written permission.
No paragraph of this publication may be reproduced,
copied or transmitted save with the written permission or in
accordance with the provisions of the
Copyright Act 1956 (as amended).

Any person who does any unauthorised act in relation to
this publication may be liable to criminal
prosecution and civil claims for damage.

A CIP catalogue record for this title is
available from the British Library

ISBN (Print): 978-1-912875-36-8
ISBN (epub): 978-1-912875-39-9

FOREWORD

In writing my life events, from the start of World War II, I hope that these will prove exciting and informative to all of you. This is a history of major, life-changing events, never just a catalogue of imagined ones... Hopefully at least one person will find reading this book useful for dealing with problems in their own lives.

In the belief that it might help those who have suffered similar life-changing events to cope even better, I am sharing my challenging experiences. Out there most of you have experienced deprivation, perhaps severe anguish, and yet survived. Depression and disability affect a lot of us, so finding a successful way of coping is the vital answer. Somehow, I managed to overcome a serious limitation, so this is the story as the events unfolded. Most initially terrible, many amusing and a few precious ones merely uplifting.

Happiness and sadness are always present in life, but it is the way we deal with those sometimes shattering experiences that help and makes us what we finally become. So, we hope you find the truth of my life entertaining (well, I survived all the drama of nearly dying at times, didn't I!) Bettina and I hope it helps to inspire you through the many difficulties you may have ahead, recover from those endured already, or those you are possibly even currently suffering at this very moment!

ABOUT THE AUTHOR

Born in an era full of drama, personal danger, and hardship, Author, Malcolm Le-Hair endured, almost from infancy, a deprived life. His parents both loved him, perhaps too much, but did not care deeply enough about each other for the marriage to last. So as a tiny boy he was faced with, on the one hand loving his mother and father to his utmost, whilst becoming aware that a third person lurked menacingly in the background. This was the terrifying, brutal step-father who usurped his father's place in the house, and beat Malcolm cruelly. He was foster parents and worse, his battle truly commenced.

This dysfunctional life eventually led to a mental breakdown! At the age of 17 he was hospitalised, again from his mother, and administered LSD without his permission, and with terrible repercussions.

Whereas this would have brow-beaten most of us, it certainly did the opposite with Malcolm. He fought back, at first only tiny fists (at the age of four) against his alien world, and – later, still always loving those closest to him despite everything – literally stood up to all his problems and eventually triumphed even over an unseen enemy - LSD and the disability it left him with!

Now discovered this is his story. His several tragedies, his triumphs, his loves, and his true friends. (One of whom has helped this story to flow so vividly from his own lips), and thus portrays the inspiration that is this, Malcolm's life of great achievement over sorrow, suffering, and the ultimate fulfilment of his lifelong ambitions.

ABOUT THE CO-AUTHOR

Malcolm, this talented and lovable Author, has insisted that he wants me to be his co-author. Having become great friends with each other in his time of need it was, for me, a joy to agree to help him in every way I could.

Therefore, I can describe to you from my own years of experience as a Chief Editor, and published author myself, that this is truly a wonderfully moving, but also totally daunting Life Story. Firstly of child abuse personally suffered by Malcolm at the hands of various spurious people. Theirs was the responsibility. When they should have been looking after him kindly not cruelly from age four upwards. His fight for survival then was a daunting experience enough. However, I also found out that these, his horrifying experiences, then led later to an era of him enduring and somehow overcoming even more terrifying suffering and life-threatening illness. Later this was caused by the experimental LSD abreaction treatment meted out to him as a teenager without his agreement or knowledge since it was being presented simply to him as a 'cure'!

When I learnt all this, my total sympathy became involved in Malcolm's future welfare and I resolved to make his full story known. As a 17-year-old, the LSD injections used on him under the guise of this false, so-called, answer for a nervous breakdown. It happened during the 1950s. What made everything far worse, the LSD was administered by a small isolated mental hospital's team. So he found himself helpless in this morass of dangerous 'cures', ending for him in acquired resultant serious Epileptic fits. Once he had a fit whilst working in the kilns at a brick producing concern and was left on the floor of the kiln wich superficially caused facial burns, from which fortunately recovered but was then banned from working in the kilns.

Malcolm suffered and bravely overcame many distressing, and cruel events (as well as the malicious people he had as a tiny child encountered). Finally, through his efforts, he achieved a Higher Management position in his main employment. This was itself a great achievement after his many, varied triumphs in dealing with disasters and surviving the Epilepsy caused by those unwarranted LSD injections.

Lessons of great help and inspiration to others of us can be learned from this, his inspiring story. That is both his wish and mine. When you read on, you will enable him to be a fountain of caring information, personal encouragement, and inspiring you in every way to face up to hardship. From this book you can if you wish to reach a great outcome in your own lives. You would, hopefully, then be prepared yourself to climb almost insurmountable mountains to achieve your very own desired goals.

MY LIFE IS MY WORD

CHAPTER ONE
1941

World War II was already in full swing when I was born.

We lived in a modest end-of-terraced house, and from what I can remember, it was simply, and comfortably furnished. My first memory is when I must have been about six months old, being hastily picked up by two loving, strong arms, and my father's kindly face peering anxiously down into mine.

In the dark of that moonless night, it was already threatening to me to hear the planes commencing their descent towards us, whining and screaming overhead as they began their relentless, accelerated dive.

The sirens were sounded in the city of Peterborough a total of 650 times during the Second World War. It is strange that Peterborough was chosen as a safe area for the evacuation of children from London because this city was among the first towns to have received an air raid. This was on 8th June 1940, when several small bombs fell on the city centre, and some shops and the town swimming pool were damaged.

This shock of the sudden awakening to a world of screeching planes, sirens and people shouting in fear to each other was enough to frighten and intimidate any child. This was because the route the aircraft would follow was the railway line to London. There they would offload a cascade of bombs designed to obliterate the factories. In addition, it would terrorise and frighten the population

Unaware of all this, and feeling secure as I looked up and studied my father's face, I was lovingly wrapped in a warm blanket. I still distinctly remember being rushed in the middle of the night to what I later knew was an air-raid shelter. We then quickly travelled only 75 yards to this large concrete air-raid shelter on the other side of our road.

As far as I can recall, this had two sections to it. There were 7-8 people huddled inside together for protection already. I am sure I can picture one person lying down, almost asleep, and another young child, afraid, crying bitterly while being comforted by his mother.

I can remember too an elderly lady who had just stumbled, visibly shaken, into the shelter. In a frightened voice, she was asking if there was the possibility of a bogeyman lurking in the other room. As this building had only one light, it was dim and dismal, and even more frightening for the child, and the adult incarcerated there for many hours. This lady was herself understandably scared. She still was feeling very vulnerable. Fortunately, other people in the shelter instantly moved to her, very supportive, welcoming her to sit with them until the *All Clear* eventually was sounded. As usual, this signal, heralded by a long, sustained blast, slightly mournful, yet to us all so welcome. It rang out for us hope in a single blast throughout the bombed City. We knew it was bringing relief to everyone who was alive to hear it. All then could feel at last they could safely return to their homes.

In the air-raid shelter, there were seats and wooden benches where people could sleep. It was cold and dusty, and not at all a welcoming place. People were smoking and chatting non-stop, relieved to be together as if to alleviate their fears. This was one of my first vivid experiences of wartime life.

The camaraderie of the people chatting with each other in the shelter seemed to me, as a baby, to be a babble of soothing voices which I could let comfortingly soak into my head and echo, surrounding me. People in those situations do not fail each other, I then discovered. They joke, trying their best to hide their own personal fears. The strength of unity in the face of the dreadfully powerful and menacing dangerous from the skies was met with a brave, almost serene spirit. This became a mixture of defiance and a belief in God, and the British tradition of looking after one another. This was at that time wonderfully strong. People, in general, maintained their faith in King and Country and their belief in God, who would save them from being killed.

I was later told that during the war, the German planes regularly bombed the city of Peterborough itself, sometimes en route to or from their homeland. They followed the well-used London Northern Eastern Railway (LNER) railway line, its rails shining below which they used as a guide for them in the night towards the capital itself. This was a richly populated and industrialised route and had more densely built and vital engineering factories. The Germans did not realise that, along that area on the left-hand bank of the rails at Peterborough, were extensive engineering factories that had already been cleverly camouflaged with black paint. Their machines, day and night, were churning out ammunition and other such vital products for immediate use by us in World War ll. The reader will later discover in this book how I recalled these memorable incidents regarding World War ll at a much later age while being medically treated with the use of LSD injections without my agreement or knowledge. I experienced mind and memory-enhancing episodes of fearful and immense proportions.

As a baby, I was the only surviving twin but suffered double pneumonia, from which I nearly died at birth. My father later told me that I had been he could see very seriously ill, and he was so worried that he fed me egg and milk frequently, and, somehow, I managed to survive this illness.

Around that time, my father had been discharged from the army because of his own ill health, bronchitis and, of all things, flat feet. Instead of serving again as a soldier, he did another even more dangerous job: driving petrol tankers around the English countryside. He delivered these critical loads that his tanker carried during the war to all parts of the United Kingdom.

I was told that my father seemed to be able to acquire sensibly all the commodities that were then in short supply. This apparently helped him to provide for his family. People traded ration coupons and goods with each other in a sort of bartering process, and my father was not one to look a gift horse in the mouth. In his endless round of petrol tanker journeys, he came across many people who wanted to make life easier and exchange any ration coupons they did not use. He took advantage of this opportunity.

Later, when I was much older, I found out that my father should never have been accepted in the first place to be fit enough to fight in the army. He had suffered many chest problems as a young child, and the lengthy training had now caused bronchial trouble, which he endured for the rest of his short life. He was eventually discharged as medically unfit.

His state of health was not helped by the frequent meals he missed in his strenuous work, and this carried on after the Second World War. This way of life, lack of sleep, and the exhausting work began having a gradual severe effect on his health that would ultimately be his downfall.

1942

An apparently small disaster – legs burned.

As soon as I was able to toddle, I remember a very painful incident, I fell on some hot ashes which had been scattered from the household living room fire and burned my legs, and I was later hospitalised for some weeks. Cinders and ashes from coal fireplaces would be thrown haphazardly onto the garden paths, in those days often while still burning red hot.

My father was out at all times of the day and night, delivering much-needed petrol to garages. This was carried out not only during the daylight but also in complete darkness. He had to be very guarded at all times, and people had to be careful not to show headlights. So shielded, dim headlights if you were a bus, or lorry driver had to be used. One could never imagine the horror of what could have happened if an enemy plane had managed to blow him up with the lorry full of fuel!

He was not always there at home at night for my mother, because he worked so hard and for such very long hours. Upon reflection, his absence would have made my mother insecure and very lonely. The loneliness may have contributed to her seeking assurance elsewhere, and yes, she did find someone who could protect her by his presence.

Unfortunately, for whatever reason, my mother later became very friendly with this man, my father's best friend, and it led to an affair. He was also married and living in a terraced house that actually backed on to our garden, and home. It was easy for him to meet my mother unseen daily.

A crisis arose. My father came home one day earlier than usual and found them in bed together. He went absolutely mad! I can still recall all the pots on the table being thrown at the dining room walls and the teapot's boiling hot contents staining the wallpaper.

Later on in my life, I was to learn that my mother's family of three strong, protective brothers subsequently came to the house, with their combined force, to warn my father off. So, after trying in vain to repair his relationship with my mother, reluctantly he finally gave up and went to live in another remote town, Banbury, all alone.

Writing this book has helped me realise and come to the conclusion that my mother, along with her many sisters, suffered the loss of their own affectionate, devoted father, who had died when they were all very young. He died of peritonitis when the oldest child of the family was about 13 years, and there were, in all, 11 children. My sick, then poverty-stricken grandmother had to take in and 'slave her fingers to the very bone' washing for other people and delivering babies. She even laid out the dead to earn the barest living to keep her family together under one roof and fed. People would not now believe the absolute poverty that they then suffered and the deprivation that widely existed in those days. My grandmother was often to be seen quietly crying because of the enormous strain placed on her, but still managed to keep her family together. I wonder how many people today could have stood up to the immense stress that she suffered daily.

My own mother remembered wearing clogs! This was the reason why leather shoes were treasured and looked after. In many cases, families existed who could not afford to have their shoes repaired, so rough repairs were done at home to save money. Cast-iron cobblers' shoe forms would have been an essential accessory in those days, and the father of the house would have been the shoe repairer. Later on, stick-on soles were invented, which helped a great deal to simplify home shoe repairs for people.

For my mother's whole family of eleven children, the absence of a father in those young years of her life clearly did have adverse effects on each one of the siblings. This particularly affected the girls. As a result, I believe, as soon as they were each old enough, and determined to escape the poverty and domination of their brothers, they sought men who would become their husbands. Then, in the absence of an active, caring father, the unrestricted, male youngsters behaved in what they thought was an adult manner, assuming they were protective to the womenfolk in the family and ruling in a Victorian and autocratic manner.

The good thing the brothers did eventually, however, was to protect my grandmother from the surly and hard-hearted officials who would come round regularly. These tyrannical men had the chance to assess which items still remaining in her home were of the slightest value, and then insisted she should sell all of these. This was very cruel, as she had so few possessions. Anything that was left of her essential items was precious to her and an absolute necessity. Instead of giving her the minimal financial aid regularly, which she so badly needed and relied on, these officials deprived her of anything sentimental she treasured.

Eventually, the men of the household would not tolerate these officials coming. The boys made it very clear that they would stop them from entering and upsetting their poor mother when what she needed instead was help, compassion and support.

Looking back, I believe most of the girls' first relationships and their marriages ended in divorce because they all needed to escape from the terrible deprivation and the circumstances they had endured for years. This later resulted in official divorces, with the women becoming more demanding of the love they needed in their next relationships. In my mother's case, four of her family eventually got divorced at a time when the legal solution was by no means a popular or safe path for a woman to follow.

1943-1945

The Foster-parents from hell!

My mother and father separated within the first three years following my birth. I was then placed in a small village near Thrapston with cruel foster parents for a while where I was myself, sadly ill-treated. The house I went to live in was a truly horrible place – a dump. A total slum as far as I can recall and the people I lived with were the same as the building... dreadful! I do not think these people would have been passed as suitable to foster anyone at all, let alone children, but this was wartime, and many things were done due to the absence of viable laws to safeguard such private agreements and the welfare of children. At that time, I was three years old, and, while being away from my mother, I am sure it was utterly heart-breaking for both of us. I now realise there was deep jealousy towards me that the new man in my mother's life felt for me and in in this respect, he dominated my mother.

The place I was made to live in was a slum, and the first night I was there I could not get to sleep and imagined faces at the window and in the dark shadows which frightened me. My so-called foster parents laughed at my frequent screams of terror. I was told roughly to go to sleep. There was not a hint of caring or any understanding regarding my fears. This was life in the country with strict and uncaring foster parents and, to survive, I would have to grow up very fast indeed now.

Nevertheless, after that had happened, eventually, the freedom of village life seemed to have an incredible effect on me. It allowed me to become more assured in dealing with people of all ages and developed within me a fresh feeling of confidence and independence that led me to become an unusually cheeky, adventurous and a daring boy in the village where I lived. I was expanding my enquiring mind, and also physically growing stronger with a sense of liberation at the early age of nearly four. The beauty of the village was that you could go around, investigate and have some freedom which, upon reflection, must have been a useful way of life building some skills swiftly. You didn't have to worry about cars or traffic as there was little of this around. I think I saw in those days more horses and carts and tractors than cars.

The family I lived with had also taken on another foster child, a young girl, at this time. Later on, a boy at least 10 years older than me joined us. For some reason, the foster-mother appeared to favour the other two children in her household. It seemed they were more obedient to her than I ever was.

At times I became a bit resentful of it all. Eventually, I rose above that feeling and enjoyed the freedom of the countryside and village amenities and the kindly local people I met on my various lonely wanderings. The fact that the family were fostering children more than likely helped them immensely in eventually obtaining a new council house, and boy, they certainly needed one.

1945-1947
My First School

I started school at four years of age. This was the village school, and, sadly, I hated it. Every minute! My first recollection of school was that it was freezing cold, and I was being given a slate and a piece of chalk, and I became thoroughly bored and even colder. One day, I walked out of school as I thought I could do better, and went off on my own around the village, where I found people who were so kind to me that they gave me cake, biscuits and lemonade and thoughtfully talked to me, so caringly that I felt suddenly cheerful once again. This was really something that I was not used to, as even though the war had now ended, there were still food shortages, but it was great. Unfortunately, a search party of teachers found me, and I was then ostracised for being such a problem child. I hated school. But, far worse, I hated my foster parents.

As a family of three fostered children, we were soon rehoused into some decent accommodation: a new council house within the village. When it came to moving to the new home, I was told, 'If you want to sit down tonight, you will have to carry your chair up to the hill to the new house.'

So I struggled with what seemed to me to be a heavy chair, resting every so often to get a bit of sympathy from locals and villagers who were out walking at the same time. Many of them had become accustomed to my presence in the village already and often had a kind word for me.

It wasn't all doom and gloom; however, it was a welcome change as our milk was delivered by a horse and cart with a large milk churn. The milkman would have a kind word or joke that made you laugh and that would brighten the day. The horse would turn its head as if waiting for an apple or a round of stale bread.

You had to go out with a large jug and get it filled up every day; sometimes, if you ran out, you could go to the local dairy and get it filled up there if you needed more. The farmers, who ran the farm and dairy, were closely related to my own dear father and would have taken me in, but for the fact that their own mother was suffering delusions, believing herself to be the Queen of England.

They also had over 200 head of cattle to milk twice a day, 365 days a year, plus over 400 acres of land to look after. Apparently, they had enough to do without taking on someone like me. There was also the fact that they were my father's relations and I assumed my mother would not want to have anything at all to do with them, being separated, as she was then, from my father.

Still, occasionally, the 'Urdy Gurdy Man' would come to the village, playing his music by turning a handle on a street organ and having a monkey on a chain to entertain us. His horse and colourful cart were uplifting to see, and we loved to hear the music the organ played. It lifted you, and I would stand there mesmerised by it all. There wasn't much else going on in the village that you could say was enjoyable, though. People wanted to relax after years of war, rationing, and the tensions it had caused had taken their toll on their wellbeing.

I can remember a couple of instances where I suffered from the evil actions of my foster-mother in particular. On one occasion, I had picked apples from a tree and ate them only to experience a bout of diarrhoea, and I eventually became weak and uncontrollably messed the bed. Although this was accidental, my so-called foster mother rubbed my face in it. This was the type of woman she was, and I shall never forget her and her dreadful attitude towards me. The woman was horrible and terrifying towards me at times.

She apparently had no compassion for me and was not fit to foster any children. Some months earlier, there had been an instance where I was forced to wear some new shoes that hurt me a great deal, being far too tight. A villager who saw my distress in walking brought me home to tell my foster-mother to change these shoes since they were obviously causing me significant discomfort because they were far too small. I had previously expressed my anguish when my foster mother first put them on but took no notice of my pain. The more I walked in them, the more pain I suffered, causing me unnecessary agony.

1946
Why Didn't My Mother Wait For Me?

Another time, I came home from school and found that my dear mother, with my stepfather accompanying her, had visited the house and brought me some new clothes. I was so terribly upset that they had not waited for me. I can imagine my mother being upset at not being allowed by my stepfather to wait to see me, but she was obedient to his wishes and was entirely dominated by this man with whom she had fallen in love. I was later teased by the foster-mother and her fostered daughter, who had enjoyed the company of my mother and her man-friend. I sought comfort by smelling the clothes my mother had bought me, hoping to catch a tiny whiff of the perfume of my mother on these.

My father's so-called best friend, John, with whom my mother now lived, had brought my mother on his motor-bike and deliberately would not even wait for the very few moments so that I could see my beloved mother fleetingly, and she could see me, her only child. Most people would agree that this was unwarranted cruelty! This type of deliberate starvation of our affection for each other was what he absolutely revelled and excelled in, but little did I know about the beatings to come, which I would later have to endure. These were far, far worse, and I could never forget them even today!

I think it was one Sunday when my mother and her man came to visit me. I can remember all of us adults and children going into the countryside for a walk. It was sweltering, and we started paddling and playing in a large stream. Somehow, I ended up in deeper water, continually going under. I was so frightened that it took many years before I overcame my subsequent terror of swimming. Even now, I will not go out of my depth in the sea or in any swimming pool. It is surprising how these one-off events that we experience earlier in life have such a marked impression on us, as I still cannot swim properly, yet my own real father in his younger days, I was told, had been a brilliant swimmer.

1946
Football Match

One day, my wanderings led me to watch a football match at the local village playing field with other supporters. Not being very quick, I ended up being winded by the ball. The man who had kicked it was very apologetic and his girlfriend promised me a trip to another town, Raunds, the next week to watch another football match, if I wanted to go. Unhesitatingly, I, of course, said, 'yes please'.

This would be an adventure for me, and I met them at the bus stop the next week and had one of the first bus rides I can ever remember having. The trouble was that I did not tell anyone where I was going. Why should I? They didn't care about me anyway, I thought. When I came home, I still got told off, as they had not been able to find me. Knowing how they felt, I thought that they would have been pleased with my absence.

I was obviously lonely all the time then, and at that period of my young life felt very isolated indeed from anyone who showed me any affection at all, so in this emotionally deprived state I grew up fast (and tough).

The other two children were obviously favoured much more than me, for some reason or other. Perhaps it was because I had a mind of my own and did not seem dependent upon my foster parents. Nevertheless, I managed to shrug it all off, and I was delighted to hear - one day - that I was going to live again back with my father, as I thought it would be far, far better than what I was currently enduring. This was an incredibly uplifting feeling for me. Sadly, however, through no fault of my own, or indeed of my father's, it almost turned into another disaster.

1947
Escape from *the Foster Parents from Hell*

Eventually, I escaped this wretched place when I went to live once more with my father at Banbury. There he lodged with a family of four. I was so glad to leave that former village and go and live with my dear father. He lived with this family in a large, semi-detached house, and it was absolutely fantastic. To me, it was luxury living.

Sad for me, and totally unexpectedly, the family he was then lodging with (and their children) turned out to be thieves. They blamed me for the things they had themselves stolen, totally unfairly. I was subsequently marginalised, and living there did not work out for me. One of the most unfortunate things in my life was that, in the not too distant future, a matter of months, I would yet again be wrenched painfully from my father, against both his will and my own, and put into a children's home.

MY LIFE IS MY WORD

However, for a short time, I was happy living with my dear father once again. The food was also far better, and I enjoyed being in a large town. This was far more interesting than my former life, and the shops were a treat - it was great fun when we two went window shopping together, and I loved having new clothes, and going to what seemed to be a much better school. This move would be the education of experiences and a new way of living, or so I had thought.

1947-48
World War II is safely over

After the end of the Second World War, I can remember us having the shell of a cockpit of an aeroplane dumped in the backyard of our garden for us to play in and for the man of the house to use some of its parts. He was an electrician. I suppose it was one of those relics of the wartime that was not wanted, but it gave us many hours of enjoyment. It also provided some electrical spares that could be reused. The other kids in the street were so envious because we all played on it and it was great fun.

One of the funnier, if more regrettable, moments I can recall was when I was walking with one of the brothers along the road where my father and I lived. In those far-off days, one seldom saw a black man. (A rare sight in this town.) I think we both sensed some slight feeling of something different as he approached us, and we started - stupidly - talking gibberish to each other. He must have thought we were absolutely bonkers. This confused the poor man, as we spoke a lot of rubbish and his English was probably perfect, and unlike ours. We were trying to confuse the man by pretending that we were also of foreign descent. He walked by thinking (I am sure) how completely daft we all were at the time. Since then, I have thought back and become so ashamed of how childishly and absolutely stupidly we behaved.

The best time in those days for us boys was after dinner at school at Banbury. We would go to a number of the bakeries in the town itself, where we would carry trays for them and, later, each be rewarded with a bag of broken cakes. These were freshly made and really delicious, and we had to eat all of them as we were not allowed to take any back into school with us.

I do remember getting a spanking from my father for something I had done wrong and crying my eyes out on one occasion. My dad was quickly apologetic and reassuring and promised me he would take me uptown and treat me at the weekend, and he kept his promise. He bought me a 'Snakes and Ladders' game and some football gear, as he wanted to have a photograph of me dressed up kicking a ball. At that time, I had no interest in football, especially after my previous experiences, but I went along with all his wishes.

I saw my father nearly every day, and he tried his best, but it was very hard indeed for him, due to the poor state of his own health as this was slowly going downhill. Some years later, his eyesight also started failing, and he subsequently lost his sight more or less completely when he was only 38. Because of his poor health, he was then placed to live in special care homes until he died at the age of 46 years because he couldn't look after himself.

I think I lived with the family and my father for over a year in all, and I went to Dashwood Road School in Banbury, but cannot recall much about it. Unfortunately, the lodging with this family did not work out because their two sons did not like me.

The brothers were much worse behaved than me. They stole from Woolworths and then falsely blamed it on me, the inference being that I was a bad influence on them. It seemed, in those days, that children from dysfunctional families were ostracised, especially those who had resided or did reside in children's homes. They seemed to be viewed as trouble immediately, and I always got the blame.

Children's Home

Much to my dad's despair, he then was forced due to this incident to place me in a children's home in a village at Horley near Banbury. Looking back, I can see that I wasn't really wanted. At least, in retrospect, that is how I felt at the time.

However, being now more mature, I feel that there was no doubt my father loved me. He did not have much free time for us to do things together at that moment because he had to work his hardest to earn enough to pay for both of us, lorry drivers did not earn much money in those days. When I later returned to live with my mother, he then also had to pay the maintenance due for me to my mother.

Fortunately, I had already had experienced plenty of 'survival training', and I did not care. This was to prove to be yet another experience to add to the story of my life. I did not know what I was really missing from my family life. Obviously, looking back, it was both parents' love and a feeling of being wanted and, better, still, a sense of being a son to someone, because I had never felt I had ever experienced it.

'What you don't have you never miss!' At least, that is how the saying goes. Years after that, you realise just all the things that you had missed when you were young, and it is too late by then to recapture those experiences. However, if I had received it, what would I have made of myself? Would I have succeeded as much as I have done, or perhaps achieved even more? What type of person would I have been? Did the dysfunctional life I was forced to experience help me to be what I am now, an actual survivor?

My dad talked to me about the children's home I was going to and how good it would be for me before I went to live there. I can appreciate his sheer frustration at that time in trying to do his best for me. Apart from getting married again or by fostering me out, he did not have any other options. I can remember having to sit and have my hair cut before I went to the home, and my dad sitting opposite, watching my every move and reassuring me that my hair-cut would soon be over. In those days, hairdressers were quick at cutting and sometimes their scissors were not as sharp, and it pulled on your hair. My father seemed at the time to be preoccupied and just discussing with the hairdresser if I did, or did not have a double crown. The hairdresser reassured him and said you can take it from me that your son will not go bald.

Admission to the Children's Home

When he delivered me to the home, my father, bless him, promised me he would come to see me. I think our parting was just as hard for him as it was for me.

My father was still working as a lorry driver and, for some reason, did not come to see me much as I had then expected at the children's home in Horley Village where I now lived. I distinctly remember the acute heartache pain I felt, and the longing always to see him. I thought I had been forgotten.

At the age of seven, I got two other children from the same home to come with me on an adventure. I had decided the easiest way to get to Banbury from Horley was to follow the railway line that ran through the village for about two or three miles to Banbury. I was oblivious to its dangers. Needless to say, I really got into trouble with my dad, and with the police, and the people whom my dad currently then lodged with, and - sadly - the carers at the children's home too.

Still, I did fulfil my ambition – to see my dad! Later on, I must have been so desperately hungry for contact with my family, as I asked for my Granny Thain's (my mother's mother) actual address. I had been told about her by my father. Dad told me she was a lovely lady, and when I got back to the home I wrote a letter to her with an address of 'Granny Thain Walpole Street Peterborough', and it got to her with no number on it! Joy! The Post Service was excellent in the old days. It must have pulled a few heartstrings to read the envelope itself, as very soon afterwards, I was told I would be going to live again back with my lovely mother. However, as far as I can recall, I wasn't told I was going to live with my mother at Peterborough until the very, very last minute. I can remember we were just starting to prepare for Christmas at the children's home by making decorations, and it seemed to be such a happy time. However, after I left, I remember that a house mother there kindly and thoughtfully wrote a letter to me to tell me how Christmas had been at the children's home. Today, officials would have inspected the premises where I was going to live, however, and would have condemned it, then refused my transfer to it. They would not have been considered to be in any way suitable.

Great Adventures and Distressing Incidents

Looking back, I did have great adventures at the children's home, on occasions with the matron's son. We used to help the farmer fetch the cows that were nearly ready to give birth in from the fields some three miles away. That job was hard, as every time you passed a field, the cows would want to go off and into it to graze on the lush grass. We quickly learned that it would be better if one of us went ahead to close the gates in advance to stop those problems arising.

Also, happily, we had magpies that would eat out of our hands. When I first went there, the matron's son asked me to go with him, as he wanted to show me a bird's nest. We ran through the fields following the path of a stream, and he stopped and pointed to a snake swimming on the top of the water in the lake. We carried on where we came across a pond with a tree stretched over it and a large birds' nest at the very end, which we could see contained four eggs. We left it alone. Later, we returned to the home, and I was beginning to get used to living in a children's home. It had its various benefits. After all, we were all in the same boat – it seemed every single one of us was not wanted by society.

On another occasion, bluebirds, which I had never seen before, nestled in the walls fronting the children's home and we watched them tenderly and caringly raising their young. The birds seemed so beautiful and caring. I can also remember getting stung three or four times by wasps and the carers not being very sympathetic at all to us. However, lessons were learned. I was inquisitive, and I suppose a bit fearless in my own way, but I had learned a useful lesson about wasps: they sting, and it hurts.

Many children who came to the home were very distressed indeed and needed a lot of help as they had been abused mentally, physically and some of them, I was later to learn, sexually abused also. They cried such a lot and did not want to talk to anyone. In some instances, they had endured such a great deal, and it was good they had been rescued from their distress and abuse undoubtedly suffered before living in the children's home. A lot of them were undeniably withdrawn as a result, but that could have been because of the effect of war, and depended on what other experiences they had gone through in their lives.

The boys lived in an annexe in the grounds but joined the girls each day in the main house, where they lived, for communal meals. The whole place was built of stone, and, by today's standards, would have been a very desirable residence for conversion into flats. In the last seventy years, I expect that this property has been sold for conversion to a domestic dwelling. There was a stone wall that fronted the property where bluebirds nested and brought up their young, and again we would go there and have a peek at these lovely, tiny fledgelings as they developed.

Harvesting was not like it is today, as there were far more manual workers on the farms then. I can remember men sitting around the edge of the field's perimeter, waiting for rabbits and pheasants to run out so that they could be shot. In those days, wild rabbits were plentiful and helped to feed so many people. Then there were times when the farmer would decide to slaughter a pig for its meat. I remember when I lived at a village near Thrapston, where I was fostered, and a man and his wife washed the intestines of a pig to make chitterlings.

Another unexpected experience occurred to me. One evening, in the dark, I had to accompany a girl of about nine or ten on an errand to the local church. She lived at the children's home, and we went to visit the vicar at his vicarage. This was one winter's evening, and I can remember it was dark, and having to walk through a cemetery surrounding the church to the vicar's residence. Upon reflection, she must have been admitted to the home for care because of having already been sexually assaulted, as she tried to do precisely that to me! Sadly, this was something that it appeared she had frequently done to other children.

On another occasion, a young boy was brought in, and he did nothing but cry his heart out. The staff had tried to do their very best to comfort him, but with little success. I was then asked by the home assistant to sleep beside him and try to calm him. In those days, youngsters from children's homes were somewhat frowned upon by members of the general public, for some reason. However, most of the children had experienced a tough life already before attending the home, and some, or most, didn't let it bother them at all. I was in an environment where it had been right in one way for me because I had become used to more or less constant change for most of my life, or had at least learned to adapt and put up with it. However, although I did not know, far worse was about to come into my life!

I suppose, looking back on this time, my father didn't have much choice as to what else he could have done to cater for my needs, but the home was as good as anything I had been brought up in so far. In fact, as far as kindness was concerned, it was an improvement. It was just that, in my case, I had a mother and father whom I loved, but I rarely saw either of them. Now, I know if I could have my life over again, I would have preferred being brought up all the time in a children's home. This is because then I would not have suffered those adverse experiences that I was forced to endure, and the terrible periods of loneliness. I found it so hard getting used to being without my lovely mother or my ailing, but very caring, father.

I have said before, on the other hand, would I have developed into what I am and what I achieved if I hadn't had those experiences? Indirectly, those experiences I suffered more than likely helped me to become what I am now.

1948-1949
Going Home to Live with Mother

I remember a row of cottages on the other side of the road opposite the children's home. I became friends with a sweet, elderly lady who lived in one of them. Before I went back to live with my mother, I called to let the elderly lady know I would be leaving shortly and this lady was so pleased for me. Both of us waved fondly to her from the lorry in which my father had come to pick me up as I left the home.

On the day of my return to my mother, my father put me on the right train and watched to see me off. It was a horrible, wet, dark night when the train drew into Peterborough East Station. I had been put on a passenger train inside the guard's van with the guard and sent to Peterborough. My mother went by mistake to the wrong railway station, Peterborough North. She then had to make a lightning dash to the other one so she could pick me up from Peterborough East station. The delay was very upsetting for me as I was just sitting on my own waiting for her, thinking I had been forgotten.

It was a cold, dark, miserable night, and I can remember my mother with a scarf tied around her head, which did not suit her. She put her arm around me reassuringly as we boarded a double-decker bus. This was driven over the river bridge on the way to my new, as yet unseen home. Even going over the river bridge seemed a trial to me. I think my fear of water had resurfaced. I did not like being near streams or rivers or even travelling over them but eventually got over this fear. The omens for my move to live with my mother were not at all good, and I soon found out how very right I had been to worry.

The conditions where my mother now lodged with the man (whom at one time had been my dad's best friend), together with his own elderly mother, were absolutely ghastly: they were poverty-stricken, Dickensian living in rooms of the shabbiest type. There was no electricity, only gaslight, a few candles, and a living room fire to warm the whole of the house. Irons had to be heated upon an ancient, rickety gas cooker. This was essential, as the bedrooms and beds were so freezing cold. It was so primitive everywhere you looked. A zinc tub was filled every Friday, and we all took turns to have a bath, topping up the same used soapy water to keep it hot. Mother had the first turn at the bath. Draught excluders and door curtains littered the house to try to keep the cold out. It was so totally backwards compared to what I had been used to living in, and it was very depressing to me. Somehow, the house was telling me what a grim future still lay ahead for me. After all, I was used to so much more comfort than this. Even in the children's home, it had been much, much better than this. I was ashamed and depressed to be living here.

The place was drab and, where the fire was, the wallpaper had suffered from previous scorching, presumably from the heat of the fire. It was miserable, with its dark brown painted doors and skirting boards and picture rails. The doors were draughty and, in some instances, did not close properly. The worst of all was the candlelight you had to use to go to bed. Shadows danced around the walls, haunted you whenever you used a lighted candle, and then sometimes, in your haste to get to bed, some of the hot wax would run down your arm, scorching the skin. However, I had the thrill of being with my lovely mother to console me!

It was so primitive, and then I would have to face that bedroom window with what seemed to me to be faces peering at me. I would hide under the bedclothes, sinking into the feather mattress, which was warmed by my body and so cosy after only a few minutes. In the winter, I would have to take a pottery hot water bottle to bed. It was a lifesaver! Later on, we had rubber ones, which were far better, of course. Water had to be heated up with kettles on an old, dilapidated gas cooker.

REFLECTIONS

Looking back, I now realise that the only good thing about it was the love and affection of my beloved mother. She was, at last, there to love and to talk to, or so I thought. However, it wasn't long before I realised that my stepfather-to-be did not approve of me. He was apparently very, very jealous, and I may have reminded him of my father, his former friend. I was glad I pricked his conscience, and hope that it hurt him. It probably made him think of his actions, because his own marriage had apparently broken up, and he could not have his own son living with us because his first wife would not let him do so. This was a bitter pill for him to swallow and made him even more cruel and resentful.

I soon found more was expected of me in helping in the home. Getting up early in the morning, washing and dressing that was for starters and more was to follow.

This was more than I had ever done before in my whole life. It was essential that I got up early at six in the morning. Also, I had to be dropped off by my mother at the top of the street by 7 am as she went to work. I then walked along Walpole Street for about a mile or more to the house where my Grandmother Thain lived. She would kindly look after me during the day before school, and all day in the holidays, except times when I went to help my mother on her round, while she was working all day long.

Walking along that particular street was a bit intimidating at 7 am in the dark winter mornings with lorries and cars flying very close by, and dozens of people on cycles going early to work. It was far, far busier than the quiet village life to which I had been so accustomed.

Granny Thain's Welcome

The winter mornings were dark and cold, and the welcome warmth of my granny's fire awaiting me was much appreciated and needed. When I arrived at her house each weekday morning, she welcomed me with a cup of her strong Orange Label Tea and another round of buttered toast. This was a welcome reward after the cold or rain. I still remember her loving arms around me and a tender kiss on my cheek. Granny's fireplace was an old-fashioned, shiny, black one, with a blackened kettle always near the boil on it. The teapot that still contained warm tea, sometimes too stewed to drink, was alongside. She did, however, have a gas oven in the kitchen for cooking the meals.

My grandmother was still very poor, so poor that I can remember newspapers being used in place of tablecloths and being torn up in place of toilet tissue. However, this was something to read whether you were eating breakfast, or sitting on the toilet! Monday was wash day, and her copper in the kitchen would have a fire roaring underneath it. She would boil her whites, with a small blue bag which contained a piece of dye to enhance the whiteness. She would pay me a few pence to help her. I had to use the 'posher' on the clothes which would help to release the dirt while making sure the clothes could become as clean as possible. This was in the yard, and I used it on the clothes that were soaking in the tub. It moved the clothes around and released dirt or stains. It seemed that whites had to be white before they were allowed to be hung on the washing line. There was a sense of pride in the spotless washing produced by the hard-working housewife. It was then thought a sacrilege if your laundry was not as sparkling clean as it should be.

Thankfully, her sons and daughters realised the extremely deprived and hard life their mother endured daily, and they had also suffered. As she had made so many sacrifices all her life for her children ever since her husband had died so young, the boys when they grew up made sure her coalhouse never ran empty of fuel and ensured that her larder was well-stocked with a variety of food for her.

My own mother had to go out to work. She was employed as a baker's roundswoman for the Co-op, delivering bread to people to an alternating 'round' of customers, and then collecting the money at the end of each week. Sometimes, the customer wanted to pay her there and then. It was interesting to note that, in those days, people avoided being in debt or having a debt slowly mounting up for them to pay.

She had to get to work early as she and her baker's roundsman had to load the bread onto the shelves inside the cart before they went out delivering to the two rounds of customers. Alternate rounds were operated, as most people only ordered or needed bread every other day.

Mother's First Argument with John (my stepfather)

Within the first two days of coming to this grim slum to live at the early age of seven, I can remember an almighty row between my mother and the person who was the deliberately awkward stepfather-to-be. As the days passed, however, I realised that far, far worse was to follow. My mother was now in despair, and we ended up walking the streets together one particular night, walking through the cold and rain and getting soaked for about two hours. Before returning home, rain-sodden, miserable and very late at night, we were both seriously distraught. For once in my young life, I was nervous thinking about how my coming to live with my dear mother had perhaps caused terrible distress for her. The step-father-to-be didn't really want me there at all, and he made that known from the start. He continued to act this way every single day for the whole time I lived there. This seemed to be the story of my agonising life then: never being wanted.

The move to this new way of living quickly upset me, and, for comfort, my mother, fortunately, taught me how to pray to God and receive His reassurance.

I wasn't used to this way of life. On our return home, I remember my mother telling this man she lived with that he had to get used to me and to accept me whether he liked it or not. This was comforting to me, but no doubt precipitated the ultimate terrible revenge which he took on me at a future date.

However, on the brighter side, my mother also bred lovely looking tame rabbits. 'Blue Beverens', she called them, and I had to help her feed and clean them out, and even do the same for the chickens, along with collecting their eggs. Also, I looked after the dog. I liked taking the dog for a walk. It was very comforting when she greeted you and, bless her, licked your face affectionately. When I came home from school, she would come running up to me, and it was so warming when she greeted me. You sensed a comforting feeling that your dog loved you, even if no one else in the whole wide world seemed to at that moment in time.

I had to go to Sunday school. It was nearby, at the back of our house, and was called 'The Assemblies of God'. They held weekly services on Sundays, morning and afternoon. I suppose this was one way of getting rid of me, so my mother and her man friend could have some peace. Unfortunately, I was not the typical school child. I had been brought up so differently, and was one who would question the teacher and, if ignored, could sometimes misbehave. I would deliberately ask questions that had nothing to do with the teachings of the church, and this made it awkward for people to even answer me.

Mother's Cooking

My mother would always cook a delicious roast dinner on Sundays. We would be fortunate enough to enjoy my mother's delicious cooking. Then we would have what was leftover cold on Monday with bubble and squeak, chops on Tuesday, lamb on Wednesday, sausages Thursday, fish Friday and a fry-up on Saturdays. My stepfather's mother, who was in her late eighties, also lived with us, and she would help my mother to prepare and cook these tasty dinners. She was very reserved at first and took her son's side over everything. Fortunately, later, when she had got to know me much better, she softened significantly towards me and then became much more understanding and supportive of me.

Mother cooked wholesome and tasty dishes (except for cauliflower, cabbage and swede, which I hated). I had been forced to eat these when I was in the children's home and can remember spitting them out into my handkerchief. I can remember going to the wet fish shop on a Friday and getting cod steaks and white herrings, which my mother would cook for us. They were delicious, and she would save the soft roes and eat them for her tea with a round or two of crusty bread. We all felt that mother was the one entitled to the butter ration during wartime.. She made sure there was not a modicum left since she would carefully scrape the remaining morsels off the greaseproof paper the butter was wrapped in those days.

It wasn't long before I was introduced to doing jobs in the house; setting the table, washing and drying up, clearing the ashes out of the grates, chopping wood to light the fires, and shopping for items that we had run out of. In time, I learned to set and light fires, and helped with the ironing, sweeping the backyard, peeling potatoes and other vegetables for dinner, and feeding the rabbits and chickens. I was initially only too pleased to do it, as I knew I was helping my mother. Regrettably, in time, it became much more of a chore, especially in the winter, as I then felt the extreme cold myself, due to the severe lack of heating in the house. I felt the cold all over my body, and in my hands and in my feet in particular.

I seemed to suffer from the effects of cold weather and still, do. In those bleak and deprived times, I had to use old, worn-out socks with holes in them as mittens to keep my hands warm and wore thick woollen scarves that covered my neck and wrapped around my body to keep it as warm as possible.

My mother taught me how to light a fire, and I felt proud that she trusted me to do this. I was pleased that I could do that for her after she had returned from work. Doing her job in all weathers, she needed the house to be warm when she returned.

Affording a chimney sweep was impossible, and we had to go to the dangerous extent of setting the chimney itself on fire as poor people did in those days, to clear the soot so that it would eventually drop down!

Life seemed to be so primitive living there, but, above everything else, what mattered to me the very most was that I did have my beloved mother by my side every day again. That was so precious to me, and I had to look on the bright side.

As my stepfather knew a lot of farmers since his firm collected potatoes from them, we, fortunately, had a regular supply of pheasants, hares and rabbits, along with vegetables and other produce that came from these generous, kind farmers. We also had our own eggs our chickens provided and, believe it or not, I could never remember having eaten a fresh egg before. The only form I could remember had been dried egg powder, which came in tins during the wartime and was used in cooking. It was only when I first tasted a boiled egg for my breakfast and dipped the bread fingers into the yolk that I really discovered how delicious these were, and liked them so much. My mother would poach, scramble and fry them with mushrooms, bacon, sausage and fried bread. I loved this food. If my mother got up early, she would provide a cooked breakfast for each of us, which was great, especially in winter.

Shed Explosion

One Sunday afternoon, my stepfather was in the shed at the bottom of the garden when there was an almighty explosion. He had stored some empty cans of petrol there and was doing something with a paint burner when the shed somehow caught fire. He only just got out to safety in time before the petrol can exploded, along with other inflammable items, and flames shot up in the air about 50 feet. The shed was destroyed, and my stepfather burnt his hand. I can remember an upturned copper hood flying up into the air from the force of the explosion. It woke the neighbours up from their Sunday afternoon nap, and the local daily newspaper even had a report of it later that week.

When my mother had a spare day, we would spend it walking together in the countryside collecting blackberries and mushrooms. One day, my mother saw one particular mushroom the size of a dinner plate. She very carefully lifted it and put it in her basket with a load of blackberries which she and I had already picked.

During one of the school holidays, I managed, unfortunately, to break a bone in my arm while playing with a gang of friends and had to have it put into plaster at the local hospital. I must have felt a bit sorry for myself, as I managed to sit outside the local shops receiving comfort from all who came by there to buy goods. As I remember, I managed to pick up a few pennies so that I could buy some liquorice sticks. Upon reflection, it seemed as though I wanted someone to show some expression of concern for me, possibly to replace the emptiness I then felt, and to compensate for the parental love that I was not then receiving, well, hardly any.

Although we had plenty of pheasants and rabbits to eat, the one thing my mother would not do was to draw them, as the smell from their innards made her feel sick. She left that to my stepfather-to-be and his mother, both of whom seemed to be used to it. We were fortunate to have a company across the road where you could rent a bin and store game and other meat in a freezer. I believe it only then cost five pounds a year, and it was well worth it, mainly as my stepfather was provided with the wealth of game from various farmers that he had dealings within his role as wholesale potato manager. He also had the chance of going shooting with some of them when the season was on. Sometimes, a pig was shared with someone else, then cut up and deposited in our freezer bin for consumption at a later date.

MY LIFE IS MY WORD

I remember one morning hearing my mother screaming at what she saw outside in the yard. It was the biggest rat I had ever seen. It looked like a young coypu, which I believe are now extinct in this country, and it seemed at least two feet in length, if not more. Even my stepfather was hesitant as to what to do. By the time he had gone outside with an axe to kill the animal, it had disappeared down a hole where an old well had previously been concreted over. To reassure my mother, boxes and boxes of broken glass were then soon poured down the hole, and it was re-concreted over so that it would be difficult for any animal to find a way out of the well.

A Good Hiding

It was not long after this episode that my mother told me off, and I turned around and retaliated verbally towards her from the top of the stairs. Immediately after this, I can remember suffering a severe beating with a wooden hairbrush. My mother lost her temper, and wouldn't stop hitting me on my head, hands, all over my body. I felt the anger that she had to let out. It took a long while before I wanted to even speak to anyone at all. I well remember this beating, and I always will.

I then realised something terrible. The wonderful friendship I thought I had with my mother did not seem as though it was to continue, and I was so distraught and suddenly frightened of the future, and then I also became very nervous. Now I had not one but two parents to contend with. My mother had apparently lost control of herself, and, strangely enough, I saw this same reaction happen in many of my mother's relations, such as her sisters and brothers. I believe at this particular time, she may have been under pressure of a different nature, probably from her own necessity to over-work, exhaustion, or from the various demands made by my stepfather-to-be.

Divorce and Abuse

Having considered the reactions of all the girls in my mother's family, I am now of the opinion that they had all been deprived of the example of their loving father. He had died young, suddenly of peritonitis. This must have been a dramatic shock to all eleven of them since I am led to believe that the eldest was at the time only thirteen.

After his funeral, it is evident from what I was told that the aggressive young male members eventually ruled the household, and consequently, the girls suffered from male domination. The girls must have also needed someone who would be protective and would promise them a far better life. Eventually, some would realise that they might have inadvertently jumped out of the frying pan into the fire, and that is why some of them got divorced from their first husbands.

It seemed in those days that children were not protected from physical abuse as well as they are today. Also, physical abuse seemed so familiar wherever you were living and was meted out swiftly and painfully when children misbehaved. A hard slap on the legs or around the ears or head was typical, and in some instances I have seen a child get a good hiding in public to show who was in charge. This sadly seemed to be the order of the day in those times. I am sure many children suffered severely because of this, and possibly such behaviour had its repercussions and was repeated when they, later in life, had children themselves. On the other hand, they hopefully decided to bring their children up in a more loving, supportive, and responsible way.

When I was old enough, I joined the Cubs, and learned a few more survival skills. It had been planned that we should go into the country to put our map reading skills to the test. The dense fog came down that particular night. It was smog, like thick, green swirling smoke, creeping around corners of buildings and you could not see very far in front of your face. Within a short time, the leaders decided to call it off as they considered it too dangerous for us boys. The smog was so severe that there was no traffic around at all. It had all stopped. It was very wise that action was later taken to reduce the pollution with the Clean Air Act 1956.

Fortunately, we are today beginning to realise how much we have polluted the air and water around us, and, hopefully, essential steps will be taken to redress the damage caused to the environment and to human health, as well as to animals and wildlife.

1949-1950
I Threatened my Stepfather!

Life was not very happy during these years, and I do not remember them with much joy. I was so frequently ill-treated by my stepfather, and he would use a stick or his hand on me by giving me great clouts around the ears which he had the very strong arms for, also on the back of my head. His nickname at work was 'Lofty'. This was because he was about 6ft 3in tall and weighed about 18 stone. You would never know when he was upset as he would just suddenly, without warning, lunge out and lash out with his hand and hit you! This made me very frightened and nervous as you never knew when to expect the next blow, or indeed why he had lost his temper. This shock meant that I was always living, from the age of seven onwards, on the very edge, in fear of being hit by him.

He was, fortunately, a hard worker. He was initially a driver, and later became floor manager of a large wholesale potato merchant. I believe he was given the job of floor manager because he would be able to handle the drivers verbally if they should become difficult. A burly, strong man, he could pick up a hundred-weight of potatoes with each arm and at the same time. When I look back, however, at that period of my life, I was really terrified by this great hulk of a bullying man, and just being near him was enough to make me white with terror. I think this was when my nerves started to be severely under constant threat of a bad breakdown.

After being made a manager, my stepfather had to have a telephone installed so that drivers who had accidents or broke down could contact him for help. I could easily hear him. Sometimes he would become quite aggressive on the phone to a lorry driver and would shout at him. This could happen during the night or early morning and was part of his responsibility as a manager. In the night, this interruption sometimes woke me up and disturbed my sleep seriously, and it seemed as though he was always there as a terrible hanging threat, continually at the back of my mind.

At home or near him, I was forever waiting for something to anger him again, even the slightest incident. His constant moans and groans about what I was doing affected my confidence and added to my very real fears. It was like a cloud of hate always hanging in the air, and it was as though I was not wanted there.

I think I began to lose my self-confidence and possibly became even more extremely wary and apprehensive, more than I had ever been before. Just being within this man's presence made me nervy. I was made to go to bed at seven and be up for six. My bedroom would be cold, and some nights I would put the coarse ancient rugs from my floor on top of the bed to keep me warm. Life seemed to be becoming a bit primitive, and it was much harder to endure.

A Scruffy Kid and A Chance Lost

Dressed in my scruffy trousers and a dirty t-shirt, as usual, I saw that my uncle Cyril, who lived with his mother near us, was getting ready to go to the Perkins' Diesel Family Day Out.

Kindly, my uncle said to me, 'Go home and get some decent clothes on and have a wash, and I will take you to the Show.'

I jumped for joy and raced back, but no one was there at home so I could not get in. I managed to get a wash at my next door neighbour's house and turned my t-shirt inside out, thinking I would be presentable. Much to my dismay, my uncle refused to take me, because of how poorly I was dressed, and I was so upset.

On another occasion, my stepbrother had come to visit his father and both of us went round the back of the house as it appeared no one was in. The kitchen sash window was held by a nail and with a penknife you could release its hold raise the window and get entry.

In so doing an oil lamp was dislodged which crashed on the kitchen sink. This made me very frightened of the consequences I would doubtless suffer.

As expected, when my stepfather and mother came home, he was livid with anger and went for me, but, fortunately, my mother stepped in and said to him, 'Your son was also involved, so if you are going to hit one, do it to the other, too.' He quickly withdrew and then very reluctantly decided enough had been said, and we got off.

The physical bullying continued, however, and I could stand no more. One day, in one of his worst rages, he nearly broke my arm, and I ended up hiding under the breakfast table to get away from him. When he had stopped his rantings and ravings, I confronted him with what he had done and told him I would go to the police if he hurt me any more.

I don't know where I got the nerve to say this, but if I hadn't, I am sure he would have done more damage to me. Upon reflection, I would obviously have had a better life in a children's home without being forced to live under these terrifying circumstances. There had been so many such incidents where he had hit me on the head, slapped my face and raged at me. But this had to stop.

Of course, all this worry, and the severe bullying was not doing me any good. I had never ever been treated like this before, except when fostered much earlier in my life, and that had been terrible, too.

After this incident, my mother was very worried, as a large bruise had developed, and my arm swelled up, and I think I bumped my head trying quickly to crawl under the table to get away from him. My mother thought he had fractured my arm, as she was anxious, and she stuck up for me.

After this episode, things seemed to settle down for a while, as I believe my mother gave him a good telling off, explaining to him the possible criminal proceedings he could face if he continued this bullying. But then, after a few weeks, he developed another way of ill-treating me. One day, he just decided to crack an egg on my head. 'That will do your hair good,' he said, and he laughed. He had a sick sense of humour. My mother then gave him another warning in no uncertain terms.

The physical bullying then stopped, and his complaining later became mental torture. It was clear I was not wanted and that he hated my presence, daily telling me off for the very least thing.

My mother's new partner had separated from his wife and son, and he had chosen to live with my mother. He had a wife, and a son of the same age as me, so you would have thought that he would have shown restraint and concern for his own family.

He chose not only to leave his own family but in so doing ruined my father's family by my mother leaving him and my father suffering because he lost everything, his wife and his son.

These personal changes in his life had such an effect that my father failed to look after himself and this gradual deterioration in his health contributed to his terminal illnesses. The deterioration in his health eventually led to blindness and his having to live in a special residential home and later the result of my father's so sad and early death.

My stepfather, on the other hand, as it turned out, actually died of a heart attack just two years before my own father died of bronchial pneumonia. They both died at age 46 and had been, for many years before the affair with my mother, good friends to each other.

In those days, women were ostracised and made to feel different if they were cohabiting. I can well remember people shunning my poor mother because of this. People would cross over to the other side of the road so they did not have to acknowledge her. Such things are so different today. This is obviously a great blessing and an improvement in people's self esteem.

My own father had done nothing wrong at all, and would not admit falsely in court that he had committed adultery himself just so my mother could get a divorce sooner. Why should he? Therefore, they had to wait seven years from the date of my father parting with my mother before a divorce was granted.

I realise now, thinking back it must have been very distressing for my father; on the other hand, he may have still clung to the belief that he would, one day, be reunited with my mother.

I became inexorably and increasingly nervous about being left anywhere alone as I was losing confidence in myself. My mother and stepfather would go out drinking at the weekends or socialising in the evenings, and I would become very nervous about being left without anyone in the house. It seemed as soon as they went out I would start hearing or imagining noises, and I suppose my vivid imagination took over. The house creaked, and I would listen to sounds as if someone was walking up the stairs, and then see what appeared to be a face at the bedroom window. I had never been left on my own at night before, and I found this upsetting and would not be able to sleep until either the parents or my stepfather's mother herself came home.

I believe my stepfather was upset because he could not have his own son, who was a little older than me, to live with us, but that was not my fault. There was not enough room at the little house. Although, whenever we had people visit us, my mother's partner would adopt a very different attitude in front of them and leave me alone. I can remember one Christmas his son came to the Christmas afternoon celebrations, and it wasn't long before he and I ended up fighting. He was spoilt by his father and his own mother, who gave him money whenever he needed it.

My mother was unusually very good at helping me to learn and develop. She worked with a horse and cart, and all day very hard. In the summer holidays, she took me with her and made me look after the cash bag, and I had to work out what a customer owed. She also trusted me to take the correct money and give them the change.

I was also allowed to hold the reins of the horse when it was time for the horse to go home. Fortunately, the horse knew the way; all you had to do was guide it when you made a left or right turn. I recall food leftovers in those times were placed in dustbins on the pavements, and this food was collected every day to feed pigs. It would be cooked to boiling point to kill off the germs and then mixed with animal feed for the animals. Most of the Co-operative vehicles for milk and bread delivery were horse driven, so you can imagine that smart horses soon sensed that food was in the bin and got used intelligently to knock the lids off to see what they fancied to eat. It was comical to see them do this.

The good thing about the horse-driven vehicles was that you could just shout and call the horse to your side and would not have to walk back to the cart. Of course, this saved time. The Co-op used horses and carts for milk and bread delivery for many years, but this service is sadly now all but finished.

Unfortunately, my mother had an accident which damaged her kneecap badly, and eventually she had to have an operation on that knee. When she came home, she was incapacitated and needed a lot of help. In the end, she had to terminate her employment with the

Co-operative Bakery. My stepfather then made her the supervisor at his own firm in charge of the prepacked potatoes section that was now becoming popular, and she worked beside him in the same warehouse. She couldn't stand upright for long, and I remember learning how to iron for her so she could rest. Obviously, I had to be very careful - otherwise, I would have got burned - but it helped my dearest mother a lot.

Mother's Help in my Education

My mother spent hours teaching me to learn to read, spelling learning tables, jigsaw puzzles and memory games; also, importantly crosswords.

There were no other forms of entertainment in those days. It was not like now, when one can thoroughly enjoy such a variety of TV programmes, computer games, Netflix films and smartphones – everything is available. In those far off days, you certainly had visits from your friends, but, once they had arrived, you had to make your own family entertainment. We did not have much to offer to visitors, but my mother improvised with games that I believe helped quicken my skills, and improved greatly, bless her, my mental capacity to learn. It was also, as well, most enjoyable for all. We played cards, and dominoes and she taught me various games which were entertaining and, in many ways, also educational. I had to learn all my tables off by heart so that I could count in multiples. All this training was very good for me, and it set examples which could be later passed down to my own children.

My mother loved jigsaw puzzles and would have them on a large tray so she could do a bit of the puzzle at a time. She often felt like it. When I came to live with her I couldn't tell the time, and this was basic knowledge. She made me sit at a clock and visualise what time it was depending on where she told me the small hand and large hands were pointing. Worse still, I couldn't tie my shoelaces! She quickly taught me.

I was told sometime later in my life that my mother had become fed up with paying all the bills for my keep. I didn't know whether to believe this or not, but can remember having to go, on one occasion, to the Magistrates' office for my mother to see whether my father had paid his maintenance for me.

Owing to his serious health problems and his failing eyesight, he was at times not in a position to be able to work, and at the age of 38 years he was forced by ill health to go into permanent care. My mother told them then that she did not want him to pay for maintenance anymore. Even if he had wanted to, I don't think he would have had sufficient money coming in at that time to have been able to do so.

This, of course, was also a disaster for me. I was beginning to realise just how sick my father had become, and I was frustrated because there was so little I could do to help him. When I went to see him occasionally, we never talked about lack of money. At that time,

I was not mature enough to know about finance and benefits. The only advantage I saw him receive was a pocket braille watch from the Society for the Blind or the British Legion, and, when he died, they came immediately to collect it!

I can remember one Saturday morning my mother taking me shopping. For a treat, she took me to Marks and Spencers at Peterborough, which even in those days had a cafeteria. You collected a tray and selected what you wanted. This was very enjoyable, but even though it was a Saturday my mother still seemed to have to rush around as though she had lots of other work she would have to do later on and, of course, she did.

We never had any electrical appliances to help us do housework, as we didn't have electricity connected to our house. It was so very primitive!

The only form of worldly entertainment we had was a radio that had to have its accumulators charged up frequently so that it could play. I can recall us all listening to Dick Barton. It was my job to take and fetch the accumulators from the local shop, generally every week; sometimes more often, if necessary. This type of living was really very deprived and made everyday life extremely difficult for those of us living in poorly equipped houses, and I could not at that time see any signs of the situation improving.

My Mother and Stepfather buy the house

In spite of this, things were to change and surprise. My mother and stepfather purchased the house for £300 and then started to modernise it by adding a downstairs bathroom and installing electricity. We were one of the last three homes in the whole of the street to have this amenity. These were luxuries for my mother, who still, as always, worked so hard. Fortunately, for her in particular and for all of the rest of us, this made our lives so much easier. I was still, however, left having to daily endure my deep fear of my cruel, spiteful, vicious stepfather.

After this dramatic improvement I can remember us all having a bath with fresh, clean hot water and enjoying a perfect soak. It was far better than we had ever experienced before. For all of us, it was sheer luxury, especially in this house. My mother would soak herself and take an hour immersed in the bath. I can also remember her using the rainwater from a container in the garden, kept for its softness, when she washed her hair to rinse the shampoo out. It was also so beneficial to have a toilet inside the house as others now also did: before, when it had been built outside, you had to go out in all weathers if you wanted to use it.

Eventually, my mother got her first Hoover, which made life a lot easier for her, and then a much-loved washing machine. She had more time to be looking after the rest of the house. Things were moving quickly, and it wasn't long before we bought our first television. Even though only black and white, this was a 17 inch Marconi, I believe. Fantastic! We, at last, had superior entertainment in the home, and my mother and stepfather shortened their visits to the public houses where they had usually spent so long socialising.

In addition to all these improvements, my mother began to strip the walls of paper as the rooms sorely needed new decorations. The electric light we now had revealed just how dirty and poor the room décor was. Three or four layers of paper had to be removed in each room, but we didn't have the products to help to decorate that you have today. You had to soak it and scrape it, and in some places it was very arduous work. Also, some plastering had to take place where the plaster had been cut out to make way for the electricity cables.

My mother, with help, managed to get most of this done, and the house began to look much better for it.

I was also taught to put the paste on the wallpaper to help my mother decorate the various rooms.

It was around this time that my mother and stepfather decided to hold a large Christmas party at home, and they started preparing for it three months beforehand. Believe it or not, we had six geese in our back garden to fatten up especially for Christmas. After two attempts, my mother baked a beautiful Christmas cake, which she stored in a large tin. She also prepared a Christmas pudding in a basin wrapped up in muslin. We had prepared and bottled fruit during the summer that could be used for the festivities.

Most of my mother's family were invited, and the excitement built up as Christmas drew near. My stepfather wrung the necks of the six geese about a week before so that they could be plucked and drawn and hung well beforehand.

My mother, her mother, and my stepfather's mother had the job of plucking the birds, and that took days. The down from the birds' feathers got everywhere. Pheasants were defrosted from the freezer bin we used, and I believe we had invited about twenty people or more, mostly all relations, to mid-day dinner, and afterwards for a sumptuous high tea.

My mother showed me how to make Christmas chains with strips of coloured paper so we could decorate the house. It was all go, and we were each, I believe, very earnestly looking forward to this particular Christmas.

MY LIFE IS MY WORD

It would be a fantastic feast. A table fit for a king. Jellies, blancmanges, sherry trifles, minced pies, pork pies, jam tarts, cocktail sausages, sausage rolls, sandwiches, scotch eggs, roast pork, roast beef, and six geese with stuffing, roasted to perfection. Honestly, it was a real feast for all of us to remember.

1951-1952
Passed For Grammar School

Nevertheless, we still seemed to be deficient in comparison to so many people we knew at that time. Clothes were not cheap, and the teachers in those days had their favourite pupils who were often the better dressed ones, and possibly cleaner than others. Some of these were often – well-spoken, as it was known in those days. However, I just plodded on in my usual way. I was scruffy and not a teacher's favourite, or that is how it seemed to me, and I noticed that many children were not well looked after, nor were they well fed or dressed. In fact, I can remember one young boy coming to school in an oversized coat that he would absolutely refuse to take off. Eventually, and embarrassingly for him, he began to mess himself with nerves and anxiety, which obviously I do not think he could help, poor lad. Everyone was soon shown the real reason for this. He was devastated and ashamed. I personally felt so sorry for his plight and sympathised with him.

Under his overcoat, the poor chap wore only - would you believe - a girl's dress. When I think back to that situation, I count my own blessings. He had to be escorted away by the headmaster, and, presumably, his parents were later severely and sternly questioned about the poor lad's totally unsuitable state of dress and the care they apparently had not given their son. But, in mitigation, some people were destitute in those days, and those of us who had known poverty ourselves were of course entirely sympathetic towards him in his plight.

Jumble sales were always well attended, and even at these, some people would try and slip a piece of clothing into their bags without paying. At one jumble sale I went to, officials decided to count the number of items when the people left and then charge them accordingly, because so many people tried to steal the clothes.

I worked hard at junior school and soon found myself transferred to the top class. My stepbrother, although slightly older, was at a lower level. Nevertheless, I did my best with whatever we were given to do, and was reasonably confident about my own ability, as I felt that I had inherited some of my mother's and father's brains and talents. Also, due to my hard experiences at such an early age (from nearly four onwards), I had always been used to changes, challenges, and survival.

Much to the amazement of my headmaster, I passed my eleven-plus at 10 years of age. This would mean I had won a place and could go to Deacon's Grammar School. I can well recollect the headmaster, calling out my name to the whole assembly present at the junior school. However, unkindly he added, 'Just how you passed the English paper, I do not know!' He said this in front of everyone to my embarrassment. This, of course, was most unethical of him, and did not add to my already shaky self-confidence at that time at all, as you can guess.

It is strange that a respected member of the educational establishment did not congratulate me, but instead found something derogatory to say. As you can well imagine, this disparaging criticism had long-lasting effects on my self-confidence for the rest of my school life. It is surprising how accurate the bible is when it says that 'the tongue is (sometimes) sharper than the sword'.

I suppose, having lived in different areas of the country, I had acquired some of their various dialects and was not as posh in my speech as they, the grammar school teachers, wanted me to be.

I was the scruffy child and clothes were expensive, and I did not speak perfect English, having a countryside dialect (Oxfordshire and Northamptonshire mixed) at that time. Looking back, it might have been that I had also developed accents from the various country areas and places I had lived in or that I had picked up accents with those I had lived with.

Anyway, I had such experiences in my life that they knew nothing of, so this did not matter. I would be leaving this school and going to a grammar school in the next term. Fantastic! I had high expectations for my own future, but sadly this was to turn out to be so short-lived.

When I told my mother I had passed, I treasured my mother's face, as she couldn't believe it and picked me up. She was so happy and swung me around with her arms. She was so proud of me. She told me that she had passed for Grammar School herself too, but could not go to it because they were so very poor, but also reassured me by saying, 'You will go. I will see to that.'

For my success, my mother bought me a new bike at Christmas, and I took the weekly payment to the cycle shop until it was paid off in full. I knew nothing about this present as it as it was delivered on Christmas Eve, it was late, and I was then in bed. It was a real and welcome surprise to me. This was typical of my mother's loving and thoughtful kindness to me. When I started school, my mother could not afford the sports gear I needed for me to play cricket, and I tried to hide this fact and infer to the sports master that I was too nervous about playing that game. They wouldn't, however, accept this, and somehow eventually realised that it was more a financial problem, and they provided some clothes that I could use so I could still play. I did not enjoy the game, but I did not then feel left out of it, as I had before.

Although my upbringing to date might have had an effect on my accent which in those days was frowned upon, now the BBC goes out of their way to employ people with a wealth of regional accents. In those days, the BBC's Received Pronunciation, a 'posh', cut-glass accent, was the most sought-after way of speaking in the minds of teachers of English, especially in grammar schools.

Received Pronunciation was required of all announcers on the BBC. Nowadays, however, it is much more refreshing and exciting when they use announcers with colloquial dialects and strong accents from different parts of the UK. These are spoken with gusto and appreciated regularly on the BBC.

It might have been that some teachers objected to how their pupils were speaking. Even in those days, it appeared there was a certain amount of prejudice if you seemed to come from a poor home. Especially if you did not have better quality clothes too! At least, that is how I felt. This seemed to give children like me an inferiority complex. This, sadly, lasted well into my later years, but I finally threw it off due to climbing the ladder at work in my job as a professional, and a Higher Manager.

Yet that could also have been caused by the fact that I had spent time in a children's home and people in those places looked down on you as though you were potential trouble, or were not wanted for some reason or other. Due to my mother's efforts and her persistence in teaching me a great deal in her own free time, I quickly became exceptionally good at maths while with her, and at several other vital subjects, too. We had mental arithmetic tests at school nearly every day, and I almost always came top. If I didn't get them all correct, I would be mad with myself. There used to be IQ test papers in those days that were available in the comics, and I used to do well solving those.

Apparently, my English could not have been that bad, as I had passed to go to grammar school. I started there in September of 1952. Leading up to then, I can well remember that during the school holidays I tried on my new school clothes and became very excited. For once in my life, I felt a little proud of what I had achieved. I had never had clothes like this before, and I believe my mother had to get a provident cheque out so she could afford them. I also had to be bought a satchel to carry my books and other requisites I needed, such as a compass, protractor, ruler, pens and pencils, and a rubber.

I had expressed an interest in learning to play the piano to my mother, but the nearest I ever got to this aim was when my dear, thoughtful mother bought me one from a customer for me to practise on. However, my hopes were dashed. As the piano came in through the front door, my stepfather inspected it, and then so sadly for me made sure it immediately went out through the back door into the yard to be dumped. His excuse that it had woodworm. I was distraught, as you can imagine! Again, I knew it was that he was jealous because my mother had wanted me to learn to play the piano. I eventually recovered from this disappointment, as I loved to hear a piano being played by others, and desired to acquire such an incredible skill, wanting to create for others such lovely music. Fortunately, I have always retained my love of listening to piano and orchestral music.

My mother, I believe, introduced to me this love of music. She definitely instilled in me an enduring passion for listening to it. Like her, I adored hearing the popular operas, and Mantovani. She also revelled in the musicals that were popular at that time and of course still are. She took me to see Johnny Ray. Eddie Calvert and many more similar stars were of course a delight to listen to. She had an extensive repertoire of music that she enjoyed, and I was influenced by this.

1951
A Fantastic Holiday

One of the great luxuries and surprises that came out of my passing my eleven-plus exam was that I was given an exceptional treat: a surprise week's holiday spent, believe it or not, with my stepfather's sister, Doris, and her husband and son. George Weedon, her husband, was in show business, and they lived in Streatham, London. Aunt Doris was a choreographer and George a musician. Both were colourful characters and extroverts, but kind and beautiful people to spend a week with, a week I have never, ever, forgotten.

They owned a comfortable flat in Streatham. As the door was opened to me and I walked up the stairs, I was gobsmacked by the size of their lounge. It was at least 30 feet long and 15 feet wide, and adorned with beautiful furniture and a grand piano to die for. It seemed I had stepped into another world and it was so exciting for me to be staying there. It was to be a week filled with surprises, I was later to find out. I was given a bed settee to sleep on, and it was so luxurious, much better than the bed I usually slept on at home. You could see the beautiful gardens and open parks and spaces from my window.

That afternoon, I had my first outing, and was taken to the then-famous Lyon's restaurant for an afternoon tea as a special treat. It was a thrilling experience I shall never forget. It was all silver service and linen tablecloths. These were snow white, and there was gleaming silver cutlery, and the surroundings were beautiful. We ate superbly filled cucumber and salmon, egg and cress, wafer-thin ham sandwiches, and delicious cakes, all of which were to die for. Being waited on by waitresses in frilled aprons and caps was terrific, too, and the staff, I believe, could see that I was sitting absolutely enthralled by it all. I was in a different world, and more was to follow that week. Doris and family clearly lived well and enjoyed the trappings of their success.

The next day, Doris's son and I were taken on a car ride to a canal with locks on it. It might have been Camden Town, but exactly where I cannot remember. It was so exciting, and many other people were visiting this area. However, a big treat was in store as well, since that particular evening we had been invited to a party, and what a party it turned out to be! It seemed like I was the guest of honour, as everyone wanted to talk to me and ask me questions about myself and the well-known grammar school I was going to. The people were so lovely and kind, something I had rarely ever enjoyed before, and I loved every minute of that holiday. I had never in my life experienced such popularity! The guests at the party seemed to know each other, and as they were also so flamboyant, I could only assume they were either actors, musicians, dancers or people in some way associated with the theatres at different venues where Doris and George performed.

I can remember Doris's husband coming home one day with a score of music and then shouting to his wife to come to listen to the latest he was going to play. I cannot remember what tune it was, but sitting there in that lounge and looking, enthralled, at him playing that grand piano was an unbelievable experience for me. I love to hear someone playing a piano and marvel at the skill they have, and, in fact, I also feel so envious of this impressive skill they have acquired. A grand piano is one of the most beautiful-sounding musical instruments that I know.

Various outings to places of interest took place during that week, and I had one of the most enjoyable weeks of my young life. When I got home, I could not help talking about it to everyone, even to my stepfather's son, who never had himself been invited there. I think I was trying to make him jealous, which was, looking back on it, very wrong of me! Some years later, I was to learn that Doris and George ended up on Broadway itself, but still retained their flat on at Streatham. George also at one time appeared as a pianist in a film. It was only a minor part, but they were clearly doing well. My holiday had been an experience of a lifetime, and a precious one that I will never forget.

My First Day at Grammar School

As it happens, I do have now three music teachers in my Le-Hair family, one of whom, Anna, is a concert pianist. There are also numerous cousins involved in operatic societies, and in drama groups, so apparently it seems as though music and acting play significant parts in our family, (on my father's side.)

It was near the time when I started my new school, and I can always recall trying to get my mother to buy the finer Worcester trousers for me, but all she could afford were flannelette ones. This material was inferior and easily snagged and would not keep its creases. The first day at grammar school, new pupils were *'ragged'* (teased and tormented), and I had my school cap stolen and fought with the culprit; in doing so, I fell on my knee, and flannelette split apart on my trousers.

The new headmaster saw what had happened and got hold of us both by the scruffs of our necks and said, 'My office at 2 pm.' Having just arrived at this school, within the first day I was on report, and I feared the worst. Yet, when we saw the headmaster, he was quite the opposite of what I had feared, and he gave the other person a thorough dressing down because he had been at the school a year, unlike me, and he should have known better. He set an example, and said the next time the same happened it would be the cane.

For once in my life, I was so ashamed of this dressing down and then had the humiliation of telling my mother what had happened on my first day. She could not afford new trousers, so I had to go to school with them patched up. I became very conscious indeed of this, as I had to wear them the whole term before I could get some new ones.

The constant bickering and moaning of my stepfather-to-be was intended to be upsetting, and I went out at night to keep out of his way. As a result, my homework and schoolwork suffered badly. I disliked him profoundly and of course still feared him every day. In one particular row, this time with my mother, I told her that my stepfather would die first before my father did.

I can remember coming home from school and kneeling in the toilet, praying that the Lord would keep me safe. I became so frightened of my stepfather then that I started to shake with terror, especially when I was near him and he raised his voice and shouted as was usual at me.

Awarded Top Prize for Selling – a Step in the Right Direction

Having settled at the school, all of us were asked to sell magazines for a garden fete, with a prize for whoever sold the most. This was one thing I knew I could do well, and I sold over a hundred. This in their eyes was wonderful, but all I did was tell people who bought them about the raffle, and a number was on every programme and would be drawn during the day of the garden fete. I sold them as raffle tickets and won the prize for selling the most. The next year, I sold nearly five hundred by knocking on doors all over Peterborough with the same message and explaining that the funds would support Deacon's Grammar School. People in Peterborough were very supportive, and I won it that year as well. Most people approved of the grammar schools in those days, especially in the neighbourhoods where I selected to try and sell these tickets. They were the well-to-do areas.

Visits with friends to Peterborough Cattle Market were educational in that you could buy certain things for a very modest price, and could also sell items. My stepbrother had a starter motor, which was in pieces, and as he could not put it together he offered it to me, and I readily accepted. I quickly assembled it in some fashion so that it looked like it should be and put it into the cattle market sale the following Saturday. It sold for a few pounds, which provided for my needs for a couple of weeks. You could also buy chickens for a very reasonable price and sell them to neighbours, making a small profit.

The problem with the cattle market was that there were some disgusting people around. One, in particular, was what you would today call a paedophile, who weighed about twenty stone – he was as fat as a pig, and looked like one. He had a garden hut situated within the cattle market. One day he tried to get hold of me, as he had done with several other friends of mine, but what he didn't realise was how loud I could shout and how difficult I could be to deal with. Anyway, whatever he intended to try to do to me, a policeman came over in time to see what he was then up to. The copper gave him a stern warning about his behaviour and he never ever bothered me again. In those days, you had to be careful of such people, as there were many around. In fact, it was possibly just as bad then as it is today.

I can also remember in the market, the poor, large sows for sale that had possibly come to the end of their useful lives. They were so difficult to move about, and men had electric shockers that would eventually guide them to the pens before they were sold for slaughter. These animals were massive and could quite easily do serious damage to you if you were not careful.

I would make money another way from swapping things at school that others did not realise were valuable. One day, I traded a watch case that was in my opinion made of gold for something else: I believe it was an old fountain pen. On Saturday, I went to the local jewellers and offered the watch case for sale. He offered me a derisory amount for it. I quickly told him it was 18 ct gold, and he then relented and gave me, I think, four times what he had initially offered.

I was so pleased with myself and with the money I made, because it would be my pocket money. A week later, when the boy's mother had come complaining to my mother that her son had stolen it from his father, the boy's mother replied that she, the mother, would get to the bottom of the story when her son returned from holiday with the school. The tragedy of this situation was that her son, while on holiday in Switzerland with the school, sadly drowned by accident in Lake Geneva.

1952- Choir Practice

Upon starting at Deacon's Grammar School, it was not long before I joined the choir to try to become involved in school activities that were possibly more noteworthy than others. My voice range was judged as Alto, and I think there were four other pupils singing in the group with me. Choir practice was at times tedious, but our teacher was very patient with us, and eventually our voices made a reasonable sound. This was because his training exercises helped us to improve our singing and to harmonise with the rest of the choir.

One week he dropped a bombshell on the choir, saying we were going to sing 'The Messiah' by Handel. This piece of music would take about two and a half hours to sing, and was very hard to learn, and tiring. Attention to detail when reading the music and practice was essential, as not only were we going to sing it but also present it as a performance in a nearby church. Hours of training were necessary.

One of the problems was that the Alto group were not very strong, but I was supposed to have the best voice and to make sure my voice was heard. Well, we eventually managed it, and we received favourable comment in the local newspaper. The church was packed.

Summer holidays came, and you can imagine the shock when I had been sent to another aunty, uncle and their family for two weeks. These were my mother's sister and her family. This was, I later learned, so my mother and partner could get married. When I was told by my aunty on the last day I was with her, she said that I was now to accept him as a father and be kind to him. Upon hearing this, I was naturally full of rage and deep anger. She, like many others in my mother's family, did not know just how badly he treated me. If my mother and stepfather-to-be had thought anything about my feelings, they would have told me beforehand. Also, they could have included me in their wedding celebrations. I apparently wasn't wanted there, or ever, or that is how it then seemed to me.

Mother Admitted to Hospital

It was not long afterwards that I came home from school one afternoon and found my mother in bed, looking as white as a sheet. I saw a bucket almost full of what seemed to be blood by the side of the bed, and ran immediately to our next door neighbour for help. An ambulance and a doctor were called, and my mother was whisked off to the local hospital for emergency treatment. I now believe that she had had a miscarriage or an unlawful termination of some kind. When I reflect on this situation, I somehow think that my mother did not want those years of poverty ever again, or that she thought my stepfather was not suitable to father another child, especially following the way he had treated me.

I was glad I was there and in time to save my mother, as I do not think my mother would have survived otherwise. This was a terrible time for me, and because my mother had to stay in the hospital, I was sent to my grandmother Thain's until she was discharged. I was shocked to see my mother looking so very ashen, and ill, and then being carted off in an ambulance, with no knowledge of how she was progressing.

Earning Pocket Money

At that time, I didn't receive any pocket money, so I had to earn it myself. I soon realised that you could collect rags and metal and take them to the scrapyard, and could then be paid money for it. Later, I learned that you got more for woollen rags, and if you sorted them out this would increase the amount you received. I ended up with a wooden truck, which became so useful in helping me earn pocket money.

Later on, after repairs to make it even more sturdy and towable behind my bike, it was used to collect some slack from the coal wharves when an icy winter had depleted all stocks of conventional coal. I then used it to collect logs from the old trees left in fields. Wherever I could find wood of any kind that could be used as fuel, I gathered it, and so became quite resourceful in the variety of work I could do, and was never out of pocket, as neighbours were quick to buy from me. People used the slack by mixing it with a little cement so it could be bonded, and formed small blocks that could be put onto the fire.

Also, I started doing an early morning paper round during the week, and even a Sunday one. However, in the bad weather, I found it hard going, and bronchitis that I had suffered from affected me, so when the winter weather came I decided to finish the paper rounds and find a different way to earn money.

That particular winter, the weather was terrible, and I remember battling the cold and rain, and then the wind took the newspapers and they blew all over the place. In trepidation, I returned to the newsagents' very upset at what had happened and told him I could not do the job any more.

I Am Taken Seriously Ill

That bad winter, when we had snow on the ground for at least six weeks, the cold really got to me, and I finally collapsed and had to be put to bed. It was serious, and the doctor visited me every day for the first few days. I had to be nursed by my mother for two weeks while staying in bed. The doctor then visited every two or three days to check up on me, as I had been so very seriously ill. My mother could not afford decent gloves for me, and I had had to make do with old, used socks on my hands, with a hole cut out for my thumb.

A fire had to be lit in my bedroom, and the doctor's instruction was that I must be kept warm. I remember my mother nursing me and buying me comics and sitting on the bed as I was so very ill. I had previously, as a baby, suffered double pneumonia before I was one year old, and that had left me with weakness, and now I had terrible bronchitis. After about four weeks, I was allowed to go out, and the first place my mother took me was to get a new overcoat and suitable gloves that were warm and waterproof. These would stand the cold and lousy weather we suffered from in those days. I chose an overcoat that had a removable lining, which my mother approved of.

It took a few weeks for me to fully regain my strength, and my mother made sure I had plenty to eat as I had lost a lot of weight. She gave me great dollops of malt, which I loved, and spoiled me with foods I liked. All this, of course, was wonderful of her.

Surprise, surprise, we then bought a new colour television. When it was installed, we all sat there in amazement, mesmerised, watching it. It had so much better a picture than the black and white. That is, until I used it and broke something!

My mother and stepfather had gone out for the evening, and I was there with my stepfather's mother and decided to change the TV stations. A clip on a switch came loose, and catastrophe followed. I had accidentally broken it. Try as I might, it would not work, so I went to bed worried to death as what would happen to me the following morning. I decided to tell my mother and stepfather at the breakfast table, and all hell broke loose. I was so frightened that I was nearly peeing myself! That's how he would get at me. However, fortunately, his mother, for once, intervened firmly and said it could have been anybody, and because it was morning she explained there was a chance that it could be put right before the following night. Also, she said, I had owned up to it and could have kept quiet. I was so pleased she had intervened.

On The Market

Eventually, having fully recovered my health, I found work on the Saturday fruit and vegetable market in Peterborough. By working all day, I could earn more than on my paper rounds. In fact, I became quite popular with the traders setting out the fruit and vegetables and serving customers. In those days, I was quick to learn, and soon had excellent verbal patter that brought the customers to the stall. I worked for a Mr Woodbine, who sold dozens of Webs Wonderful lettuces. He later started selling tomatoes and celery as well, and I became the quickest person to unpack and to present a box of tomatoes to the purchasers.

These would be packed in a small wooden box, and you had to take the tissue paper that these were wrapped in off each one in the top layer to show how red, ripe and firm the tomatoes were. We always had sold out entirely by dinner time, so I had time on my hands.

I loved this job, and I am sure my demeanour must have been noted by a local stall trader, a sweet lady called Mrs Woolley, as one day she stopped me and asked if I would work for her on Saturday afternoon. To this I readily agreed. Mrs Woolley, whose family had been on the markets for years, befriended me and encouraged me to work for her in the afternoons selling her high-class fruit and vegetables. She was about fifty years old and unmarried, and took a great liking to me, and she managed to get me additional work in my summer holidays. This was with her well-to-do and high-class friends, who paid well, which pleased me even more.

She also taught me some of the tricks of the trade, as it were, in the sale of fruit and vegetables. The bad fruit was never thrown away, as she took it home, peeled and cut out the bad or over-ripe pieces, and made a fresh fruit salad for her aged mother and father and herself. Nuts were seasonal in those days and only sold at Christmas time, so those that were unsold would be stored and mixed with the next year's nuts. Most of the stored nuts would go bad, but, by combining them with the following year's, people didn't realise. In those days, grapes came in barrels with small cork chippings to keep them fresh and to stop them from bruising. They were far more expensive than today.

Disability in its Most Cruel Form

One day, while standing at the stall, I had the shock of my life when I saw something move under a market stall just opposite. I went over and saw it was a legless man with - of all terrible tragedies - two blocks of wood for hands so that they did not get sore and so that he could just about manoeuvre himself. His lower body was protected with - would you believe - part of a rubber car tyre so that he could just about push and shuffle his poor body along. It was so sad to see such a very severe disability.

After eating what I think was an apple, he shuffled off and disappeared into the crowds. The memory of his distress and his sad helplessness stayed with me for many, many years afterwards. I still remember him now, and it guides me to try my very best to do helpful things for other people and especially for those disabled.

I was, on one occasion, trying my hardest to buy my mother a suitable birthday present, and saw a lovely, fancy shopping bag in a shop near the top of our street. I ordered this bag and told the owner I would call and pick it up on a Saturday evening on my way home from the market. I also purchased some flowers, a large bunch of big chrysanthemums, which she loved, and a box of chocolates as well. I think my stepfather was upset at the display of love I showed to her, as she was delighted with them all. It was just a small appreciation of my fond love for her. When I look back, the shopping bag was nowhere near suitable for her, as it would not have been big enough and was far too fancy for my mother's taste.

While I was doing well at the age of twelve with my work on the Saturday market, I still felt that I needed more chances of earning some additional money, and found a part-time job in a wholesale grocer's. After all, I was growing up fast then, and it was necessary for me to increase my income. I could go to this job after I had finished school in the afternoons, and I worked from Mondays to Fridays.

I found the new work at the wholesale grocer's boring until I happened to watch the butcher boning hams that needed cooking. He knew I was interested in how this was carried out so skilfully, and he showed me how to do it. I wanted to learn as there was so much involved in this process. Also, lard that could be rendered down from the hams being cooked correctly. This subsequently became an additional income as I could sell this to our neighbours.

I also needed money because I had started smoking, which I found obviously costly. I liked to have a milkshake now and then and some nut cluster toffee, and to use a decent fountain pen to write with. Very soon, I became an unofficial assistant to the local butcher, and could bone a ham as quickly as he could. I did, however, have a few accidents cutting my fingers, but, eventually, learned to keep them out of the way. If Health and Safety laws had been around in those days, all of my work experiences would have been banned, and I am sure the company nowadays would have been fined.

Doing the work like I did was right for me, but, sadly, with all the rules and regulations there are today, I doubt whether the opportunities are available now to children as young as eleven or twelve. I am sure it did me a lot of good, and it also inspired me later in life. Looking back, I believe it was an education that was very beneficial to me and my future career, and that it would be helpful for many children to have a similar stimulus today. Of course, this would hopefully not be as desperate as my particular situation then was!

Dreams and Aspirations Faded

While I was overjoyed at first at passing my eleven-plus, the dream very quickly faded. The thought of being in the house whilst my dreaded stepfather continued to stop me from studying and from doing my homework was so frustrating. I just wanted to get out of his way, so I arranged to join at first the Boy Scouts, which allowed me the chance to get away from him for two weeks on holiday in Wales at minimal cost. Later, I transferred to the Sea Cadets, which also allowed me to be out of his way and gave me some peaceful respite from his continuing cruelty. While the reasons may have been right, when I reflect back on this, I still should have tried harder myself at school studies, especially with homework, as I could certainly have done better. The trouble is, you are given your chances in life and have to be aware and recognise that this is a golden opportunity at the time. You must persevere and make the best of it.

One of my worst experiences was having to go to the school dentist. I could not remember going to a dentist before, and did not know what to expect. He decided to take out one of my back teeth, with me being unaware of how he was going to set about doing it. He gave me an injection, and in his haste started to pull the tooth out too soon. The injection had not taken effect, and the pain was so excruciating, and alarming that I lashed out, but he quickly rebuffed my attempts to escape the unbearable pain. He then pushed me back in the chair, eventually pulling the tooth out with such great force and pressure and an agonising jerk. It was so screamingly painful!

That episode stopped me from going to any dentists at all for many years. If I had a bad tooth, I would just crush an aspirin into the root to stop it hurting until it finally killed the nerve. Eventually, I had to go to a dentist to have these teeth taken out, and I was informed that private dentists would do this and give you a pain-free gas instead, and it would be paid for under the NHS. This, at the time, seemed a far better way to me, as they did it under the NHS and neither my mother nor I had to pay.

My Father's Severe Eyesight Problems

When only 38 years of age my father was sent to the famous Radcliffe Infirmary, Oxford, since he had suffered from deteriorating eyesight for several years. He then also became ill with thrombosis, and sadly went blind relatively young. He was eventually admitted to a nursing home in Leytonstone. My father had suffered all his life with bronchial problems, made worse by a short but damaging spell in the army before he was discharged due to bad health. Life for me continued to be still difficult at home, and it got me down because my father was suffering, and there was little I could do at my age to help him.

1953

I visited my father in Oxford one weekend. As before, he was in the famous Radcliffe Infirmary, and was, I believe, very depressed about his fast failing eyesight. I had to stay in student lodgings as it was the summer holidays. This was in a large house, and it was a shambles. The furniture was deplorable. The only good thing about it was it had been arranged for me to have my breakfast in a house just across the road. This arrangement turned out to be great. The people there were not only highly intelligent and kind, making me feel very welcome and comfortable, but the breakfast was excellent. I can remember also having a simply enormous cup of tea too which they had kindly made for me.

I always had, for many years, significant difficulty in being able to travel the considerable distance to get to see my father, as he lived a fairly long journey away and you could not get to it very quickly, so my mother had to rely on her friends, who would take me periodically to see him. The cost of travel was too much for her to be able to provide, as much as she wanted to. Of course, I also wished to write to him as well. It was not very satisfactory, but now I am older, and, I hope, wiser, I realise that I should have asked the authorities that he be moved to live nearer to me so I could have visited him on a more regular basis. I am sure we would and could have had an even closer and more supportive relationship. Now, I often ask myself, 'Why didn't someone help me and advise me at that critical time in my young life?' I shall never understand and always much regret our lack of sufficient contact. I loved my father, and, despite his severe illness, he cared deeply for both my mother and me all his life. Each time he saw me, he asked how she was. It was all very, very sad. I do not think he ever got over their separation.

At one stage in my life, I was able to visit my father on a small number of occasions. One particular time, he had been taken from the residential home where he lived in Leytonstone to Whitechapel Hospital, and was in an oxygen tent. They used in those days such contraptions to hold the oxygen in the air around the patient's face and body to ease breathing and chest infections.

I sat there all weekend in an armchair beside him, with hardly anything at all to eat, and then came home on the Sunday afternoon on the train. I was all on my own, and at that time was reluctant to ask for anything for myself. A nurse eventually kindly brought me a sandwich, which was so thoughtful of her. However, my father recovered enough to later go back to his former nursing home.

1954
What I had Tried to Achieve at Grammar School

I tried my best, or so I thought, at grammar school, but still had my great ups and downs. One day I ended up having a big fight in the park after school. A large number of pupils gathered to watch, and, at one stage, I seemed to be winning when I landed a punch that hit the side of the opponent's head. Bones in my hand were broken with the strength of this blow, and the fight ended with both of us seeing the damage that had been done. I still have a bone that is badly bent in my right hand.

I was too frightened to tell my mother what had happened, and slept with this painful broken hand all night. It was so painful it woke me up in the night when I moved around in my sleep. In the morning, I knew I had to go to the hospital, and I went on my own. They asked how I had managed to do it, and I said I had hit a wall. They quickly replied that if I had there would have been grazing visible. After having an x-ray, they said it needed it to be reset. Then they had to contact my mother, who was still working at the bakery near the hospital, as they needed her signature before they gave me gas. I managed to recover and go to school late. I was glad it had been reset, as it had been excruciating during the previous night. A couple of weeks later, when I returned to the hospital, I was told off because school friends had signed my plaster and I had got it wet, and so the nurses had to strengthen it. My mother found a cover that she could place over it to keep it dry and clean.

1956

I remember visiting my father (now blind) one day there when drainpipe trousers were the fashion. He was very perceptive. He asked me if I was wearing them. As I didn't answer, he felt the bottom of my trousers with his finger tips and told me of his disgust at me wearing such sorts of trousers. Besides that, he did not realise that I did not earn enough money in those days to even keep myself and pay some part for my board to my mother.

She had kindly paid for me to go and see him by again asking a friend to take me there by car.

Mrs Walker – An Angel

While my father was in this home for incurables at Leytonstone, a dear, sweet elderly lady, a Mrs Walker, was admitted. She was partially blind herself, and became so friendly and devoted to my father, whom she then called her 'son'. When I went to visit, she would arrange for me to have tea and cakes with her. She genuinely loved my father, and came from a devoted Quaker family. Before my father actually died, she gave me her husband's copy of a book her husband, an author himself, had cleverly written. It was called 'Death Flies High', and she also gave me a poem he had written, 'The Unfailing Friend', both of which I still cherish. It was as if the Lord had placed an angel there to care for my father, and that gave me an enormous amount of comfort, knowing how kind she was and that she had been there for my father before and, most importantly, right up until the very end, and beyond, when he died.

MY LIFE IS MY WORD

The minister used to come and visit them both, and Mrs Walker was pleased that my father took part in the small service they all held together. She really loved him as one of her own. Mrs Walker was also unable to care entirely for herself, but made sure that she did so much always for Dad. She also wrote little letters to me as well as she could. One of the things she told me was this. When the local vicar came in to give a small service for them, he kindly whispered to my father, 'Len, you do suffer, don't you?'

My father bravely replied, 'Not so much as Christ did on the Cross.'

When I look back, I realise just how selfish I must have been then, but, I am sad to say, that when I visited my father on the odd occasion he did not seem as pleased to see me as I would have expected him to be. Now, I realise that he was depressed since I could only visit him occasionally because I lived so far away from his nursing home.

However, now that I am older, I much regret all that I could then have done for him, and didn't. My father had now become totally blind. In this home, they kept him mostly in his bed in a single room, for some reason. It might have been perhaps because he was too much of a danger walking around on his own.

1957
GCE Disaster

Whilst waiting for my GCE results, which I dreaded as I knew I had not done well, and since my name was not in the list published in the local newspaper, I realised that and I assumed I had not passed any subjects. To this day I do not know how I really did, although the results would still be available. After leaving school that summer, I took on a job as a rose budder, but found that it was back-breaking work. To add salt to the wound, it was in the midst of one of the hottest summers for years. If it wasn't your back aching, it was your fingers, having to tie the rose buds to the briars with rafia. It has now all been simplified with preformed plastic self-adhesive type wraps that are much easier and better to put on; also, they stop the rain getting into the plant. In addition to this, at the time you were always thirsty because of the summer heat and had to drink plenty of water, or, when you could afford it as a treat, some lemonade.

I stuck the job itself despite the pain in my hands and also in my back for six weeks. These were possibly the hottest six weeks of that year, and then I had an interview for a job as a salesman at an outfitters in Peterborough and started work there. It was a tedious, pitiful job of having to put clothes such as socks, shirts and pullovers in the correct order in the stock room. I helped to unpack new stock, put it away, and dusted down the shelves. I apparently was not the person that fitted their expectations because I could see the silliness in the way the other two senior salesmen behaved. They were so childish. It wasn't long before I was sacked from the Fifty Shilling Tailors, and, believe or not, it was because I wore one of their own suits which had drainpipe trousers! They did not think it suitable for me to wear these as a salesman. Mind you, I suppose they were right, but they didn't know that I didn't have anything else appropriate I could possibly wear, but I could not tell them that as I did have some pride.

After having been sacked by my previous employer, I then resorted to becoming an apprentice turner at Peter Brotherhoods, where some of my ex-school friends also worked. Some of my friends from the sea cadets were employed in apprenticeships with the same company. I was set on to work, and my pay was two pounds, sixteen shillings and ninepence per week! It was pitiful, and I had to cycle four miles there and back every day in the cold, rain, and hot sun. I suppose the exercise was good for me, and I was able to give my mother some board money to help her.

My attempts at working a lathe were not very successful, but I tried and joined my friends on the day release so I could start my apprenticeship in the right way. I carried on with my apprenticeship, trying to do my best, but I wasn't perfect and needed help many times. However, the lathes (called Herbert No 7) were old and not easy to do intricate work with. Still, with what happened within the next few months, I was very soon to have to terminate my apprenticeship.

When it came to public holidays, my friends and I would go camping at the Ferry Bridge or near the Staunch lock at Peterborough. I was so glad, as I could get away from my stepfather. My mother by this time had begun to realise the terrible effect my stepfather was still having on me and she provided plenty of food to take with me, and a couple of pounds if I needed it. We went in the summertime and had a good time; the river was always pleasant to be beside, and sometimes we went fishing as well. It mostly was an enjoyable, relaxing few days, and I had escaped the wrath of my stepfather. Looking back, I really do not know how I managed to cope with my dread of his beatings, even though they had now ceased since my threat of what I would do if ever my stepfather beat me again. However his anger and lashing tongue still put me on edge whenever I was in his presence.

1958
Stepfather Dies Suddenly

It was September 1957, I believe the third Sunday of the month. My stepfather had left early that morning to go to a big fishing match. He had been appointed as an official steward. Strangely, when he left the house that particular day, before closing the front door, he appeared to turn and smile at me. My mother was expecting him home for his dinner at mid-day, but, as he did not turn up, we ate ours first, and then waited for him. About an hour later there was a heavy knock on the door, and there stood two police officers, who asked if they could come in. I led them to the room where my mother was sitting wondering and worrying what had happened.

My mother, startled by them, stood up and asked what the matter was, and she looked extremely nervous and agitated. She then quietly asked, 'Has he been taken ill? Let me go to him.'

They asked her to sit down in her chair and said they had some news about her husband. She immediately said,

'Is he ill? I can get his tablets now and take them and go to him.'

They replied that he had died suddenly and could not be resuscitated. My mother instantly collapsed into her chair, her face so ashen, and then she began crying incessantly. My stepfather's mother, also sitting there, suffered similarly and started weeping.

I ran out of the house to my next door neighbour and then up the street to a distant cousin on my stepfather's side to tell them all what had happened, and asked if he would run me in his car to my grandmother's house so I could fetch her to comfort my mother. He did, and we took my grandmother back with us to my mother so that she could look after Mother and be there to comfort her and be with her. A doctor was called, and he prescribed some tablets and did his best to help my mother get over the sudden and terrible shock she had suffered.

My stepfather had died suddenly at age 46 from a heart attack while taking part as a steward in a fishing match. He had been suffering from Angina for some time, and, because of his heart condition, he had been stopped from moving sacks of potatoes or doing any lifting at all when at work. It is strange, because away from our house, my stepfather seemed to be a different person. He was well-known and well-liked by most of

MY LIFE IS MY WORD

those people who knew him from his pastime activities and from his work.

He and my mother regularly played darts and dominoes in a variety of public houses and, apparently, they drank but not ever to excess. After all, my stepfather was the warehouse manager and in charge of the lorry drivers. Because he was so well-known and his death was so sudden, the evening newspaper printed an obituary about his life.

After an autopsy had been performed on him, my mother continued to be distraught. She wanted his body to be brought home and placed in the front room to be viewed by people who wished to pay their respects. It seemed that this was the custom in those days. We had many visitors over the next few days, and my mother arranged for the Co-op to be the undertakers. There was no expense spared for his funeral. My mother was in a vulnerable position, and was only extravagant due to the fact that some insurance policies they had were then maturing.

Because an autopsy had been carried out, time had now elapsed, and his body began to smell, and the resulting odour (which was the distinct smell of death) was one of the worst you can experience. I went to the pharmacist to see if he could tell us what to use, and he suggested a saucer of vinegar be placed under the coffin. This did alleviate it so that it was bearable. After the funeral, my mother had the room fumigated as this smell still lingered unpleasantly.

On the day of the funeral, wreaths were being brought to the door every few minutes from various florists, and they ended up being laid out on the pavement and all along the hall until the funeral cars arrived. Because he was so well-known, there were over fifty wreaths at his funeral, and it seemed like as many cars again that followed in the cortege. The police who knew him too had placed *no waiting* signs up to the street as they wanted to allow plenty of space for the funeral cortege. The police realised that this would be a big funeral and did their best to help in this matter. After all, my mother was only 38 years old, very young to face widowhood, and she needed a lot of help and assistance. She was in a daze with shock, and felt deep sorrow and complete disbelief at what had happened.

Afterwards, my mother reflected on the cost of the funeral and realised that she had spent too much money. It was very easy in those days to get carried away after the loss of a loved one. She had ordered a marble headstone for him as well. It was fortunate that they also had some savings available, in addition to the insurance policies.

After the death of my stepfather, although my mother had plenty of potential suitors, she was still in shock and needed time to grieve. The bills also had to be paid to maintain the house, and, in effect, she was subsidising me somewhat, too. In those days, there was very little support for people in a situation like my mother's. She had worked ever since she was old enough to earn a living, and my mother was used to that. Therefore, there was very little that she could do at this time to assist me in visiting my father.

With my mother so distraught, it began to affect me too, and I became seriously ill and shocked at all the sad events that seemed to be happening. I was also very depressed about the words that I had shouted at my mother in a temper some months earlier. I had said, 'My stepfather John will die before my own father'. Two weeks earlier, my mother had said to me that my own father was dying and would not get better and I had then just retaliated at her.

My mother suffered an additional problem in that neither of them had made wills, and the stepfather's estate had to go through Probate so that everything could be done that was legally required.

Many times my mother advised everyone she knew to make a will, as she did not want them to have to go through all the financial problems she had herself suffered when she could not access the money needed.

Years later, when my mother married again, and I then had a second step-father, she told my wife that they had each made a will and that it had been placed on deposit in a deed box at her bank with other vital documents. That is why it seemed so strange, years later when Mother herself died, that no will was found. In fact, even if she had not left me anything, I could not believe that she would forget her own two grandchildren, whom she loved so much.

1958
Serious Mental Breakdown

At sixteen, I had finished school and wanted so badly to earn a living. My search for a suitable job was not at the beginning successful, nor was it appropriate. What hampered me was that I did not seem to have any energy. Although we had lived well when at home and had at that time wholesome and tasty food, my body weight was at that time really deficient. This was partly my own fault, since while at school I had spent my dinner money on cigarettes instead of food and had gone without my school dinners for a couple of years, which had a damaging and lasting effect on me. Mind you, I had tried to make up for it when I came home by eating much more, but that didn't seem to work. I had only left school some months earlier, and my appetite was not sufficient to make up for all the meals and nourishment I had gone without. I was not keen to exercise apart from cycling to and from work, and creeping depression took its toll on me.

I felt this getting worse, and fell into a deeper depression, which made me feel helpless. This was due to the situation I was in. A sombre atmosphere pervaded the whole house. While, of course, I was glad in one sense that I no longer had to contend with my overpowering stepfather, I was also at that time anxious about my mother's precarious health. I had, in fact, in my mind replaced him with another fear about my mother and her own fairly fragile health. Because of the antagonistic nature of my previous long, acidic relationship with my cruel, abusive stepfather, my mother, who still adored him, had found it difficult to confide in me, or even want to talk to me at that particular time.

Clearly remembering what I had said earlier to her about my stepfather - that he would die before my own father - and possibly resenting me for saying it at that particular time, she perhaps didn't realise that I had only retaliated because she somehow seemed to know that my own father did not himself have long to live. I knew there had been more than considerable friction in my relationship with my stepfather, but I do not consider that it was ever my fault, although I was then beginning to think that it might have been.

This attitude my mother had did not help me, especially at this time when I was depressed and suffering from an actual nervous breakdown. I visited my doctor to tell him about how I felt but he asked so many confusing questions, suggesting that I should see a psychiatrist. With my mother, I went to the psychiatrist the very next week at Peterborough Hospital. After asking me many more questions, then examining me, he suggested to us that I should be admitted immediately to the psychiatric wing of a particular mental hospital in Lincolnshire, Raueby Mental Hospital, formerly used as an asylum.

Serious Situation

Little did I realise that I was to be subjected when there to experimental LSD treatment so quickly, and the terrible effects this would have on my health for the rest of my life.

One advantage, however, was that it was not far away from where we lived. This hospital had a separate, self-contained psychiatric unit where the psychiatrist said he believed they would be able to help me. Within a matter of days, I was taken there by my mother and her co-worker in the company's Land Rover. They dropped me off at the psychiatric unit itself, and then drove off. My mother, crying her eyes out, looked from the car window back at my lonely figure standing there.

At that time in my life I did not feel like talking to anyone at all. After being shown where my bed and clothes cupboard was and the ward I was to sleep in, I sat in the lounge on my own. I was a very quiet, subdued, and also very lonely figure without anyone to talk to or with whom to commiserate. I could recall my grandmother in the past had said, 'Oh! men in white coats came and took one of our neighbours to Rauceby Mental Hospital.' That was the same hospital complex in which I now regrettably found myself. The separate psychiatric wing was housed in a small number of somewhat oppressive buildings. There were only places here for about 50-60 patients. The building was split into two, with different sections for male and female patients waiting to be treated. I believe it had nearly 500 patients in the main wing. The majority of these, I was led to believe, were ill from the effects of various wartime experiences they had suffered, and those born with defects at birth who also needed permanent nursing.

Although we had lived well in the past when at home and I had good food, I was now very underweight indeed, and had very little energy. Apparently, this continuous under-eating had harmed my health, and the effect was not helped by the very exhausting, tedious physical work I had to do when I first left school. I was working hard in a rose garden under a blistering summer heat and perspiring a great deal. This, later coupled with the many miles of cycling each day while working as an apprentice, added to my feelings of tiredness. After leaving school, my appetite was very poor, and this meant I was already thin and undernourished, which the staff had later noticed at the hospital. In addition to this, the emotional turmoil of my present situation had increased my suffering to a great extent.

After noting that I was not eating much, the male head nurse spoke to the doctor, and I was put on a course of insulin injections. This would be in addition to having the LSD treatment which I had just been prescribed and then told, without any warning after a session of group therapy, that I would receive that afternoon.

I was asked to attend sessions of group therapy. This is where topics were discussed that any of the patients could introduce for others to review. I later found out from these meetings that, dependent on what was being considered by some patients, they would then be chosen for special treatment. One person, who admitted to being a homosexual, was castigated by me, and as a result, I was the one who was selected for early treatment.

The insulin certainly gave you an appetite, and within days, I became hungry enough to begin eating the food that had been prepared for all our meals. In fact, after two or three weeks on this insulin, my appetite had improved so much that I started putting on weight. I noticed this when we were routinely weighed each week. I began to eat a more varied diet, and I realised my health was improving.

At this point, it is relevant to note that homosexuality was not made legal until 1967. It was 1958 when I was in the hospital, and although people were all too well aware of what was going on in the outside world, many people's attitudes were not necessarily in favour. Besides that, I was a Christian and, although not practising then, I still prayed to God, and had a background of grammar school religious indoctrination, which told us that such practices were considered at that time to be wrong. Consequently, the law stipulated that homosexuality was illegal.

It was only a matter of the very next day, possibly because of my expressed views, and after this incident of my opinions at that time being revealed, I was told to change into my pyjamas and be in a bed in the treatment room at about 2 pm. I did this, and a doctor came in and told me he was going to inject me with a drug that would make me feel more relaxed. This injection was carried out, and he said he would be back in half an hour to see me again. A male nurse watched over me during this interval of time, possibly thinking that, if the drug adversely affected me, medical aid could be quickly summoned.

LSD - NHS Experimental Abreaction Treatment

This experimental drug that I had been given at the hospital was by injection into my arm. Appalled, later in my life I was to find out just how dangerous this had been and would be for me, and how it caused me consequently to become an epileptic, suffering from serious fits. I believe that it had almost been fatal for me. It was LSD Lysergic Diathalmide, and, believe it or not, although I was then seventeen years of age, I can clearly remember the name of the drug as I saw the phials with its printed label when the drug was administered . I was totally unaware I was being experimented on at the time of these injections. Little did I realise what damage this drug could do to me, nor the long-term effects it would have on the rest of my life and on my subsequent health. Come to that, I do not think the doctors knew themselves the full extent of the damage that it could well cause to their patients. Papers had been written previously about its effects, but were the medical profession aware of this? Who had given permission in law for untested drugs to be used on me, as I was 17 and a minor? Finally, had my mother allowed this? I doubt it very much. If not, who had given permission for it?

During the next half an hour, the drug relaxed me, and had the effect of making me feel happy and good about myself. During that time, a male nurse watched over me. The doctor then came and sat down and started asking me questions about my past life. He didn't have to ask, really, because the drug made me so eager to tell him about everything that I had been through - both the good and the bad. It just spilled out and flowed from my lips. The LSD made you feel as though you could remember every single tiniest thing, however far back! For example, this is when I could remember memories back to very early baby years, and childhood, such as the wartime and the planes flying overhead to bomb London.

I could, due to the effects of LSD, recall the instances where, as a baby, I had been taken to an air raid shelter even though I was very young. Then, later, the unwarranted beatings I received as a young child were also painfully and vivedly recalled. Still, there had also been the shock of the final row between my parents and the items on the table being thrown at the wall in our dining room. This particular and memorable occasion was probably, I had realised, the result of my mother's very serious indiscretion with my father's former best friend, which had led to my own parents' separating permanently, and later divorcing.

Most of the issues that I have described or will be included I can still recall quite vividly due to the lasting effects on my memory of LSD injections. The ferocity of the action and impact this particular drug has on your brain differs between each individual. For this reason, it cannot be classed as 'safe' to use in any way. It varies according to the extent of the terrifying moments a person has endured during his or her lifetime. The effects differ from one person to another to such an extent that no one can predict the final outcome. Even the fact that each person has possibly been damaged so powerfully by such harmful drugs. This could have a lasting effect on the remainder of each person's whole life being under the influence of such a dangerous drug.

After being given LSD injections, one would lie awake for long periods, e.g. from two in the afternoon one day until at least the morning of the following day. I think this went on for at very least many hours, during which time I was provided with orange juice to drink as and when needed. You still wanted to talk and talk incessantly as an irresistible force took over your mind.

The doctor then asked me to write down on paper anything else I wanted to say. I did this throughout the night, and wrote pages and pages of rubbish without ever feeling exhausted by the effort. The drug kept me awake all night until the following morning. When I got up, I felt drained and wanted my breakfast. After that, we were told to stay awake all during the day as, if not, none of us would sleep that following night. After such treatments, I suffered from a fresh and severe bout of depression, because I was psychologically and physically drained.

Another person in the group had an experience where he said he did not want to be born and, when he checked later by asking his mother about his own birth, he found out she had experienced a very complicated birth indeed. He, coincidentally, was the homosexual in the group.

LSD had a depressive effect on most of us. By the late morning, we would all feel exhausted and very low in spirit from this mentally draining experience. This was made much worse because the drug kept us wide awake for more than 24 hours. We then sat about in the lounge for another 12 hours until bedtime, when sleep would overtake us. At weekends, we were then allowed to go home, but not for the first two weeks of this treatment. There was one patient who, when he had his treatment, had been provided with an extensive range of artists' coloured chalks which he, as a skilled artist, used to explore his ingenuity in creating psychedelic pictures.

When I was allowed to go home, I had first to catch a train from Sleaford to Grantham with a group of patients from the hospital, then buy tickets for the Pullman, which was sometimes The Flying Scotsman to Peterborough. This was a fantastic experience, since it was a majestic train and, as it drew into the station, you could see people being served by waiters in smart uniforms in the Pullman coach section. The railway waiters were serving meals to these wealthy passengers. It was the epitome of luxury, and looked to me a delicious dinner.

In those days, it was a remarkably quick and reliable journey, about 45 minutes from that station to London. (It still takes about the same time nowadays all those years later!) Once arriving at Peterborough North LNER, I had a short walk to my mother's home.

After I had been away at the hospital for about three weeks in all, I found she was still behaving as though very shocked and depressed, and had been prescribed some sleeping tablets by the doctor. She very quickly informed me that my stepfather's mother had been dispatched to live then with another son, who kept a newspaper shop, as my mother considered it was their time now to look after their own mother. I believe she had had some sort of confrontation with her mother-in-law and, after the sudden death of my stepfather, she probably felt she had enough to contend with herself.

Ironically, the only one poor chicken we had left, who had the freedom of all the garden, had died. It must have been many years old, and for that reason, it was kept on as a pet and had the privilege of the full run of the backyard.

My mother suffered a bout of deep depression from her shock of her husband's death, but eventually went back to work after three months at home as there were no further benefits available in those days. I was relieved, but also suffered guilt and sadness. While I was now at last free of my stepfather, his jealousy, his cruelty and his criticisms lingered strongly in my mind. Nevertheless, I felt it was my fault that he had died, and this, I now realise, was ridiculous. My mother was still so sad and depressed, and it all got on top of me. However, going back to work helped my mother decide whom she wanted to work for, and she changed her job to becoming the restaurant manageress of a local company, Perkin's Diesel, after being given a tip-off about the existence of the situation from a helpful neighbour. This person managed that particular office, which conveniently was in walking distance for my mother, too. He and his wife knew her well, and realised what a hard-working woman she was, and so she was quickly engaged.

My mother could not face going back to the original potato company where she had worked so closely alongside my stepfather. Understandably, she, bless her, wanted a new start with different people.

This change of job turned out to be good for her. The depression slowly but clearly subsided, and she became more able to cope with all that she had suffered. The new position was right for her, too, and she quickly showed how capable she was, and became much happier. My mother was a compelling character and promptly mastered control of the suppliers to ensure the best of food and service for this new company.

I recall, in my younger days, my mother had once found an elastic band hidden inside a chocolate whirl. With sweets at that time still rationed, she was so incensed that she wrote a letter and sent the sweet back to the manufacturers with her written explanation. Questioning their quality control system, she found, in about a week, a large box of assorted toffees and chocolates was delivered with a letter of apology to her. This expressed the company's regrets to her, and their hopes that the accompanying replacements would be acceptable.

With this sort of success, it has impressed on me, wherever justified, to voice my own complaints in the future, and seek retribution and compensation. To date, I think I have achieved well over three thousand pounds in reimbursement for problems my family or I have suffered. I would urge everyone to make sure that they do the same should they find difficulties with goods received, or companies' services that justify complaints.

Many years later, I was to find that, I had been - without my permission, nor that of my mother, and at the age of seventeen - injected with an experimental, vicious drug, LSD, for 'Abreaction Treatment'. After my first treatment, I was soon allowed to go home for Christmas, and it had been arranged that I should spend this at my Uncle Roy's and with his family at Leicester. Sadly, while there, I had a severe attack, later diagnosed as an epileptic fit, which was terrible and frightened all present, especially his children. Later, I learned that this must have been the severe form of seizure.

EFFECTS OF LSD

After this seizure attack, I was physically and mentally drained and lethargic. It had utterly exhausted me and, even though conscious afterwards, I was shaken, could not walk at all steadily or well. When I had recovered somewhat, it was arranged for me to go to stay at my Aunt Doll's (one of my mother's wisest and kindest sisters). Fortunately, at the time, my grandmother was staying with her. They all thought together that I should be living in more quiet surroundings than those in which I was then. I was very weak after this particular attack, and glad to be with my grandmother, who was always reassuring and loving towards me. This was precisely just what I needed. The seizure had obviously deeply upset my uncle's family too, and they had sought advice from my grandmother as to what to do. Upon arriving at Aunt Doll's, my grandmother quickly reassured me with her usual kindly, tender kiss. As she wrapped her arms around me, giving me a loving embrace, I started to feel that I would eventually be alright again.

As it was the first seizure I had ever experienced in my life, not only did I not know what was going on but I was afraid that I would not be able to be allowed to work afterwards. Sadly, I was well aware that I had always wanted to choose an interesting and exciting career for myself. Once, indeed, a recruitment officer had uncaringly told me that as a disabled person I would be only able to live on benefits for the remainder of my life. This, of course, generated in me a terrible feeling of helplessness. So, I think my attitude toward work became rapidly even more focused than ever before, and I inwardly determined to get myself better.

1958-59 ANOTHER SETBACK -
Seizure Attack
NHS

Upon my return from the Christmas holidays to the mental hospital, I told them about the particular attack that I had suffered, but they did not think it serious enough to investigate, and this, as I much later in my life learned, was only an experimental drug given at that particular time. After this LSD and more treatments, I now firmly believe I had suffered what was later diagnosed as epilepsy, but this attack was completely and perhaps deliberately ignored by the hospital, and they continued to give me further treatments of LSD injections regularly for the rest of the time I was hospitalised there in November 1957 until April 1958.

I would have thought that, if this were an experimental drug, the details of my experience would have been reported and carefully collated, along with those of any other person who had similarly suffered adverse effects, or who had been ill after LSD injections.

I had about seven or eight LSD treatments at least, and the last one was really horrific. I was later led to believe that people hurried to my side, frantic to assist me in recovering from it. Other patients told me the next morning that there had been indeed a lot of shouting and running around as the doctor needed urgent assistance from other medics in bringing me around again. I know it was different from other attacks, as I can remember something horrible happening to me and then a total blackness. Finally, I was waking up the next morning, feeling as though I had had a good night's sleep. Could it be that I had gone into a catatonic state at that time? Or, could it be I had suffered another epileptic grand mal seizure, which I now believe was created by the LSD treatment?

A grand mal seizure is very sudden severe loss of consciousness and violent muscle contractions. It's the type of seizure most people picture when they think about seizures. A grand mal seizure - is caused by abnormal electrical activity throughout the brain.

I must have been given something else to reduce the effects that this last treatment was having on me, so the question is - what had happened at that time, and what happened as a consequence?

Abreaction Treatment, as it was known, could, with help from a doctor, allow your deepest thoughts and vague memories of your early life to come to light. This would theoretically result in a fast and free off-loading of situations and experiences you had suffered. You cannot stop talking, so you are garrulous, virtually unstoppable, and you relive incidents that you had long, long forgotten but which had impacted in a serious way on you and your brain. It is supposed to produce a cathartic, soothing effect on your life experiences. Some of these could help the doctor in resolving whatever problems you have or had. However well-meaning the medical profession may be, I still recalled what I had suffered as I could not ever forget it, nor the abuse I had experienced.

This is a resume of what the intentions of LSD treatment was supposed to do.

'Abreaction Therapy focuses on reliving a traumatic event and going through the emotions associated with them to heal and move the whole of the patient's outlook forward. Initially created by Sigmund Freud, the method gives patients a way to release their unconscious pain and escape from the memories and feelings that have kept them from moving forward.

Freud's initial belief in promoting abreaction in therapy was that, through the release of the painful emotions, the traumatic experience itself would be dealt with. The problem is, abreaction, in this case, *the expressing of emotions,* by itself does not cure anything.'

I cannot verify this, but it would not surprise me to learn that the method of administering the LSD dose was gradually increased by the hospital with each treatment, as we noted that the after effects lasted longer each time, and afterwards you felt even weaker, more lifeless and more depressed as a result. It was just as though you had experienced a grand mal epileptic seizure, which I now believe I suffered during my last treatment at that hospital.

Many people who have a grand mal seizure never have another one and don't need treatment. But someone who has recurrent seizures may require therapy with daily anti-seizure medications to control and prevent future grand mal seizures.

The following signs and symptoms occur in some but not all people with grand mal seizures:

A scream. Some people may cry out at the beginning of a seizure.

Loss of bowel and bladder control. This may happen during or following a seizure.

Unresponsiveness after convulsions. Unconsciousness may persist for several minutes after the convulsion has ended.

Confusion. A period of disorientation often follows a grand mal seizure. This is referred to as 'postictal confusion'.

Severe headache. Headaches may occur after a grand mal seizure. These can be very painful.

It is a terrible experience; firstly, two people have to help me to stand, and then I rest all day. Knowing all this, I feel thankful that I am now living a normal life again at long last.

Sadly, I believe that repeated treatments of LSD caused permanent brain damage that turned me into an epileptic.

NHS and Mental Health Treatments

The usage of LSD, Insulin, ECT (Electro Convulsive Therapy), Leukotomy and DVS and VNS, plus many others, make you wonder how this happened when there seems to be so many controls and testing that has to be done before new drugs for physical illnesses can be classed as safe for us. Patients suffering from mental breakdowns seem to be treated in an entirely different manner. It is almost as though psychiatric patients are expendable, and their human rights appear to be ignored, as is the safety of the drug or treatment which is being administered.

I had endured at a very young age a terrible life, in which I had largely felt that I was not wanted. My mother was not there in my early years when I needed her most, and, when I did have her again, she had a man hovering over her and me who was always jealous and possessive and violent, and I had to deal with his demands.

After my first LSD treatment, I became a little more relaxed, as I had become withdrawn from socialising with others. I now felt more at ease and conversed with some of the other patients. Many of them talked about their own particular problems concerning health and family issues mainly, and one was a man who spoke to me about his work as an AA driver. He told me of the terrible and heart-breaking accidents he had been called to where, for example, he witnessed the headless body of a motorcyclist found at one end of the damaged lorry and his actual head impaled on the rear end axle. He said it was horrific, and explained that seeing such motor accidents had finally taken its toll on his own now - very fragile mental health.

Another person suffered from alopecia. This is a condition where a person's hair falls out in clumps, and often follows the loss of a dearly loved person. Sometimes this is caused by severe depression, or shock or profound grief. Many others told us how life had got them down so much that they had attempted suicide. A couple of students were there as it was possible they were not reaching the expectations held by their parents, or studying was becoming much too difficult for them to cope with.

The physiatric unit that I resided in had a lounge where both male and female patients mixed in the evenings socially, and this was for me a fantastic opportunity to get to know a very pretty young girl of about 16 years old. A male nurse was always in attendance, and I suppose he could see that a physical attraction was developing, and we were then closely monitored.

It was terrific for me to be the centre of her attention, but possibly naive of me as to why she was attracted to me as I had no experience of women at this time in my life. I did not consider myself as handsome or attractive in any way and had a low opinion of myself.

Later, I learned that she was exceptionally sexually advanced for her age. Her desires were proactive, and that same night, after saying goodnight to me, she escaped from the hospital unit and was later found in a compromising situation with a lorry driver who at the time did not realise that she was only sixteen. She had nymphomaniac tendencies, and had needed sexual gratification, which it appeared she had been used to receiving from a much earlier age in her life, and that was why she was placed in this particular unit. When she was found with this lorry driver, she was transferred to a more secure unit for treatment and help.

Nearly 40 years later it was revealed that LSD had been administered to over 4000 mental patients who were not warned, nor told in advance, of its potency. The ones who took legal action subsequently were people who found out in the newspapers about the practices that had been used on mental patients and soldiers (without their consent) at Porton Down

Research in the UK. Many psychiatric patients were affected adversely by this treatment, and the effects had lasted for many years and possibly for their whole lifetimes. The accuracy of these facts can be verified by:

BBC NEWS CHANNEL 24 FEBRUARY 2006
MI6 payouts over secret LSD tests
You will see below the quote from BBC regarding this very worrying use of LSD on UK servicemen.

Porton Down Case

A 'volunteers' programme' started at Porton Down (originally) in 1916. Much, much later, three UK ex-servicemen have been given compensation after they were given LSD without their consent in the 1950s. The men originally volunteered to be 'guinea pigs' at the government research base, Porton Down, after being told scientists wanted to find a cure for the common cold. But they were given the hallucinogen drug (LSD) in mind control tests, and some volunteers suffered terrifying hallucinations as a result. The Foreign Office said the secret intelligence body MI6 had made the settlements after receiving legal advice. The out-of-court settlements were thought to be under £10,000 for each of those men.

In a statement issued later to the BBC News website, the Ministry of Defence said it did not make any admission of liability in respect of the settlements.

The statement added: 'The Ministry of Defence is very grateful to all those whose participation in studies at Porton Down made possible the research to provide safe and effective protection for UK Armed Forces.' A spokesman for the Foreign Office, which oversees MI6, said: 'The settlement offers were made to the government on behalf of the three claimants which, on legal advice, and in the particular circumstances of these cases, the government thinks it appropriate to accept.' These men had volunteered for experiments at the government's chemical warfare research base at Porton Down in Wiltshire in 1953 and 1954.

Below are quotes from the sufferers themselves.

'They stick to the old maxim: never apologise, never explain. But I think in this case they have decided to pay some money. I consider that is as near to an apology or an explanation I'll get.' Both he and fellow serviceman, Logan Marr, a former shepherd from the Scottish highlands, suffered hallucinations after they were asked to drink a clear liquid. The research was carried out after British and American governments thought the Soviet Union had developed a 'truth drug' which could compel spies and servicemen to yield up important secrets.

The fact that LSD had been given to various volunteers (without them being aware of the seriousness of the after-effects of the drug itself.)

MI6 scientists decided to test LSD, the closest thing they thought they had then to a truth drug, on volunteers to see how they reacted. Alan Care, a lawyer who later represented the three men, said: 'As far as we are aware, these are the first settlements by the secret intelligence services for a personal injury action.' He added that a request that documents relating to the case be put into the public domain had been refused.

'Some volunteers at the base did not find out they had been given LSD until some 50 years later. Thousands of servicemen and women have volunteered in the testing of defences against chemical and biological attacks at the Wiltshire military base.'

1958
Mother and Son's Relationship

Six months had passed by, and my mother wisely wanted me to return home to live with her rather than become too used to living in a hospital environment and protected surroundings. She was now living entirely on her own. Happily, my mother and I seemed to have restored our previous relationship with my regular weekend visits home.

My stepfather's mother, who had lived with us, had been sent packing to live with another son as they had had words. Besides that, my mother thought it was time other members of my stepfather's family should do their bit in caring for the old lady.

My mother decided then to help me recover from my breakdown by signing a hire purchase agreement for me to have a scooter, a Lambretta 125cc. She thought it would increase my confidence and give me an interest and help me become more mobile with the possibility of expanding my social life. It would at least help me get to work more quickly!

After discharge from the hospital, my mother, whom I considered now was coming to terms with her loss, kept her word and signed the hire purchase agreement for my Lambretta scooter. It was fantastic, and it did for a short period improve my social life, before disaster sadly and suddenly struck, and I was prevented from riding it for medical reasons.

My mother asked me to go with her to see a black moleskin fur coat, which she had her eye on and liked very much. How it suited her! I readily agreed. Indeed, I believe she had already fallen in love with it and my approval was all that she wanted. She looked a million dollars in it. From what she told me, probate had been granted, and she decided to treat herself. I remember that I then asked her to buy me a pullover I had seen in the window of a new man's clothing shop which had recently opened. She agreed.

Epilepsy Diagnosed

I resumed my apprenticeship with Peter Brotherhoods Ltd and was able to go back and forth to work, passing with ease all the cyclists on the way using my Lambretta 125cc. A few months later, after having left the hospital, I was out with my friend and his parents at the seaside and suffered another seizure, which was later diagnosed by a doctor and confirmed as an epileptic attack. This attack took place while we were on a speedboat on the sea at Hunstanton, and I was rushed to a local doctor who diagnosed it, unknown to me at this time, as epilepsy. When I delivered this doctor's letter to my own doctor, as he had known me for a few years, he could not believe it and thought I could possibly have a tumour of the brain. He arranged for me to go to the London Hospital for Nervous Disorders for an in-depth investigation. My mother thought it wise to accompany me, and I was strapped on a table that was tilted into various positions and had my brain x-rayed from every angle possible.

Whilst we were in London my mother and I took the opportunity of visiting my father. They held hands and I always believed that my father still loved my mother.

On the train home my mother said that my father was dying, but I would not accept this.

These tests at the National Hospital for Nervous Disorders comprised blood and urine tests, weight and height measurements and an electro-encephalograph, which was somewhat like a hairnet with electrical contacts fitted over your head to measure the electrical brain activity and numerous other tests on my body. Some weeks later they confirmed the prognosis was actually epilepsy.

The dangers of LSD

It never occurred to me at that time that LSD had been the original cause and had started my epileptic attacks. Some years later, I was to learn of LSD's consequences and the detrimental effect it would have now on me for the rest of my life for every single day. It is always there, and I have to take twenty tablets every day, and, should one miss taking them, you can suffer the severe consequences. As with most disabilities, it has an effect on your quality of life. You do not have the energy, as you are on drugs that have a significantly sedative impact on you. Many years later, my mother said that the doctors in London thought that it could have been caused by the injections of LSD I had been given at the Rauceby Mental Hospital, Sleaford. The National Archives report that at this exact hospital, medical records are still closed for scrutiny or investigation for one hundred years. Later, I was told that medical records were destroyed after twenty years.

Once confirmed, I was then informed by my doctor that I had to give up my driving licence for my scooter and had to retire also from my apprenticeship at Peter Brotherhoods. The reason given was for me that to operate machinery would have been too dangerous. I then needed to find suitable employment elsewhere. I had to terminate my learning, sadly, and I was called to an office to see some manager, but he didn't seem to have an ounce of compassion or understanding in him. To tell the truth, he was very discouraging. I felt life was becoming more impossible each day, and I could not envisage any better future for me.

Can you imagine how I felt? My driving licence, which I had only possessed for a few months, was so essential, and in those days, with epilepsy, you had to go three years without experiencing another seizure before you could apply to have your licence renewed. I was so demoralised and depressed at hearing this of course. When I argued with my doctor, he told me that if I didn't give my licence up, he would report me.

Fortunately, my mother had arranged that my Uncle Cyril would take over the hire purchase agreement and give me enough money to purchase a new bicycle so that I could at least be mobile when I needed this to use for future employment.

NHS, Epilepsy and Medication

I was put on the sick for six months and began to relax, not realising the terrible effects this diagnosis would ultimately prove to have on me. It affected me daily. Neither did I understand the anticonvulsant medication that I would have to take for the rest of my life, and the effects that itself would have on me all the time.

However, there was later a ray of sunshine while I was relaxing in the sun by the river Nene embankment at Peterborough. Life was beautiful again as I soon found I was attracted physically to a sexy redhead girl who happened to be close by, and who showed an interest in me. Sitting later in the café nearby, we drank milkshakes and listened to the jukebox. This allowed us to become more acquainted with each other, and it was not long before we were holding hands and kissing each other and walking home to where I lived and becoming even more intimately acquainted. It was heaven, but regrettably, it was not to last. I do, however, thank her for my introduction to manhood, and it was terrific for a few weeks until she got fed up with me. She was a very demanding lady but also enticingly beautiful.

There were at least two more girlfriends that I fell in love with who seemed, once they had found out eventually that I was an epileptic, they did not want to know me or see me any more. One of them, I never thought I would get over losing her, but when she knew about my disability that was it. She dropped me like a lead weight. It was very disappointing, especially when I thought we were well-suited to each other, but it was not to be. I had to get over it and get on with my life. Regretfully, that type of incident had an adverse effect on my confidence as one can imagine!

Depressed once again, this time I tried some churches, thinking God would help, but He didn't at that particular time. I realise now that He was waiting for me to seek an even greater need of him. I reasoned with myself, 'Why should He?' I was not a regular worshipper. I was traumatised by what the epilepsy was doing to me. I could not pick or choose any job I wanted due to my illness. I was forced to become a basic labourer. At times, owing to the drugs I had to take, I was also exhausted. Their effect slowed me down, and often I didn't feel myself. There was so little to look forward to, and life itself seemed monotonous, dismal and depressing. I had to earn a living and to adapt to the limitations of what life had in store for me.

Employment in the Brickyards

Eventually, I secured a job as a labourer at Fletton Brickyards. Whatever self-esteem I once had quickly disappeared even more. Here I was, an ex-grammar school boy, now having to do very exhausting, manual work with some of the hardest types and toughest characters in Peterborough. I had to swallow my pride and accept what life had given me. It would be up to me to sort myself out, and that took a good few years, and possibly I am still doing it now while writing this book. In addition to that, I had to cycle to work every day while still living in Russell Street, Peterborough. It was about 5 miles at least each way. This would be daily in addition to the hazardous, exhausting work I would be doing at the brickyard itself. It, fortunately, added more exercise to improve my muscles and physical wellbeing, which was essential, but I wondered, 'was the whole thing destined not to last?'

Walking into this factory and hearing the deafening noise of the presses was ear-shattering and frightening to an extent. My very first job at these brickyards was to take green, new bricks off the large, cumbersome presses and stack them onto bogeys. These were, when filled, collected by a small rail train, then transported to the kilns for 'setting' so they could be baked. No one told me, but after a few days of stacking green bricks due to their weight, your wrists become very weak indeed due to the heavy lifting, and you have to have your wrists tightly and well-strapped up to support them, and then only carry out light work for a few days. It was so difficult and painful to pick up anything at all. I got through this suffering because I wanted to succeed at this job, and did manage finally to achieve this goal.

However, afterwards, you end up having, fortunately, an exceptionally strong grip. It took me a few days to ride my bike safely, having to steer it with my wrists in this heavily bandaged state. But this only lasted a short while, and I was then determined to get back to normal.

After doing this job for a few months, I wanted one where I could earn more money and start to become a setter in the kilns. When you became a setter or drawer, you were on piecework, and you only got paid for the number of bricks: in this case, those you had set in the kilns. Drawers would get paid for what they stacked on the barrows and wheeled out from the kilns. This was a backbreaking job, but, when you became proficient at it, you earned good money. The trouble was it was piece work, so you got so much for a thousand bricks. The heat in the kilns would be about 80 degrees, or sometimes even more and you sweated. It was best to drink a lot of cold tea with no milk in it to keep you hydrated.

It was a dangerous job, as the kilns were not in a good state of repair and in the past apparently people had even been badly injured in this dangerous place. Knotholes were also a hazard, liable to form because of water after the clay had been collected. Poor quality bricks were also dumped into the knotholes, making them very treacherous. Only hard cases were able to survive these dangerous conditions and the heavy physical work involved.

During the time in which I became a setter in the brickyards and slogged at it for a year or more, I formed several friendships with others who also worked in brickyards, and we did all that was wrong. I got drunk every weekend and gambled most of my wages away. However, I did buy myself a suit now and then so that I was decent when we ended up at the dance hall on a Saturday night. It was normal for me to take a hip flask of brandy or another spirit to enhance my drunken state and give me the Dutch courage I needed to ask girls to dance with me. In those days, they were very choosy, and many times I was refused, but possibly that was because I was nearly drunk with trying to get the courage I needed. But then, anyway, I sadly was not a good dancer either!

Some workers had a short temper with certain persons at work, and I regretfully include myself amongst them. I can remember one day a drawer saying something that upset me, and an argument started, which then developed into a fist fight. I was much bigger than him and soon had him on the ground, and, in my temper at that time, I nearly hit him on the head with a brick. I was given a warning, and in the future had to be careful, as my anger had to be firmly controlled.

Being a setter, you needed to set at least fifteen thousand bricks a day, which would be equivalent to moving thirty tons of bricks with your hands every day. One day, I had an epileptic seizure at work in a kiln, and the people did not get my head off the floor quickly enough. Consequently, I suffered superficial but very painful burns to my face. I was lucky - the wounds eventually healed, but I had then to give up being a setter as the boss said it was too dangerous a job for me to carry out in fear of my developing a seizure frequently while doing this particular job.

I then ended up with a new job, possibly the most dangerous I had yet had in the brickyard: emptying the bogeys that came loaded with clay from the knot holes, as they were called. Bogeys were filled with clay in the knotholes and then transferred on rails and wires, which pulled them along to where the clay was then tipped. At first, I had to release the wet clay that got stuck in the bogey by swiftly climbing in and digging it out and then hooking up the bogey so that it could be returned to the clay pit. This was very dangerous work.

After two or three weeks at this, I then enquired about doing the actual 'release' work when the bogey first came in. Here you had to be quick and put your foot on the carriage of the bogey and ride with it, releasing the catch and making the body of the bogey bounce off a large wooden bar and then bounce back, and quickly securing it. If you did it right, all the clay would fall from the bogey, the bogey would then bounce, and you would rapidly secure it by closing the release handle and finally returning it back to the pit. These bogeys would have about two tons of clay in them as it was wet and cumbersome. It was, therefore, easier if you got the bogey to give up all its clay, as you then didn't have to dig it out. A good shovel full of brick dust scattered over the bottom of the bogey would help to stop the clay sticking the next time it came around for emptying.

1958
Mother Encounters a Flasher

My mother's depression had passed fortunately at long last, when one evening she decided to go out to her new company's social club. Returning home, she had the shock of finding a flasher jumping out from a doorway entrance. She was still in mourning for my step-father, but not at all frightened, and she took a good look at him. Then, strangely enough, the very next Saturday in Peterborough city centre she spotted the same man. Bravely, she then went up to a policeman and got him to immediately arrest this man because she could verify he was the flasher. In court, she was praised for the help she had given in this particular case.

My mother, still a relatively young woman, was plagued on all sides of her with would-be husbands offering to marry her, as she was only 38 and still a very attractive young woman. She was also very hard-working. Eventually, she married again, and my new stepfather possessed just one arm. He had lost his right arm as he had been born with a withered arm from birth, eventually having to have it amputated. He had not been married before, and had a lot to learn about life itself with a wife and a stepson. However, he had fallen for my mother in a big way and even came back from the holiday he was spending in Paris with his friends as he realised that he could not face life without her! He took me to the pub one Sunday and told me that he wanted to marry my mother and hoped that we would be all able to get along together.

Looking back for a reason for my mother's need for another man in her life, I believe my mother needed the love that she had not been able to receive when she was a young girl, and that she missed her father, who sadly had died suddenly. Most fathers would have spoilt their daughters, and she never received that type of love, so mistakenly sought admiration from men.

1959-1960
Mother Decides to Marry Again

My mother and this new stepfather-to-be had decided to get married, and arrangements were very quickly put into effect. New furniture was bought to replace some that needed it, and Horace, my stepfather, installed all his belongings. He and his brother were both unmarried and lived with their mother and father near where I worked at Fletton.

The house we lived in at Russell Street, Peterborough, was a large, old palisaded terrace house. Even though a lot had been done to it, a great deal more was needed to bring it up to date. It was very close to the city shopping area, about five minutes to the shops, and it was very convenient.

The house had many unhappy memories for me, and I persuaded my stepfather and my mother to sell it and buy a new bungalow. The house was put up for sale and quickly sold, and so we moved to the other side of Peterborough, off the Whittlesey Road, to a new bungalow and a lot nearer to my place of work and to my new stepfather's parents. It was much better and safer for me as I did not have to cycle through the centre of Peterborough. The best of it was that the price they received for the old house was enough to purchase the new bungalow.

Before we moved to our new bungalow, my mother had encountered an unexpected delay. This was due to considerable difficulty occurring with the builders themselves not having completed all the essential work. So, after being told that there would still be a significant delay, she went immediately herself to the managing director who owned the building company. I think the name was *Shelton's Limited*, and she literally forced him to complete everything in time for our move in. A very assertive and determined woman, my mother!

Being a persuasive lady, when she wanted something carried out, she generally succeeded, and was virtually irresistible. I was, of course, proud of her for insisting in this way since it enabled us to move into a fully complete, comfortable, bungalow without any more waiting.

We all managed to cope with each other. I cannot say it was all happy, as we had our moments and I know my mother was trying her best, but trouble occurred between my stepfather and me. I was very antagonistic towards this man, as I did not want to suffer again what I had been through during my earlier life from the first violent, abusive stepfather. In fact, I had made up my mind that I would not tolerate what I had previously experienced. Very defensive and quick to retaliate against any criticisms he made, especially concerning me, I made my points.

Remembering well, I had been off work sick, and, after recovering, decided to dig the garden of our new bungalow to help. When my stepfather came home that day, all that he could say was that I had picked the easiest part of the garden to dig! I was so incensed at this criticism and what my stepfather said as I had been off work suffering from the pain of a bad back. I would have thought he would have been thankful that I had tried so hard to help. His attitude took me back to the times when I suffered from my previous step-father, and, of course, I was now on the defensive yet again.

1960
My Own Father Dies and gets a Pauper's Funeral

To illustrate how nervous, touchy and erratic I was around this time, I went with a friend on holiday. I had saved up about £70 in spending money, which was a reasonable amount in those days. When I went to withdraw some, I was told by the bank clerk I couldn't, for some bureaucratic reason or other. I was incensed at her attitude and foolishly I then made her close the account and give me all of my savings. I felt as though I was being spoken to as though I was a little child, and I was in those days, upon reflection, very quick to take offence and this nervous breakdown was not cured. I seemed to have to fight every step of my life painfully at that time.

I took all this money on holiday to a holiday camp at Caister and put most of it in a one arm bandit, apart from a few quid I kept back. I gambled the small amount of money I had left on five horses with an accumulator and trebled my money. That was the last time I have ever bet. I had learned my lesson, and, to this day, will not even buy a raffle ticket or gamble on anything. I had once before lost a week's wages in a card game and resigned myself to no gambling. I considered my money was hard earned and I needed to remember that it was not to be frittered away.

Some months after returning from this disastrous holiday, later on 27 November 1960, I was told my father had just died. Having phoned from the local telephone box, I walked back, and then suffered a massive epileptic seizure, falling on the concrete path surrounding our bungalow. I fell, bruising my face badly and grazing it. Because it was a bad attack, my mother called my doctor, and it took me two days at least this time to get over it.

Until I had fully recovered, my mother would not let me go to London on my own to attend my poor father's funeral. When I arrived finally at the nursing home where he had been, the person in charge asked why it had taken so long for me to come!

My mother had already told her on the phone that I had been forced to stay at home because of the severity of the fall, and that I had also been taken ill, so warned her some delay would occur until I had recovered. This added to my sorrow at my father's passing away.

My mother, realising the strain I was under, made arrangements for me to stay with a care worker at her home until the funeral had been arranged. I seemed to be in a daze after having this particularly severe seizure, and also with trying to recover from the shock of my father's death.

I suppose it was the two together that made it serious. Travelling from Peterborough to London, everything seemed to be so rushed. Mrs Walker, who was an exceptionally dear friend that my father was very fond of and who treated him like her son, resided also in the nursing home. She was so distraught that my father had died.

Fortunately, he had been befriended by this dear, sweet lady, who was exceptionally kind to him. She was an angelic, quietly and well-spoken patient just across the hall from my dad, who had proved a great comfort to him since they met. Her actual son, I was told, was in charge of an antique magazine and was well-educated. She would sit and talk to my father every day. Coming originally from a Quaker family, she brought so much happiness and peace to my father in these last fraught and sad years of his life. Deeply religious herself, she ensured this uplifting aspect of her own life was devoted to ease my father in his loneliness and blindness. Fortunately, I now believe this gave him great comfort, as well as her companionship. He so much needed and appreciated her. It was as though the Lord had provided for my father a special angel to comfort him at a time when he needed it most.

Looking back on my own father's life, I realise how selfish I had been to him. He had been blind for eight whole years, with no relations coming to see him except me. Living on his own in a local nursing home, he was in bed most of the time, then dying at the very early age of 46. I was then 19, and sadly poor so he had to be buried in a pauper's grave. I could have done more, but didn't have sufficient daily contact with him to build a supportive son-father relationship. As fast as I earned money, I spent it. I seemed to be living just for the moment, and could see no future. Of course, this was wrong of me. Also, I had a chip on my shoulder as to how life had already treated me. There were many times I spent sitting by his bed when he had been admitted to hospital and taken a turn for the worse, but he had survived those times, and I then returned to Peterborough to my mother's.

I was nineteen and was the only relation at the funeral. I buried my father sadly and entirely on my own, apart from an almoner who represented the home he had been nursed in, and kindly accompanied me. I was an irate young man. When I got back home, I wrote to my father's relations to say I did not want to know them anymore because they had not come to his funeral, but little did I realise that they had significant health problems themselves at the time in their own family.

I do not think I would have listened to anyone. I was so upset and shocked that at 19 years of age I had and did bury him on my own. My father was only forty-six years old. The final straw was that I had purchased a wreath for him, and because it was a pauper's grave, I was not allowed to put it visibly on the top of the grave. How stupid a rule to have! So I had to tell the undertakers to bury it under ground with him, which was very upsetting, as you can imagine.

Reconciled with My Father's Family

Some 40 years later, I later learned that the kindly relations on my father's side could not come and visit my father in the care home because their own mother was at that time so seriously ill. They could not leave her because of her dementia, and also they had their large farm to look after, with 200 cows needing to be milked twice a day. However, later, when we were reconciled to everyone's delight, they told me that during the time my father was well, there had been times in which they had given my dad a holiday at their farm. They had got on well with him, thought he was a lovely man, and even though he was ill then he still made them laugh. When he was well and could drive a lorry, they had marvelled at his skills and said he could park a truck on a sixpence.

1961-63
My Introduction to Amphetamines

When I look back, it could well be that some of the problems I had might have been drug-related. I had complained about my tiredness owing to the tablets I had to take. In those days, there wasn't the variety of anticonvulsant drugs there are now. I had to take a large dose daily of phenobarbitone which, later on in my life, was reduced to a level as far as they thought could be considered safe. I was prescribed Methedrine, which is now a banned drug, I believe. The wonder of this drug is that, when taking it, you are always awake and have bundles of energy, but it is highly dangerous. I was on it for about three years before it was withdrawn, and I never realised just how dangerous it was until I became involved in my LSD legal case some 40 years later.

Methedrine, the trade name, was used as a stimulant to the nervous system and as an appetite suppressant.

Most usage of methedrine is illicit and illegal, except as outlined above. Methedrine was the proprietary name given to methamphetamine hydrochloride by a pharmaceutical company and was available for purchase on prescription until 1964. Methedrine evolved into the street name of methamphetamine during the 1960s and the early 1970s. High-doses of methamphetamine or another seriously powerful drug with the street name of 'speed' were popular drugs of choice for abuse during this time. After the manufacturer withdrew commercially made Methedrine for sale, large quantities of illicitly manufactured methamphetamine were being produced and sold on the black market from meth labs.

My mother's sister is seriously injured

It was about this particular time my mother, who was always very helpful to anyone in the family circle in need, heard the news that her sister Joan had suffered a terrible accident while at work in the dairy. Crates of milk had fallen on top of her, and the outlook was not very good. The extent of her injuries was life-changing in the fact that the accident caused her to be paralysed. After being treated at Peterborough Hospital, she was later transferred to Stoke Mandeville Hospital. The problem this created was that her husband, who didn't drive and had to work, could only visit her one day of the week. My mother and stepfather took him and their daughter down by car to help them, and I am sure, knowing my mother, she would have taken other things that her sister wanted. Regretfully, the accident was caused by her sister playing around, and was her own fault.

1962-1963

My mother did her best to kindly put on a small party for my 21st birthday, which was appreciated, and gave me a portable radio as a present. I think I got some clothes and money, but cannot remember much else about it. A friend with whom I worked and who lived near us came, and we both went on holiday to Caister Holiday Camp, but it turned out not to be a great experience. Limited entertainment was put on for customers in those days.

The problems in my relationship with my second stepfather greatly worsened now, and I did not want to upset my mother anymore. I made enquiries about retraining for another job through the local disablement officer and chose to go to Leicester, hoping that one of my relations would put me up. My mother was the one who was suffering. After a massive row had occurred, I decided to ask my Aunt Doll, who lived in Leicester, if she would let me lodge with her and her husband so I could go to the disablement training centre. Kindly, she readily agreed. I could not see any future in the type of work I was then doing and wanted to better myself.

My Aunt Doll knew little about me apart from the Christmas when I first had an attack, but was very interested in what had happened to me in my young life. She talked to me and was very surprised - amazed, even - and was so sad to hear of the problematic and deprived life I had endured when a child. For most of her own life, she had lived in London, and did not meet up with my mother for many years. She said she had known little about me at the time, and was very shocked at the way I had been treated.

When my mother and stepfather came to visit me the next time, my Aunt Doll argued with my mother about what I had suffered to such an extent, and so vehemently, that my mother and step-father finally walked out. I was later told to fetch my belongings from their house. When I did so, only my mother was there, and the atmosphere was very upsetting to me. I was shocked to have to do this, so packed everything up, and walked out, leaving my mother in floods of tears. I later realised that I had seemed to put on a very determined face to my mother, and it must obviously have been a totally upsetting experience for her too, and one which I wish had never, ever happened.

Whilst at the retraining Centre at Leicester I was persuaded to take an IQ test for Portland Training

College for the Disabled. Within a few months I then received the news that I had been accepted and would be given training in Accountancy.

My Aunt Doll then did her very best to mother me until her own husband died soon after I was finishing my actual college training.

Before going to Portland Training College, I got a job as a wages clerk at Ashwell and Nesbitt's in Gypsy Lane, Leicester. I worked there for a few months, but my epileptic seizures continued to worsen. Still more worrying than this was the insistence by the then manager that I remain at work after suffering such an attack. Eventually, they got the message that it was medically necessary for me to be taken home after each attack and to thoroughly sleep it off before returning to work.

The strangest part about this actual period of my life with Aunt Doll is that a man who lived two doors away from her was continually chastised by Aunt Doll and her husband about the hostile attitude towards neighbours and the language he used. Later on, my aunt found she happened to slowly get on much better with him, so much so, she even became quite fond and intimate with him, and I did not see so much of her, but was grateful always for what she had tried to do for me.

After her first husband died, however, the two of them then became great friends and very quickly later got married! There is nothing as queer as folk, they say.

1964
Portland Training College for the Disabled

I was offered a place at Portland Training College for the Disabled in Mansfield to study accountancy and related business matters, which I accepted. It was a residential college, and I would be there for training about six months.

It was a great place, situated on the edge of Sherwood Forest, and it had plenty of disabled people there who, sadly, were far, far worse off than me. This probably made me much more sensitive towards people with similar problems when I became older, and I am glad to say that I still am now.

It also had some attractive women around the place who were friendly. There was good food, and I quickly made friends and enjoyed it so much. The one thing we all had in common was that we were, every one, disabled. However, I was there to learn again about accounting and business practice and other relevant subjects so that I could get a job as an audit clerk. I think I gave some of the tutors there a hard time until I had settled down, but they were very supportive of all of us and wanted us to achieve. There was the most positive atmosphere of achievement in the whole college.

I enjoyed the social life there too, but I needed to earn more money, so I worked as a barman in the evenings at a public house in Mansfield and received cash in hand. The trouble was I was bought drinks, which I did not refuse, and this brought on, sadly, even more seizures. The officials got to know of me working in the evenings, and I was told I would have to pack the job in otherwise I would be reported, and was told I needed to get my head down for the exams for which I had been entered.

Pleasant Memories

We ended up seated together at our dinner table with a reticent, young man in an electric wheelchair who was very timid, shy and could be a bit tearful at times. However, we all encouraged him to laugh and smile by including him in our conversations. It was beautiful to see him come out of his shell and enjoy his time there with us. Regrettably, I cannot remember his name, but after a few weeks I was invited to spend a weekend with his family.

We were picked up by them on a Friday evening, and everything went exceptionally well. They appreciated what we had all done for him and couldn't have been kinder. They thought there had been a remarkable change for the better in their son and wanted to give me a good time for my part in achieving this for him. On Saturday, I was presented with my dinner, and it had the unusual ingredient of a sheep's heart, which I had never tasted before (and have not ever eaten since). I managed to eat some of it, but in the evening the whole family with their disabled son took me to a large local pub or working men's club and got me drunk. This was because they were so pleased that their son had made friends and had begun to be a much more fulfilled, happier person. They attributed this to knowing that I, and the other students who had also sat with him, looked after him to good effect. He had become a more confident and happier person in every way.

They were so thankful to me and the others for how we had all helped him to achieve this.

This experience made a long-lasting impression on me, and I have always been, since then, very interested in helping those people I have encountered who were obviously in need. This has resulted in many valuable and precious friendships developing during my life.

When I came back, I found a young woman who had joined the college. She was beautiful and lovely, not just to me but to many of the males at the college. Eventually, I cannot remember just how, but we became very close friends and then spent much time together and enjoyed every romantic, amorous moment we could capture together. The college was set in nearby woods, and we would have a wonderful time. Her hair was as red as the sunset, and her body had curves in all the right places. I could not help noticing her eyes, captivating smile and her long, beautiful red hair.

Whilst at Portland College, unbeknown to me at first, my mother and second stepfather were sadly involved in a significant, fatal car accident. Two people in the other vehicle were killed as a result, and my mother and stepfather were also admitted to hospital, both with serious injuries.

Mother's head injury was such that she had a severe concussion, which meant her staying in the hospital for several days. This accident, and its impact on her head, I am led to believe, eventually caused the brain tumour from which she died some ten years later. The accident was reported on TV, but, fortunately, I did not see the full horror of it all.

However, it was not my stepfather's fault; the error was the driver's in the other car. It was a terrible shock to eventually find out about it. In a way, it actually started the healing of my own fractured relationship with my mother and stepfather.

The two of them had ended upside down in one of the many dykes that drain the Fenland, but, fortunately for both of them, there was little, if any, water in it at the time or they could have drowned. However, they were strapped in by their seat belts, and it was difficult for them to escape, so they had to wait for help. They had been in threat of drowning, and hung upside down for hours before rescue. My mother helped support her husband who only, you remember, had one arm!

She was for some considerable time also trapped in the car. She then had to try to somehow release herself from the seat belt, at the same time she was helping to hold Horace up. He was trapped by the belt, and not only was he suspended upside down, but, as he unfortunately had only one arm, he could not free himself at all. In retrospect, this might have been his saviour as he could have been paralysed since there were hidden neck problems too, which revealed themselves at the hospital only just before his discharge.

NHS Failure after Car Accident

My stepfather was seriously injured, but the extent of his injuries were not been fully established until his discharge from the hospital. At this time, he collapsed when getting ready to leave the ward, and they found he had fractured his neck. In the hospitals defence x-rays were not the most perfect of equipment and had MRI scanners been invented then I am sure the outcome would have been more beneficial to my stepfather.

He underwent an 8-hour operation and had to endure for a whole year a solid plaster cast with a metal frame from his head to his waist.

My mother had suffered a severe concussion, and after three weeks was released from the hospital, but many years later the consultants told me that they thought that this injury was the most likely cause of her brain tumour. Eventually this led to her early death at the age of 53. If this was the case, then it seems people who suffer concussion should be always be recalled for re-examination for a long period after such accidents. This would be an excellent preventative precaution to take.

It appeared that my stepfather had been driving along the main road when a car from a side road came out without stopping and hit him. My stepfather's car ended by being pushed upside down in a dyke and the other vehicle, unfortunately, hit the parapet of a bridge with such force that it killed its two occupants, a man and a woman.

This accident brought home to me just how short life can be, and after meeting my mother, who had already been discharged and was overjoyed to see me, we then visited my stepfather, who remained in hospital. I apologised to him for how I had previously behaved, and from then on I respected him and treated him as a father until the day he died.

My mother, upon me seeing her after such a long time, was relieved and strangely elated. Recovering from head injuries caused by this terrible accident, she had been discharged after three weeks in hospital, but still did not seem quite her former self. However, we had all been reunited, and past hurts were forgotten. This was a great comfort to us both. I realised I had been unusually hard in the way I had behaved towards my mother and towards my new stepfather too. After experiencing this disaster, I vowed to myself I would never ignore them in this way again. It had undoubtedly hurt me as much as them, and it was childish of me to behave in that manner. I deeply regret this now, of course.

My mother and stepfather, who were not responsible for the accident, eventually received compensation for their sufferings, but had a tough time as my mother had to nurse my stepfather for a long time until he could cope on his own again.

My stepfather had to undergo the operation, and was encased in plaster from his head to his waist, with a metal frame running through the plaster to limit movement of his neck. This was to keep his body in the correct alignment position for better healing, but he found it very uncomfortable. When the hot weather came, he found it even more difficult, as his body itched and the only thing he could do was to use a long ruler to scratch and relieve his discomfort on his back.

By this time, I had passed the Institute of Bookkeepers exams and Royal Society of Arts exams with credits, and was awarded a First Class Diploma from Portland College. This enabled me to obtain a job as an audit clerk with a firm of chartered accountants after returning to Leicester.

Unfortunately, my Aunt Doll, who had by then been widowed, as I was finding out, had decided to get married again.

Much to my dismay, I had to come to terms with the fact that I was not wanted at her house any more by the new man in her life, and so I had to find a place to live. The cost of such bed and breakfast was not affordable on my meagre wages as an audit clerk, and I began to go without meals so I could manage financially. Eventually, I was taken ill with pleurisy and became quite thin, pale and weak. I needed to change my employment to earn more money so I could at least keep myself in a decent state of health. No one, of course, had realised this, whereas my aunt Doll would have done so had I been still living with her, since she was such a caring, loving and perceptive person.

I became a warehouseman as I didn't feel I had the necessary training yet to become a qualified audit clerk. As it was, the job was slave labour on a pittance. The company expected me to carry on working as soon as I had actually become conscious again after just experiencing another seizure. This could well have been brought on by their unreasonable expectations of me being able to manage an ancient telephone system that was at least fifty years old, and not at all fit for purpose. This was in addition to the job of preparing accounts for a sole trader, who was one of their clients.

However, the wages at the toy warehouse company I discovered were significantly better, and during this bout of pleurisy, I managed to visit my uncle, who only lived half a mile from where I was lodging. He and his wife, seeing how ill I was, were sympathetic and readily offered me accommodation with them at a much-reduced affordable rate, with meals included, which was much more acceptable for me and appreciated. They had three children themselves, and these were good company for me when we all sat down at night for our dinner.

My Uncle Roy and his wife had these three children, two girls and one boy. The boy was ruined, the elder girl was so bossy, and the other girl was so timid. Her mother inferred that her youngest girl, Susan, was the problem. However, I could not help but take a liking to Susan and help her with her school work. Her older sister was very quick and sharp and needed to learn some manners while this younger, gentler sister was very much in need of support. The constant bickering by her mother took a lot of her confidence from her but, having suffered much the same harrassment in my own life, I then readily became her defender. Later on, she went on to become the manageress of a council OAP home. Then, after redundancy, she obtained a senior position in the packing department at a large well-known clothing company. Even today, I still communicate with her by email and telephone as she now lives in Spain happily with her husband. She was very much like her father, always working and earning money to provide for her family.

I Meet my Wife To Be

Now that I had been reunited with my mother she was worried about me, and notified me of the existence of an epilepsy club in Leicester. It was there, on my initial visit, that I first met my wife to be. My future wife, who was classed as disabled because of her childhood epilepsy and had found it difficult to find work, decided that keeping a home would be enough for her for the time being. I can remember standing at the reception when a gentleman and this particular young woman came into the club. He, her uncle, had brought her on his motorbike, and, when he saw me, he said, 'There's a nice young man.' Eventually we managed to get talking to each other, and I asked her if I could walk her to the bus stop at the end of the session. She agreed. We talked for quite a long time and arranged to see each other the following evening. She had been overprotected by her family, and had little, if any, confidence in herself. She lived with her mother, who was a single parent, and also her uncle. He worked for the local electricity company as a labourer.

Tricia and I got thoroughly acquainted, and within a short time we got engaged. Her Aunt Molly put on a little celebration for us with a lot of family relations on Tricia's side coming to celebrate. We now had both agreed to plan for an early wedding. It happened a bit earlier than scheduled, as Tricia became pregnant, and I looked forward with some trepidation as to how we would manage to cope financially. However, her mother thought that it would be wise if we lived with her until we could get a place of our own, to which we readily agreed. It was a suitable arrangement, as we stayed with them for over a year. Tricia still had attacks, but tried her best to cope with the housework and the apparent demands of pregnancy, married life and, later, our first young child to look after.

1965
Our Wedding

Tricia and I had a church wedding at Leicester thanks to my mother-in-law and her brother, who gave us £500 which paid for the wedding and reception at a hotel nearby. My Uncle Roy, who had given me a home when I needed it so much, was my best man at my wedding. It was a small recognition of his kindness to me. I recall the many times as a young man when he lived with his mother, Granny Thain, and I used to tease him while he was having his dinner. After so much aggravation from me, he would get up and chase me.

After our wedding, my stepfather came back the next day and took us in his car to my mother's so we could have a week with them as a sort of honeymoon. My mother and my new step-father let us have the run of their bungalow during the day while they went to their respective jobs. Tricia and I had a few days out but also took advantage of resting and relaxing together happily.

I think a lot of people thought we were very brave or even foolish marrying with our specific health problems, but we ultimately proved them wrong. Both having the same disability helped us to understand each other's issues, possibly more than other married couples could ever have done. We had no other choice but to help each other. My wife could not cook very well at first. However, her mother was an excellent cook, and her Sunday dinners were delicious and very much appreciated.

Because of my wife's epileptic illness, she had missed essential schooling and found it difficult to even add up. I persevered with her and taught her maths sufficiently well for her to budget and shop economically. Over the next few years, I improved her cooking with gentle persuasion and praise, until she eventually became an excellent cook.

With both of us being disabled and our attacks being so regular in our first years of married life, even with the drugs we both had to take, it was an effort to see any better future. Fortunately, we had found out that my wife was pregnant, and now had to plan for this and to do our best to prepare together for parenthood.

We decided to accept their generous offer, and so lived with my mother-in-law and her brother, Fred. His health had been severely affected by serving in the Second World War. However, bless him, he managed to carry out a simple labourer's job, and helped his sister by contributing generously to the costs of the running of the house.

As far as my own progression in my career went, I had become by then a warehouseman in a toy wholesalers, and this, strangely enough, was a job which at that time suited my abilities much better, plus I earned more money. I worked hard, was conscientious, and when my bosses knew I had got married, they gave me a reasonable wage increase. To them, I was becoming an asset that they did not want to lose me, so Michael, the director, encouraged me to carry out stock control in my spare time and paid me over-time. He was a charming, supportive man, and we got on exceptionally well together.

Looking back on this period, I think, after working in the brickyards, I had become hardened to physical work at this particular time in my life. This, in fact, suited me. I did not have any specific aspirations at that time, but this was to change dramatically very shortly. Michael knew that I was a hard worker and could eventually complete orders more speedily than others. Upon reflection, I now realise that the time spent in the brickyards had significantly increased my physical strength too. This was a great asset. Also, I seemed to have developed a knack of recalling accurately whether or not we had stock available of certain products. In some cases, I was able to remember the actual finite quantities.

1966-67
Richard, our First Child

In February 1966, my first child, Richard, was born. It was a very traumatic time for my wife, as she was in labour for thirty-six hours in all, and really suffered so much pain. She ended up having stitches and needing daily healing salt baths after returning safely home. The delivery had really sapped her of her former energy, and she was also very sore and exhausted until her wounds healed. She was initially upset as she had wanted to breastfeed the child herself, but her milk did not come quickly enough, so we had to purchase National Dried Milk.

It was later on in life I was to find that the Primidone tablets Tricia was prescribed and was taking at the time for her epilepsy should have been changed when she became pregnant, as these seemed to have a severe effect on my first son's mental development. Most importantly, however, was that this delay in delivery could also have caused possible oxygen deprivation at his birth. Regretfully, much later on in our lives, we were able to establish that he had a severe disability. After years of being told he had behavioural problems, it was only in his late forties that we were able to finally establish that he had suffered for so much of his life from Asperger's Syndrome.

Fortunately, being able to continue living with Tricia's mother and her uncle, we both had the assistance from them helping us in the initial year of bringing him up, and we certainly needed their enthusiastic and constant support. The baby always seemed so hungry. At three months old, he was eating rusks with his milk, and by six months he was enjoying Weetabix. For the first three months Richard would wake up at three in the morning for a feed, and I would have to go downstairs in the cold to make a bottle for him. It became very exhausting indeed for me, as I had to leave very early for work. We were so utterly tired on Sundays after dinner that we would both go to bed in the afternoon to catch up on our sleep. For many people, this would not be a problem, but when you each take quite powerful medication, as we both had to do daily, it was one we could both do without.

However, in the meantime, the boss's son wanted to help us. He realised that we were hard up, so he kindly chose a perfect way of helping us. He picked up a magnificent new £250 Royale pram for only £35. The pram had slight water marks on the inside from a small, negligible tiny amount of fire damage, and this was not noticeable when you put in sheets and blankets. Anyway, it was a snip. It was a very beautiful pram in cream and blue. Later on, we bought a sunshade for it, which really set it off. Importantly, it was one of the most elegant and beautiful prams, and lasted for both of our sons' early childhoods.

We continued to live with my mother-in-law for just over a year, and my wife, although she still had attacks of epilepsy, thought that she needed to live in her own house and begged me to find her a house we could rent. She felt that if she didn't stand on her own feet then, she never would, and we both had to pull together. The house was too small, and my wife, who had been virtually used by her mother as a cleaner, felt herself to be inadequate when living there. Because she could not work, she yearned for a home of our own.

1967
Our First House

I was told by a member of the staff where I worked that a local terraced house had become recently vacant, and I contacted the landlord, who was pleased to let us have the house for a nominal rent. However, he said he would have to increase the rent from nineteen shillings and sixpence to one guinea (which is £1.05), but that he would put a new backdoor gate up for us as we now had a child. It was fantastic. We were so excited, and accepted his offer. Also, it was not far from the warehouse where I then worked, so I would not have to cycle so far.

We were so excited to have this - albeit somewhat rundown - house, and family friends came and helped us to move in the contents we needed and make it ready for us to live in comfortably. My uncle who had been my best man came to wallpaper the living room and did other essential work to make it habitable. Again, this was an absolute godsend.

I can remember buying our first table and chairs, which only cost £5 from a market stall at Leicester. This set was metal-framed and covered in plastic. We had a three piece suite given to us, and my wife had a double bed, dressing table and wardrobe. I had saved enough money to buy a new cooker and a washing machine, and we were now starting our real married life at last. A cheap carpet lasted about two months before we had to discard it. I can remember buying six dinner plates from Leicester market, only to find they were all chipped when I reached home. Since I lived within walking distance of the market, I quickly took them back and confronted the seller, who seemed somewhat shocked, but I got my money back. I wonder how many others he had conned that day?

The fact that we were only half a mile from Leicester city centre was an excellent opportunity for window shopping after the shops had closed. We would walk around with our pram and dream. Owing to my wife suffering epilepsy as well as me, we had to help each other since she was well enough to look after a child but not also able to perform a job.

It was enough work and worry for her to look after our first born and the house. Shopping was easy. In those days, you had a book and gave it to the local grocer, who delivered it that same day. Bread - those lovely, white, crusty, nutty loaves – all of this was obtained from the local bakers. Our next door neighbour would thoughtfully ask if we wanted some bread when she went to buy hers. It was all good, wholesome food. The butcher would look after his regulars, and we would eat a lot of liver, sausages, homemade food and stewing steak.

We always looked forward to my mother in law preparing us a lovely Sunday dinner. Her cooking was terrific - a delicious beef roast with Yorkshire pudding, roast potatoes, onions, spring cabbage, peas and gravy. It was all so delicious, as I still recall I looked forward to it every week.

NHS

The problems of coping with married life were a shock to both of us; we had to look after ourselves. It wasn't that we were lazy - far from it. We both had disabilities that required taking strong medication that in some cases sapped our energy and had a powerful sedative effect on both of us. While living at our first house, I was taken seriously ill and became very dehydrated, and the doctor had to be called as I was too weak to move from the bed.

The doctor carried out various tests on me and prescribed some horrible medicine that I had to take. He found difficulty in establishing what was wrong with me at first and eventually said it was *encephalitis*. It left me very weak, and I was off work for a whole month, but the boss still generously paid me. When I returned, he kindly said I was only to work six hours a day for the first month, and I was glad he did this as it was very humane of him. A good, kind man.

However, I managed to pull through, although it was clearly severe: a clerk I spoke to in the office said that she knew someone who had endured that particular illness and had been confined to a wheelchair for a total of six months altogether.

At our first little house, I had promised I would take my wife on a proper honeymoon, and to fund this I had decided to help out at one of the local public houses part-time. However, before we enjoyed this holiday, we had some excellent news that we were to be housed in a new maisonette on the St Matthews Estate at Leicester. This was because our terraced house was scheduled to be pulled down for slum clearance.

Part Time Work - Barman

Getting to grips with an additional job is hard work, as is being on your feet for 8-10 hours on Saturdays, and sometimes on Sundays, too. Working three hours some nights also takes a lot of effort, especially when you get up early for the day job at an exceptionally early hour.

Returning to my regular weekday job on Mondays was hard work, too. I enjoyed this, but it was tiring and difficult work, especially at weekends when matches were on because we were near the local football ground. As a result, we would have many supporters come to have a drink before the game. I managed to save most of this money and decided to take my wife on the promised belated honeymoon at a hotel in Jersey.

She and I had never had such a holiday as this, and we both looked forward to it. My mother had arranged to look after Richard for us while we were on holiday. She was in her element having her grandson to herself for a whole week. During that time, she managed to get him to walk, as we found out when we arrived back from our honeymoon.

I cannot remember which airport we flew from, but I will never forget the plane itself. There were all these passenger jets taking off, and we were waiting for ours when an announcement came about our Dan Air flight. A plane taxied along to pick up passengers, and it was an absolute relic of the past. People stared at this... one could only call it a wreck, and some laughed, just to then be told this *was* the plane we would be travelling on. It was cramped, and the passenger seats were positioned at an angle and so very uncomfortable. However, by the grace of God, we reached Jersey safely.

Our holiday exceeded all our wildest expectations. We had a lovely hotel room and a waiter who could not do enough for us. On the day of our departure, the money had nearly run out, and we had to be very careful as to what we actually spent. We finally arrived back home after a delay in finding that my mother and stepfather eventually had had to leave the baby with Tricia's mother, and could not wait for us. However, my mother-in-law had looked after them and then taken over the babysitting. She was pleased to tell us that Richard had started to walk at last. My own mother had cleverly taught him to walk by giving him a football, so if he fell, he would only fall onto the football, and would not hurt himself.

Ever since we had moved to our first home, my wife had become very friendly with the local vicar. He was called the Reverend Bernard Badger. He was a wonderful man, and an extremely well-educated individual. My wife, not having experienced much religious instruction or education, was so moved by him, and became a practising Christian. He was like a father to her, and visited us many times, helping us in our biblical understanding. We both went to church on Sundays, although at first it was a High Anglican Church, and it was at times difficult for us to follow the services. However, this introduction in our life was to support us through the various difficulties and problems that lay ahead. We were later confirmed in a lovely church by the Bishop of Leicester and did our best to follow a Christian way of life.

At times, it was difficult to honour the Sabbath and to follow Christ's teachings, but it helped my wife very much and gave her the strength throughout her life to cope with various problems. These were sometimes regarding health, and we also experienced financial and social issues in our married life. Even though it was a long way away, we used to push the pram to our church on a Sunday morning en route to Tricia's mother, which was about seven miles away, then we did this again in the evening. It was good exercise for both of us.

We obviously could not drive, both being epileptics, and had to abide by the restrictions placed on us.

Besides that, we did not have the money to buy a car, never mind run it. It was a hard life for both of us, but being young, and in love, we managed, and my wife grew in strength and developed as an attractive young woman, mother and wife.

1967-1969

Having now moved to our maisonette, I had to give up my additional job as a barman, but to earn the extra income to provide for my growing family, I then took on the role of part-time insurance salesman and collector in the evenings and on a Saturday morning. My wife was now expecting our second child, and we urgently needed the income. The cost of living was increasing, and our clothing wore out and needed replacing. We had a maisonette that needed some more furniture, and I was the one who had to work my socks off to provide for my family.

Initially, I went out in the evenings to sell insurance with a manager to get the hang of it, and quickly became adept at earning a reasonable additional income, which, of course, helped. I realised, however, that if I worried about money and paying bills too much, then this could have an effect and consequently bring about one of my severe headache attacks. It was, therefore, better for me to earn money and not to worry. On Fridays and Saturdays, I collected insurance premiums, and on Monday dinner time I took my takings into the office with my insurance books.

Later on, during the week, I collected their premiums and repeated the exercise. I had found a nearly foolproof way of selling insurance to houses that had been sold or re-let and would introduce myself to the man of the house suggesting that he took out an insurance policy to cover his life for the sake of his wife and family for such a small amount of money. They were interested that the cover was good and possibly crucial to all the family. Later on, when they had settled down, I would suggest an endowment policy for his wife and contents cover on the house. Generally, they readily agreed, and felt I was a friendly, helpful advisor, and my insurance book for the area increased well.

After a couple of years, I had become disenchanted with the way I was being treated in my warehouseman's role. The foreman seemed to be growing quite antagonistic towards me for some strange reason and, eventually, we ended up having a severe disagreement about stock levels. A delivery driver had recently been caught by the boss stealing, and was arrested, prosecuted and sent to prison. The boss addressed us all the next day saying that if we wanted anything, he would much rather give it to us than send us to jail. He was most upset. I believed that the foreman was well aware of what was going on, and it eventually resulted in us both, that is the foreman and me, not being able to work with each other.

In a heated discussion, I then resigned and went home. I felt I had endured enough from the foreman in the way he treated and spoke to me. Besides that, I figured I could do better for myself and obtain a more rewarding job. My mother-in-law, who worked in the canteen at East Midlands Gas (Emgas), thought I should apply for an office vacancy, but I dismissed the idea. I should have listened to her then, as you will find out later in this book.

The problem this precipitated turned into a dire situation indeed. I became anxious and had a massive epileptic seizure which is known by the medical profession as a 'grand mal'. This resulted in the doctor coming to see me. He issued me with a sick certificate, but this would not pay the bills nor feed my family, so matters got worse and the doctor was called again. He told me that he thought I should go on the sick for the rest of my life, which at that time shocked me, and I became very depressed. The reason I had suffered this attack was because of the worry of providing for my family and paying all the bills. A turning point in my wife's self-confidence then occurred. As the situation had made me so ill, my wife, bless her, had to go to the social security to get them to pay us what we were entitled to receive so we could just about survive and cope. I had to work for a living, and that was the only way forward. It was far easier to work and not worry than to sit at home trying to think about how you could manage on so little.

I quickly realised that if you want something, you have to work for it, and that work was right for me. In fact, most of my married life I have done a full-time job, and part-time jobs too (sometimes three) to increase my income, and I applied that principle when I was married as it saved me from worrying and had the benefit of the exercise in doing the rounds of my clients kept me fit. Walking around streets knocking on doors canvassing for insurance, and later in my life for cavity wall insulation, kept the wolf from the door and increased my income.

The sad thing about it was that I allowed my wife to indulge herself with the children whom she loved. I loved them, but I had to pay the bills, so I did not see them as much as I would have liked while they were growing up.

I ended up having three weeks off, and frequently scanned and read the evening papers to find another job. I eventually found one that would keep the wolf from the door, but, owing to my disability, it was not that easy. You see, I had to be honest with my employers as to my health problems in case I should be taken ill whilst working for them. I ended up later as a warehouseman in a shoe stiffener manufacturer. I had about seven difficult women to look after as they had to pack the merchandise. They were some of the most trying and awkward women you could ever have to deal with. They argued, shouted, screamed at each other and called each other names, so the place seemed like bedlam at times. You had to get used to their antics and ignore them in their 'calling' of each other, while never, ever even slightly siding with any of them. It turned out, fortunately, to be proper training for my future career when I moved to East Midlands Gas (Emgas).

One morning, going to work I endured another serious epileptic seizure while riding my bike, crashing into a cast iron street lamp. I ended up with my head and face black and blue with bruising and enduring a significant headache. It was good that you only felt the pain after a seizure. Police contacted my wife and let her know what had happened, and I was taken to Leicester Royal Infirmary, x-rayed and checked out, and then kept in for the night. Not one person inquired about me from the stiffener factory, but they had a shock when they saw me on my return to work. They were horrified to see the state of my face and the many blackened bruises.

This job did not last long, as after a couple of months, a large lorry came with about thirty tonnes of cardboard boxes that I had to manhandle and unloaded. I never received any help from anyone and, as I got near the end of unpacking it, I was fuming. I did not mind hard work, but this was slave labour due to the complete ignorance of the manager. At the end of this job, I went to the manager and told him just what

I thought and what he could do with the post. Not one person had offered to help me. I walked out and went to the labour exchange, and asked for details of jobs that were suitable for me.

1969 – I am Just 28
Labour Exchange - What a Disaster

About half an hour later I was in the labour exchange, and was then called to the front desk. A young man of only about 18 years of age briefly and somewhat carelessly, thoughtless of my feelings, told me the only job they had for me was as a toilet attendant. This to me was an insult, and no consideration had been given to my achievements and past extensive, varied and sometimes perilous work history. I was livid, and I quickly informed the young man that I had spent six months studying for exams, and what I had achieved. I told him in no uncertain terms where to stick the job, and I didn't mince my words.

People stared at me as I walked out of that office and, as I left, suddenly I noticed an entrance next door that said 'Professional Vacancies'. I went in and asked if they had any jobs at East Midlands Gas (Emgas) to which they replied, 'Yes, do sit down and let me take some details from you.'

I recalled that my mother-in-law had previously suggested this company, but I had ignored her. I had come to the conclusion that it would be better in the long term to take a job like this as it would provide some security for my family. This had come back now to remind me, but I also believe the Lord was involved in this as well.

They told me that I would have to take a numerical test at their offices. The receptionist reassured me that I would easily pass this, and that the organisation were always pleased to employ disabled people if they could. The company was proud that it used more than the average number of disabled and looked for ability rather than disability. However, I do not think this message had been heard by everyone, as you will see when I was interviewed for another position some years later.

A week later I went for the test, passed it and was offered a position as a general clerk in the metering records department. A letter of the appointment arrived a few days later, and although the money was no better, I would be included in the pension scheme. Looking ahead, this information was very reassuring to my family and me, especially at this time in my life.

The offer had lifted me, but as I did not have a proper suit to wear for work, I had to find a way of buying one somehow. Savings were non-existent, and I had to sell even my tape recorder and some other electrical goods to a second-hand shop near us to be suitably dressed for office work. The only suit I could afford was a green tweed, and it was a colour I was not that happy with, and I do not think I have ever worn that colour since. It was so loose that I had to wear braces to hold my trousers up.

My first day at work came about, and I had previously bought a small wheel cycle which came from my part-time insurance work, and it was a necessity so that I could get to work. I chose one of the latest models to join the new entrants that would be starting at East Midlands Gas (Emgas). It was inspiring, but I was apprehensive, and a whole new world seemed to be opening before me. In reality, this became part of my life for the next twenty-five years.

The one thing I can remember is that my first month's wages amounted to £69. I had to feed a family of three and an expectant wife on that and pay all my bills: no wonder I had to do a part-time job as well.

Adapting to clerical work and trying to understand computers was confusing to me at first, but I had spent years pushing myself and adjusting to different jobs, and the fact that I now had a job and could provide with my part-time insurance agency work was in itself satisfying. Worry and not enough sleep, and occasionally forgetting to take my medication, all contributed to me still having attacks, which incapacitated me for at least twenty four hours each time they occurred. It took me years to learn from my mistakes. I now have a strict routine every day to reduce these attacks and have been free for twenty years plus. Thank God.

I remember a woman supervisor who was so strict and spoke to me when I first started learning as though I already knew exactly what she was talking about. I am afraid I didn't, and had to go back and ask for more guidance. Regretfully, I found she became more relentless and expected too much from me, and spoke to me as though I was stupid. This must have upset me, as I started being severely affected by her attitude. Unfortunately, this caused me to have a seizure and fall on top of her. The next thing I knew, I was waking up in the first aid room.

Each time I always had grand mal attacks. Twenty-four hours was the maximum I would allow myself to be off work, irrespective of how bad I felt. I then forced myself to go to work the next day and manage until the weekend, when I had a break and could rest. When you are unconscious and have to be carried out to the sick bay and put to bed for an hour so you can recover, it is embarrassing. Even more so, when your son and wife come to pick you up and walk you to the car to take you home. Later, they undressed me and bathed me. Since I always perspired and peed myself in these awful, embarrassing, uncontrollable attacks and needed a complete change of clothing as a consequence, it was very difficult for me.

I would then be put to bed to sleep it off, then would get up and go through a period of deep depression as to why this should happen to me. I thought it was unfair. It was a cursed disability with the general public having little if any real understanding of epilepsy and seizures, and my fellow clerks never realising the physical pain and actual mental anguish that you go through. I had so many attacks that people in the early days used to put something in my mouth to stop me from biting my tongue.

The main problem was that the energy I expended when having an attack sapped me so much that it would last nearly a week before I felt better and fully recovered. When I think of some of the excuses some people gave for being off sick, like a toothache or a headache or, 'I have the flu but will be in tomorrow', I hope I set an example to them and to others by persevering with the pain and lack of any energy to force myself to go back to work quickly. In some of these attacks, I could even chip or break my teeth or disfigure them. Sometimes, I bit my tongue, and it would bleed. With blood coming out of my mouth I also suffered a great deal of bruising from falling. All this was exacerbated by the depression and exhaustion I suffered afterwards when, after a long sleep, I became more conscious again of my surroundings.

In the end, frustrated with dentists and my consequent appearance, I had thirteen teeth taken out in the hospital. It was a horrific experience as I can remember coming round while they were taking the last two of my teeth out! People would not believe me and thought I imagined the whole agonisingly painful experience. Strange as it may seem, years later I read of patients who had suffered similar experiences, and investigations had proved that the anaesthesia equipment had been faulty.

The problem the next day was that I could not move and the doctor had to be called, and he diagnosed severe shock from having my teeth out and said that with rest and painkillers I would eventually recover.

I ended up with twelve or more stitches in my mouth that same Christmas, and I also had an abscess. I found brandy seemed to soothe my pain but, in the end, had to go to Accident and Emergency on Christmas Day, where a doctor said, 'This will hurt.' I nearly jumped through the roof. He had whipped my stitches out, and the poison from the abscess started to be released, and run out, and he then prescribed antibiotics. I then went home to our Christmas dinner only to find that after having my teeth out I was hungry but could not chew or eat anything. However, I eventually got my false teeth fitted, and came to the conclusion that I should have persevered with what original teeth I had, as false teeth can never replace your own. Your gums shrink, and your false teeth have to be replaced periodically, or mended and even sometimes stuck in with temporary paste to keep them in place.

During my first few years at East Midlands Gas (Emgas), these experiences were to a degree stressful.

This involved getting to settle down to this type of work. It was a significant change for me, possibly because of my disability and the adjustment from a very physical work role to a more sedentary one. Eventually, I was given the difficult job of finding gas meters that had been erroneously deleted from the computer records. I gather now that no one would want a post like this, but it turned out my saviour, since I was able to question clerical staff in other sections which would, in some cases, show me where the record had been deleted and how this had happened. It was an excellent way for me to learn, and I found that I quickly became more proficient in my job, more useful to the company itself, and I became acquainted with the right people who could advise me.

The other added advantage of this job was that I had to visit various sections to obtain the correct information, so some physical effort was needed, and this walking also benefitted my health considerably. The walk between offices was more beneficial in a tangible way.

Previous Company Asks Me Back

This job improved my knowledge of how the gas billing system worked, and helped me considerably to understand the work I had to do. I had done this work for about six months when a director from the toy warehouse company that I previously worked for approached me again and took me to my local pub to see if I would come back and work for them. He had presented a bunch of flowers to my wife and some chocolates. I at last felt appreciated, and realised that, for once in my life, I was wanted for the effort I had put in. However, after talking it over with my wife, I refused their request, as I felt that the job I was now doing at British Gas had far better prospects, conditions and security, and these prospects were the makings of me.

This decision then made me realise that I had the chance of redressing my educational failure at grammar school, I had attained RSA and Institute of Bookkeepers exams with credits, and a First Class

Diploma in a variety of subjects at Portland Training College for the Disabled, with credits. Even though my results at the grammar school were not brilliant, I had benefitted from the four years spent there, and I had been able to put that education to good use while working at East Midlands Gas.

Over the years, the company has provided the additional education and knowledge for its staff, but only if you were prepared to develop your own abilities. I used this opportunity to grow from a junior clerk to a higher manager. I was eventually able to gain promotion to far greater heights than I or others could ever have realised at that time. The one thing this job gave me was to open up opportunities, to make the best of myself and my particular skills. It also provided a pension and some security at that time. I wanted to provide for my family and look after them.

Owing to my previous health problems before starting work at East Midlands Gas, I was excluded from their sick pay scheme. However, at the time, I was certainly fit enough to contribute towards the pension and have those rights. My health record should have been reviewed within my first year but it was not until some years later that this was finally satisfactorily sorted out. It was only when in a heated discussion with a manager that he realised that I was not paid if I was off sick. He realised that this was totally unfair, sorted it out, and that gave me even greater security. He said that I should have been paid sick pay when off ill and would be from now on, and it was an error on the company's part.

1969
Our Second Son

My wife was now expecting our second child, and was suffering fainting attacks. I had to take time off work, especially towards the end of her pregnancy. Physical activity was very tiring for her, and I had received a letter from work at that time informing me that if I didn't return to work my employment would be terminated. This was a real shock to me. I would have expected some compassion at this time, but had to devise a way of returning to work.

I was agitated at receiving this letter and had to think about what to do. My mother-in-law could not help as she had to work, so there was no other way but to get my wife admitted to the maternity hospital early. I had a talk with my wife and said we have to go to the maternity home tomorrow, and that we would walk it.

'I expect because of the distance you will find it tedious and faint,' I said, and she did. As her delivery was not far away, they decided to keep her in because of her blood pressure being up. This allowed me to return to work. This action may seem hard, but I couldn't think of any other way of resolving the matter.

We had another disaster during her pregnancy, as my son Richard developed measles. Once the doctor knew, I had to rush to the hospital to get an injection for my wife to stop the fetus from becoming damaged. All was well at Andrew's birth, but, later on, the school established he had colour blindness. Is it just a coincidence that measles if left unchecked can cause blindness?

My wife had at one time while pregnant fallen from the top of the stairs. It was when my mother and stepfather had been visiting us. Thankfully, she and the baby, after being examined, were alright. My wife had been ill a few times when I had been at work, and I can remember one day returning to see, through the french windows of the maisonette, my wife lying on the carpet and our son, Richard, patting her face. The last few weeks of her pregnancy had been very trying, but she eventually delivered another son, Andrew, a brother for Richard.

Tricia had tried to breastfeed our first son, but her body did not produce the milk needed in time. She had prepared for it, and the milk was on tap when necessary. We had decided it was a far better method than the bottle because she used to fall asleep feeding Richard with a bottle. Andrew did not wake up at night, and we managed to get a good six hours of sleep each night.

Malcolm Le-Hair and Bettina Croft

I was relieved that at last our second child had been born and the fact that my wife could breast feed him did not subject us to the tiredness and depression we suffered with our first child. Physical demands with another child to look after can quickly bring on depression. We had to be careful as Social Services could be employed to judge whether we were in a fit state of health to look after our children.

Epilepsy

Many people regarded something like epilepsy as a 'mad' illness. This mainly was due to some people not only suffering from epilepsy but also other mental and frightening illness, including additional brain damage that compounded their problems. However, if people really knew just how many well-known persons suffer from this disability, they would find that they are some of the most intelligent individuals in the world: professors, doctors, writers, musicians, actors, painters and even members of the Royal Family.

Here is just a small selection of the many thousands of famous people who suffer or did suffer from epilepsy:
- Vincent Van Gogh
- Susan Boyle
- Elton John
- Katie Hopkins
- Edgar Allan Poe
- Martin Kemp

- Theodore Roosevelt
- Agatha Christie
- Lewis Carroll
- Charles Dickens
- Prince
- Michelangelo
- Florence Griffith Joyner
- Tchaikovsky
- Prince John (of the Royal Family, who died aged 13)
- Fyodor Dostoevsky
- Rik Mayall
- Richard Burton
- Julius Caesar
- Handel
- Peter the Great
- Socrates
- Sir Walter Scott
- Alfred Nobel
- Isaac Newton
- Joan of Arc
- Muhammad
- Margot Hemingway

An amazing example of famous, talented people!

Not many people would realise that you also can often suffer depression after a seizure. It was not only that, but the pain you received as a result of falling and banging your bones against something hard and unyielding, like a desk or a floor, was terrible. Bruises were an issue, and sometimes I got a cut and a sore tongue from biting it, which took time to heal. Plus, people do not see those injuries, but I felt them, and this could be very painful for a few days. When I had an attack, it was a grand mal, which in most instances would not give me the time to get onto the floor before becoming unconscious. Another issue was that I would sometimes let out a scream which could frighten some individuals. I would shake, and the physical activity I expended drained me of most of my strength and energy.

There were a couple of times when I would experience an aura before my seizure. An aura is a beautiful, exhilarating feeling that comes over you, and then, suddenly, it's gone, and you lose consciousness. However, I have only experienced this about two or three times in my whole life since I have been epileptic.

It mostly would start with a feeling of ecstasy, then your leg shaking, and you had a split second to save yourself, but generally, it was very hit and miss, and more of the latter, as you eventually lost control of your body.

The idea was to get yourself onto the ground before you lost consciousness to save yourself from falling and hurting yourself badly, but I was rarely successful at avoiding this fall. One time I had an attack at work and was arched over a chair, and hurt my back badly, which I felt for many weeks afterwards.

However, being a sufferer did provide me with the knowledge and compassion of just what others in the same situations could and did suffer. Some years later, a new female clerk was introduced to my section, and, in my interview as her manager, she said so quietly, as if ashamed, that she was an epileptic, with some nervousness in her voice. I quickly set her mind at rest by quietly saying to her, 'Do you know what, so am I, so do not worry one bit!'

I can understand her reluctance in telling anyone.

WhenI had been courting a lovely, beautiful girl in my younger days soon after I had been diagnosed with epilepsy, once she found out I was epileptic she did not want to know me at all from then on. I really fell for her and suffered heartache that took me quite a little while to get over. Some years later, this was repeated with another young woman. In those days, people were not educated about this disability, or, come to that, a lot of other problems of a similar nature. There is possibly still some ignorance today.

1970
First Promotion

I had now been promoted to the position of Accounts Clerk, a step up from my previous job in Meter Records, and had only been there just over a year. Progression in seniority, and also a welcome increase in salary, followed!

My family had grown, and Tricia was beginning to enjoy life with our sons. She was a good mother and wife, and her cooking was improving. However, money was in short supply, so my part-time insurance evenings and Saturday mornings for the Liverpool and Victoria Insurance Company were essential aids to our funds. My additional job was necessary to provide extra income. I had to work harder to sell policies, as this also supplied me with a commission, which could also double your earnings.

One Friday, I remember coming home from work, and there was an awful smell in the kitchen with something that had evidently been cooking in the oven. After taking it out, I discovered it was a chicken my wife had bought from Tesco's that very day. My wife could not smell it, but I certainly could. Not having had a brilliant day at work, I took it out and put it in a carrier bag with the receipt and sped off on my bike to the first store Tesco had opened at Leicester. I asked to see the manager and then took the chicken out and placed it under his nose. It was actually green inside with mould!

He immediately realised that I was upset and had good reason to be, and said someone would visit me the very next day. I left him my home address and, true to his word, a tray of pork pies, bacon, fresh ham and sausages and other fare was delivered in recompense. We were eating exceptionally well for the next week or two.

I can remember my mother, after the war when sweets were rationed, returning the toffee that had an elastic band buried in it. Within a week a parcel was delivered which contained a variety of sweets and chocolate, and an apology.

A Good Samaritan

Unfortunately, Tricia, through looking after her mother's house, was very strict about keeping our home clean and all of us having clean clothes daily. This then made the laundry a big job, especially with two young boys. The only problem was that our washing machine decided to give up the ghost and I just didn't have the income to provide another. Fortunately, her uncle Fred, who visited us regularly and had lived with her mother since he was young, saw my frustration. Even more importantly, in his kind heart and thoughtfulness, he saw and appreciated my wife's distress.

He left earlier that particular day, saying that he had to go uptown. I told my dear wife I would see what I could do after I had finished my Saturday insurance work. However, by the time I came home her uncle had returned and said he had ordered and paid for a new washing machine, and it would be delivered to our house on the following Monday. He indeed was a good Samaritan, and came to our rescue many times later in our married life. I was glad to be able to repay him some kindness later on in his life. To me, he was one of the good Samaritans in my life, for whom I had the utmost respect.

Our son Richard had developed a double rupture as a child, and walking was becoming very difficult for him. He had to have it operated on, and, while it was worrying for us, we knew he needed it to be done. He very quickly recovered, and soon found he could now walk again and ride his tricycle.

In the maisonette above us lived an Irishman and his family. Unfortunately, his walking around with hobnail boots and bouts of drinking and sometimes shouting made it difficult for us to sleep at night. In the end, I asked the doctor for a letter as it was very trying for my wife. We took it to the council offices asking for a change of accommodation. We were then able to move nearer to Tricia's mother and uncle and could then all help each other. It was ideal for Tricia, as many of her relations and aunts lived in the area and she would rarely be on her own.

A Move to a Council House

Soon after we moved into the new council house, my mother and stepfather came to us with carpets and started helping us to sort the house out. My mother seemed glad that we had moved into a house with a generous garden for the children to play in. I was also pleased as it was easier for me to get to work living in that particular location. What was especially useful was that it was easier for my mother and stepfather to drive to this new house; they did not have to drive into Leicester as they could come on the ring road, which made it much easier for my stepfather. I also had the chance of fellow workers giving me a lift to work if they saw me waiting at the bus stop at the top of the street. Apart from saving us a lot of money on bus fares, it meant less standing in the bad weather, which was not, of course, good for my health.

I had to give up my part-time job once I moved. This was because it was too far to go on my bike collecting insurance payments and trying to sell more policies. British Gas was going through a difficult time and was getting ready for the conversion to natural gas. This was the largest peacetime exercise that any company had ever undertaken, and would take at least three years to complete. Conversion to natural gas would, in lots of cases, renewed the existing gas appliances because they were in effect refurbished so that they could burn Natural Gas.

Opportunities now occurred so that I could make up the losses of my part time earnings by applying for promotion to Accounts clerk.

Fortunately, I was lucky enough to have an excellent team leader, who quickly showed me the ropes, such as how to deal with customers on the phone, and also those that wrote in complaining or enquiring. I threw myself into this particular role and enjoyed the customer contact.

However, my wife's health gave me cause for concern, as at times she experienced periods of extreme tiredness. I could see that she was suffering. I would then take over the housework and other essential jobs that needed doing. Sometimes I would have to put her to bed, but she would eventually recover. She was not used to working so hard. Looking after two children, a husband and a house was more than enough for her.

1971
Promoted to Senior Clerk

My learning quickly developed and I became very proficient at dealing with this promotion. I put a great deal of effort into ensuring customers were contacted promptly by telephone and by follow-up letter. Also, I was dealing swiftly with far in excess of the number of queries and replies each day that was expected of me, and this quickly became noticed. Many a message received was, in fact, a thank you from some customer who was grateful for the way their enquiry or complaint had been dealt with by me. All 'thank you' letters were passed to senior managers for them to see and comment on. It wasn't very long before I was promoted to Team Leader at East Midlands Gas (Emgas).

Being promoted to Team Leader then gave me opportunities to develop my management skills, as my team had four accounts clerks, one who would be my deputy when I was away. The trouble in East Midlands Gas (Emgas) at that time was that it was very beauracratic and those in authority became accustomed to, and tampered with, that form of management. Having been in some different jobs before coming to East Midlands Gas (Emgas), I had already experienced other ways of managing, and it did help me considerably. A lot of the staff who worked at East Midlands Gas (Emgas) had come straight from school and had little, if any, experience of working for another company, so I was able to use that benefit to my advantage.

Already in my life, I had experienced a wide variety of jobs and experiences. I believe that one of its benefits in my case was that ideas readily came to mind about ways specific tasks could be done more efficiently. I started to put my thoughts to managers on memos, copies of which I kept. However, sadly, I became very frustrated when I found they were being ignored, and then finally decided that I should put them into the Suggestion Scheme, where at first they still, however, failed to reach anyone important's attention. Not to be disheartened, I continued to put these ideas forward. Finally, becoming more adept at identifying the benefits and savings that these would make for the company, I would get a cheque now and then, which was helpful to me in providing the little luxuries for my family.

I found a better way of developing ideas for the Suggestion Scheme. One important one was to look what other utilities were doing and, if necessary, adapt it. What's the sense in reinventing the wheel?

My ideas worked, providing us with extra cash, not much but welcome when you had a family like mine. I also wanted to do as much as I could for them, being a devoted husband and father.

With natural gas conversion fast approaching, the accounts sections were reorganised to cope with the extra workload we were to then endure. Later, further opportunities arose for a significant promotion. I readily applied for one of the positions available and, much to the amazement of other staff members, who had thought about applying but hadn't bothered, I was fortunately successful.

I heard that they were frightened to accept all the detailed responsibilities, whereas I was not in the least scared of taking on more responsibility.

1972
Promoted to Unit Leader in Doncaster

I had another increase in salary, and, due to my somewhat meteoric rise through the company's ranks, I became Unit Leader of the Doncaster Section, which was, however, the smallest region. I again worked extremely hard with my staff and customers and especially in dealing with the arrears of work that all sections had inherited. Staff turnover was very high, as in those days the wage rates were better in other companies but not the actual working conditions. East Midlands Gas (Emgas) was exemplary in that respect. However, my staff were appreciated, and, wherever I could, I did my best to see they were each individually promoted for the benefit of the company as well as for themselves.

Our section quickly managed to clear the arrears of work, and a more relaxed and happy atmosphere developed as a result of this. Senior managers noted the success our part of the section was continually generating, and one morning I was called to see my senior manager, who suggested that I should become responsible for another district, which was noted as having problems with its staffing and consequent work arrears. As there was some rivalry between the geographic divisions, I refused it at first. Upon this occurring, the manager told me that if I didn't take it, I would not get any further in my career - and he really meant it.

He suggested that I go away and think about it, consider my whole position, and try to realise the splendid opportunity this would give me and not disregard this golden chance. Finally, he added that he wanted me to let him have an answer the following morning.

1973-1984
Promotion to Unit Leader, Mansfield

I was shocked at his threat, and was then joined by his assistant manager, who spent some time with me doing his best to prove that he was not the horrible person he was now portrayed. Instead, he was one who would give me every assistance necessary to sort the section out and bring it up to date. In fact, he said, 'If you need overtime I will arrange to ensure that for you, and for staff that you need or want to remain at night and/or Saturday mornings from eight till twelve.'

I relished the idea that I could work overtime, and the next morning agreed to change sections. It had more clerks, more customers, but of course also many more arrears of work. The following day I accepted the challenge to become Unit Leader of Mansfield Gas Accounts.

The start of overtime was a welcome addition to my salary, and this was to carry on for three years because we had natural gas conversion and decimalisation to come. In both of these exercises and situations, we also had to educate ourselves and to explain the changes to our customers. We found that the use of standard phrases that could be used when dealing with customers on the phone or in sending explanatory letters was a welcome help to all of us. With decimalisation, I contacted my old toy company and found they had metric conversion biros containing all the information, which had a quick reference table hidden in its casing that could be brought to view. This, of course, would be useful, and time saving. Very soon, I had sold a couple of hundred to many members of staff. This then helped the persons concerned, as well as the company itself.

Mansfield section seemed a hostile environment to be in at first, as the staff were initially suspicious of me. Fortunately, as it turned out, it was not long before they did realise that they had to get on top of the work. Their attitude towards what I was achieving slowly warmed, and they became more enthusiastic.

Staff very quickly got my message to improve their attitude and to work harder, and they rose to the occasion. Even my friend, Dave, who had been brought over from another section (Hire Purchase), was responding well. Usually, when staff were transferred, it seemed as though a black cloud hung over them until senior managers were satisfied with their individual output and quality of work. I was perfectly happy with Dave. Both his attitude and his work were such that one day

I took Dave's work over to a senior manager as an example so he could view and inspect the high quantity and quality of Dave's output. In fact, I got along with him so well that later Dave became my best friend.

We were blessed with a new starter person, Philip Reid, a shy man but with impeccable manners and an incredibly grateful attitude towards us all. He found it difficult at first to look you in the eye. But, Oh! What a funny man he was when he got going. You could not help but like him and feel sorry for Philip all at the same time, but writing came naturally to him as he was an author and skilled at writing. He was with us for a couple of years, liked his pint, and was an able table tennis fanatic. He was a secretary or chairman of the Table Tennis Association and was well known for the work he had done promoting the game. He had at one time been a close friend of the Shah of Persia and showed me the silk embossed cards he used to receive. After Philip Reid had left, he returned about some months later, having kindly promised to bring me personally a copy of his own book on Victor Barna, who was then a famous table tennis champion. The book Philip wrote contained details of Victor Barna and his many successes in winning fifteen world championships, amongst many others. The renowned maker of table tennis bats, Dunlop, had asked him to write the book, and I believe he did it in three months, and it was then put on sale. The book he gave me had a thoughtful inscription written in it to me, in his beautiful, if not really elegant, handwriting, which I still cherish to this day.

His inscription was:

To Malcolm
The best boss I ever had (Too good for this place)!! Philip Reid

Dave, My Best Friend

Dave, who had rapidly become my best friend, had his eye on a young woman called Glenys who worked on the same section, and she very soon became his girlfriend. Dave lived up to his image, and it wasn't long before he was dating the best looking woman in the accounts section within East Midlands Gas (Emgas). Having become friends of his, my wife and I arranged to go out as a foursome for a meal with them. Later on, they would meet at my house and play with our children. His wife would chat with Tricia, and we all became eventually very close friends.

As our friendship developed, they stayed at our house most weekends as we all enjoyed one another's company. We would go out and have a drink and a meal together, sit and watch television, or just talk. In these pleasant times, we would get to know each other more intimately, and the friendship grew. We would talk for hours about work, friendships, you name it. It all added to our enduring happiness together, and we became closer than ever. Eventually, they became engaged and started making plans to buy their first house together near where we lived. It wasn't long before I helped him to sort it out so they could get married and settle down together.

Previously, my wife and I had a long weekend at the seaside with them, but the weather was not very good, and Dave was forever hungry, so we were often stopping to eat at different places to satisfy his needs. I did not have the money that he had, with him being single, but Dave was cautious with money and had already saved a lot.

To improve both our promotion chances, we then started studying for an HNC conversion course, and, regrettably, it nearly finished our friendship. Sadly, this was through me listening to caustic comments made by others about Dave, and I regretted this. Because my mother was so ill, I could not spare the time to study, and because Dave did and passed and I didn't, I then temporarily terminated our friendship. It was more than a bit childish and a jealous part of me, and I later profoundly regretted this.

In our earlier days, we had had a night out with our wives at a foreign lager bar in the centre of Leicester. We had a fantastic night, but the minute I stepped into the fresh air, I just keeled over. I was helpless. Dave and my wife had to put me to bed. Dave was stronger than me. His rugger training and drinking prepared him for such nights as this. The next day he laughed his head off at the state I was in. How he drove us home that particular night, I do not know.

About this time, Tricia's uncle, Fred, who lived with her mother, was involved in a motorcycle accident which severely damaged his leg. He kept complaining about it, and I told him that I had arranged for him to have a chat with a solicitor to see if he was entitled to any damages. His case was settled out of court, and he seemed happy as to the amount he received. His injury kept him off work a long while, and he could not look after himself. I decided we should move and buy our first house to be near him.

Having noticed a terraced house around the corner from where Tricia's mother and Fred lived, I enquired about it, and we eventually bought it, as Tricia's uncle gave her some more money for our deposit. Living in such close vicinity to him, Tricia was able to go and visit him during the day, and I was able to bathe him and take him to the public house at the weekend. He absolutely loved this as he could then try to indoctrinate the regulars with his political views.

My mother was at this time frequently ill with stomach pain, until it was established she had an ulcer and needed an operation. My mother fortunately recovered enough to carry on her job, and both of them started to enjoy life again. I know at one time in her life she had used pure lemon juice to help reduce her weight, and she never seemed right after using it. Perhaps the acidity of this affected her adversely.

The horrific car accident that they had already suffered and the compensation they received allowed them to be comfortable, although my stepfather and my mother had always saved when they had money.

My mother adored our children, and I am sure would have not let them out of her sight if we had lived nearby, so they visited us as often as they could to see the boys. My stepfather had only one hand, his right one, as his left arm was withered, and after twenty years he had been advised to have the arm amputated when he was twenty one years old. When driving, it was understandably difficult for him during changing gears using a false arm, but he managed it. I am sorry that for some reason I stopped him from buying an automatic gear change vehicle when he wanted a new car. He would have found it a lot easier, but I suppose I was like a lot of men in this country who at that time – I did not like the idea of automatic gear in cars in case the driver did not manage the same control as with using a stick shift.

However, that view has significantly changed in my case, as I now believe automatic cars are the best thing since sliced bread. In fact, I think they're much safer, as you cannot stall them and can concentrate more on the road, having better control of the car as you have two hands on the wheel most of the time.

Moving next door to Tricia's relations was excellent and helpful for us all. Tricia was used to living like that, and her mother and uncle, aunts and cousins would regularly call to see if we were alright. It was also good that I could look after her uncle Fred, as he needed help in bathing and washing his hair. This was due to his frail health, his eventual immobility through a road accident. Because of this our friendship and respect for each other grew and he enjoyed my company when we went for a drink together. I was a sort of protector to him as, sometimes, when I accompanied him to his public house venues, his socialist views expressed strongly could lead to him being verbally abused by other drinkers. However, he would quickly shrug this off.

My Mother's Brain Tumour Diagnosed

My mother was then taken seriously ill, and her doctor, who had visited her three weeks previously, believed that she was suffering a nervous breakdown. Eventually, it was established she had a brain tumour, and it was, moreover, found to be inoperable. My stepfather had asked his own doctor to visit her. Within a matter of minutes of arriving at her bedside he diagnosed this severe condition and told my step-father that it could well be a brain tumour.

She was immediately admitted to hospital, and over the following two weeks, my mother descended rapidly into a coma, or was deliberately put into one to avoid the pain. After two weeks, I became apprehensive because nothing seemed being done to treat her, and I firmly told the staff this. Eventually she had an operation at Addenbrooke's Hospital, a famous Cambridge research hospital.

Some time later, after having had her operation, we were told we could see her, and for a time she seemed quite reasonable in her responses, but I sensed all was not well with her. They had relieved her from a severe headache by making a hole in the side of her head so this tumour could actually grow out. This then reduced the pressure on the brain, which was causing the headaches. Upon leaving her bedside, a doctor ushered us into a small room and told us that she had an inoperable tumour and only weeks now to live. Within the next few weeks, we were to see a tumour as big as a small cauliflower grow swiftly from the side of her head. My mother was only 53 years of age at the time. The specialists believed that the cause of the tumour was the concussion she had suffered in the car accident she and my step-father had been involved in some ten years earlier.

I travelled to Peterborough from Leicester by train every weekend so I could visit her with my stepfather. It was the least I could do. Besides that, my step-father needed as much support as possible. He was devastated by it all. However, he did also have my mother's close friends to comfort him. They lived in a bungalow nearby.

With my mother in the hospital having such a fatal illness, I could not do my homework, and had to withdraw from my studies. Fortunately, she was eventually moved back to Peterborough Hospital. It was very tiring for me and very depressing. It was good that although my wife and I had our faith and had both become practising Christians the thought of losing my mother at a very early age was for me too hard to accept.

It was good that my mother was in a coma, and I hope she never felt the headaches that she used had so often before suffered from so excruciatingly. My stepfather and I would sit by her bedside, but there was little we could do except tenderly hold her hand and talk to her in the hope that she would obtain some comfort, hear us and know that we were all with her, surrounding her with our love and care. Eventually, the tumour grew and became very noticeable to other visitors, and my mother was moved into a room on her own. My stepfather visited my mother every single day, and so he was more aware of my mother's deterioration than I was and possibly was able to accept her inevitable passing away more quickly.

I would regularly say my prayers every night by the bedside, and would sometimes fall asleep because of the strain that daily life was placing on me. My stepfather would take me back to the railway station to return home.

One night I was so tired out that I fell asleep on the train and ended up late at night at Birmingham station, and had to get a taxi back to Leicester, arriving there in the early hours. I was awoken by a big, burly African lady, who was one of the cleaners. She gave me the fright of my life. I was becoming mentally and physically exhausted with everything; work, family demands, helping and looking out for my wife's uncle and my own mother, as well as Tricia's mother, who was living in the next street.

Praying was comforting and the least I could do as a Christian, and I can say that I would not be where I am today if not for my belief in God. Being Christian has over the years given me great comfort and strength and helped me in my life, as you will no doubt gather after you have finished reading this book.

With both myself and my wife suffering epilepsy, we were allowed a telephone with the line rental paid for by the state. This was very helpful, especially at this period in my life with my mother so gravely ill. I would phone the hospital every morning and ask how my dear mother was. I could also contact Tricia if I was worried about her and to see that she was alright.

One night, in despair, I prayed that the Lord would release my mother from her terrible, painful illness. Seeing my mother every week getting weaker and not being able to do anything to help her or even have a conversation with her was incredibly depressing. I asked the Lord to take her home. As it happened, my prayers were heard. The very next morning, I could not bear the thought of ringing up to see how she was yet again. I went to work only to be told at 10 am that my mother had passed away during that night. My stepfather was waiting to take my wife and me to Peterborough to make arrangements for her funeral.

1974
My Mother Dies

As my mother was only 53 years of age when she died of this tumour of the brain, I became terribly depressed and upset, despite knowing that some months earlier we had been warned that she had a terminal illness. It was still, in the end, a terrible shock. I believe it had been more so for me because I had been deprived of my mother's company for so much of my childhood and young life, and was as a result so vulnerable that I had to make myself tough at such an early age. By deprivation, and without my well-loved and caring mother, I had endured years of longing for her presence, and now she had died so young.

I had missed my mother so profoundly, and now, in an instant after her terrible illness, she had been wrenched from me at such a young age. Having to share her with a cruel, jealous, possesive man deprived me of the lack of motherly love I had missed at that vital stage in my life. I was always worried about her health. This was especially so when I was married, as I didn't see her enough of her to maintain the loving motherly relationship that I had wanted, and that I know she too had wanted.

A sad fact persisted, however. Because of my wife's mother and uncle and their needs, most Christmases were spent with them rather than with my mother. I realised it would never be that she would ever now share a Christmas dinner with us!

My mother died on the 5th December 1974. There was also a bread strike on, and my stepfather was worried about being able to provide food for all the friends and relatives who would come to the funeral. I asked my stepfather to take me to the Co-op bakery in Peterborough, and I went into one of the offices and told them I was Edith Bilsby's son. This was my mother's married name when she had worked for them. They quickly remembered my mother, sympathised with me and asked what they could do. I told them that she had just passed away and I would need some bread. They quickly supplied me with six loaves and said how sorry they were to hear about her death. They remembered her well, and also remembered me too as a young child. They assured me that if I found we needed more, I just had to let them know. Everyone was so kind.

It was a terrible shock when I found that my mother had not made any sort of will. According to my stepfather, there was nothing - no will at the bank, no will at the house. My treasured mother had told my wife and me when the two of them went on holiday some years previously that all the documentation was safely in a deed box at their bank. When I asked my stepfather about this, he said there was no such will, and that he, therefore, inherited everything himself. He took Tricia and me to his solicitor to confirm this. I could not prove there had actually been a will as wills were not registered in those days; however, steps are now being taken to ensure they are registered but this is still voluntary.

The only reason I feel sure my mother made a will was that, when my first stepfather died, she had to undergo the official probate procedure herself. This was such a long, drawn out process that she would not have wanted anyone close to her to be likewise forced to go through such a painful time, and have to do this while so full of grief themselves. Nevertheless, he said he would give us £1000, which I accepted reluctantly. I was upset that my mother had not left a note or loving letter for me to read, nor mentioned even her grandchildren or me with mementos of the past that she knew I would have wanted. This was naturally upsetting. I also hardly had any good photos of her, even though she was stunning and photogenic, and also looked marvellous for her age. Regrettably, it was as though I did not exist. This in itself was very depressing to me, and it was very hard to accept, but I had to. I somehow had to make an excuse for her and had to resign myself that the tumour she suffered from had affected her thinking before she died.

The loss of my mother was a serious matter. To enable me to carry on working, I had to take Prozac, medication afterwards recommended to remain on it for three years. My mother had meant so much to me, and, every day, knowing she was not now there was so depressing. At first, upon waking up in the morning I would recall that I had lost her. It was such a dismal start to the day.

I loved to see her when she occasionally came to visit us. It hurt me so much more because I had not seen enough of her during my early years, and now her life had been cut short, and I wasn't going to see her again. Words cannot adequately express the feelings you have when these situations happen. Tricia used to say to me that I worried too much about my mother, but perhaps I sensed the genuine possibility that I would lose her, like I already had my father, at an early age. In fact, I recall a nightmare I had many years before she died when I had seen her in a coffin, and that vision continued to plague me.

However, I made sure the money I received from my stepfather was invested well, and decided to move and buy a semi-detached house at Wigston Magna. I didn't want to see this money being frittered away.

Reconciliation

It was two years later when it was the firm's dance and my best friend's wife, Glenys, came up to me and said,'Malcolm, don't you think this has gone on long enough, because I do not want the quarrel to carry on?'

Thanks to Dave's action, and his wife endorsing this and speaking thoughtfully to me, we were reunited, and our great former friendship became very long-lasting. Quite unexpectedly, Dave decided to ask me to be his best man at their wedding. I was only too pleased and honoured. The wedding day was fantastic. Great weather, lovely reception and a memorable day for all followed.

Our friendship was, thankfully, restored, and Dave and I began to see each other again. I was so pleased this had happened. We remained close friends until Dave so sadly died of a sudden heart attack, as you will read later in this book.

East Midlands Gas (Emgas) went through many changes, and at one time in our region we had the equivalent of nearly a 100 percent turnover of staff. It was an exceptionally bureaucratic organisation, and wages at that time were better in other companies. We went through so much change with natural gas conversion, which affected the calorific value of gas, and this had to be explained to customers.

These two massive exercises created hours of work and arrears built up until so we were allowed to do overtime in the evening and Saturday mornings. This added to our wage packets and was a very welcome bonus for the hard work we had put in. For once in my life, I was beginning to save as I intended one day to move to a larger house for my family. At this time in my life, houses were one of the best investments for anyone to make, as they appreciated in value because of inflation.

Natural Gas Conversion and Decimalisation

At East Midlands Gas (Emgas), we not only had to educate ourselves but also customers some of whom had great difficulty in understanding the new change to decimalisation. Not only customers, of course, but come to that some of our staff did as well, in explaining the effect it had on their accounts. Natural gas had a higher calorific value than coal gas, and, by rights, your usage would be less and should show in the meter readings, but the cost of each therm (a unit of gas) would be dearer because of the increased calorific value (heat content).

Eventually, these massive exercises placed considerable pressures on all of our staff, but conditions were changing. Some employees received a promotion from their current position to the next grade because of the additional demands, and because the wages at that time were not as good as those which could be obtained elsewhere. At that time, staff could leave and easily walk into another job with just as good, if not better, conditions.

Driving Lessons and Test

I had toyed with the idea of driving my own car earlier, and now it was necessary for me to have a licence again to be able to progress much further in my career. I would require a driving licence, and I had previously started taking lessons.

I was determined not to take my driving test until I really felt adequate and as fit as possible for this. So, I had, during the previous 18 months, received many driving lessons from the instructor, as I had stipulated that I needed to drive with confidence in my own abilities. I certainly did not want to drive while in any way ill-prepared, primarily for fear of hurting someone else, either pedestrian or another driver. However, the person who taught me was very loud and strict, and held a fantastic record for his pupils achieving passes. He really taught me to drive, along with essentials such as learning how to complete a three-point turn and reversing correctly. During my second lesson, when I seemed to be using the accelerator a bit too much, he directed me to a dual lane carriageway. He then made me use the accelerator to overtake several other cars and vehicles. He scared the wits out of me, and then said, 'Have you now got it out of your system?'

'Yes,' I quickly replied.

His own son was later on awarded the title of Lorry Driver of the Year. It must have been his father's marvellous influence.

I persevered with this instructor for 18 months, and on the actual day of my test, he took me for a lesson beforehand and threw the book at me, singling out every mistake I made. By the end of the lesson I was in the frame of mind that resulted in my attitude becoming: I will show you, mate. I had chosen to take a lot of driving lessons because I felt I needed these, and I am so thrilled that I did.

After I had finished my test and told him I had passed it, my tutor was elated and said to me confidently, 'Malc, I knew you would!'

Senior Officer

However, things were to change, and I was promoted from being just a unit leader to the position of a Senior Officer, with an increase in salary. This promotion also came with the provision of a company car to drive and the provision of private health insurance. This time I chose a Montego car, a gleaming white estate which I thought at the time was a beautiful car. My Maestro car was sold, and money deposited in the bank.

Working at East Midlands Gas (Emgas), I was by default selected to go on a potential higher managers' course at Stratford upon Avon for three weeks. Another person had been chosen initially, but was unable to go, and I was selected to take his place. It was frighteningly heavy going, but the Lord was in my life, looking after me, and I survived. One or two of the would-be managers could not cope with the revealing aspects of the course that highlighted their own inabilities. Not looking at the course constructively, these particular members of staff gave up the course and just went home. They left because they did not feel like going on with it. These also felt that it was not doing them any good. I personally found it was an exciting but hard three weeks, with after dinner speakers and plenty of team working as we were split into groups.

We had numerous tasks as a team to undertake, and it was interesting to see the diversity of talent British Gas had in its employ. Talking to others on the course was in itself educational, and many new contacts were made by us all.

Managers came from different regions of British Gas - that in itself was good, as we were able to compare the various jobs we all had. We were wined and dined with the best of food and the highest grade of speakers. It was especially educational and served its purpose, as I was later (in fact, some considerable time later) promoted to a higher manager's position. I would then be one of only seven hundred in the country and felt I had achieved something far more significant than I had ever in my life before expected. I well remember the words of the warning given to me by that doctor some years earlier, saying those ominous and deadly words, 'I will put you on the sick for the rest of your life as 'disabled'.' I could at that particular time have given in, but I was not going to let my disability do that to me. After all, I had some pride! I had fought the disability that I suffered from, and have continued to do so for most of my life.

I remember attending an earlier interview for another position, and a manager asking, 'You are disabled, aren't you Malcolm?'

I had to think up something very quickly, and the Lord intervened, inspiring me with an appropriate, witty, answer – in reply, I said in a calm voice, 'So what!' I qualified it even further by adding, 'You know, most people take one or two weeks off for when they have colds. All I ever take is an odd day when I suffer a serious seizure, or similar. I then force myself to return to work the very next day!'

Other managers present in the interview room nodded approvingly. It is not the disability but the ability that an individual has that matters. I got the job, but it seemed I had to continually fight this disability.

In 1977, I was promoted to Unit Leader at Leicester, and did my best to repeat my previous successes. This turned out to be a welcome regrading to Gas Accounts Officer in 1979, and I was then promoted to Senior Gas Accounts Officer in 1982. All this brought to my family the additional financial benefits because of a corresponding upgrade in my salary.

Also, an increase in pay was given to many staff as a significant number had left owing to the severe pressures of work, and at that time alternative employment could be found with higher wages.

1969-1994
Promotions

At East Midlands Gas (Emgas), I had worked my way up from Junior Clerk to Senior Clerk, Team Leader, Unit Leader, Senior Officer, and eventually Higher Manager. I took on the roles of Assistant Gas Accounts Manager, Planning Manager, Project Manager and Court Manager. Every interview I attended, I was selected. This was because I was very ambitious, and I worked hard and knew I had something useful to offer.

We had previously moved to our first detached house at Enderby. This was in a beautiful spot in Leicestershire, and I was beginning to find that extra money was needed to satisfy the desires of my family. Curtains, new carpets and then a replacement car for my wife and on top of that a holiday in France had not only to be organised, but also had to be paid for, so we needed additional finance.

When it came to the home improvements, I am useless at DIY, and have to earn money to pay for it to be carried out. The increases in salary I received covered my new mortgage and travelling costs, and there was little else left, so I had to also work part-time so I could provide the luxuries for my family. I had pushed myself this time, and it would take some effort to get on top again, but I had to do it. I was always the sole provider!

In those days, a lot of people thought that when you purchased a new home, everything was okay, but it was not, and I had trouble with the gas fire the builders had installed. East Midlands Gas (Emgas) condemned it, and it was supposed to have been put right, but another visit by the gas fitters and it was again condemned. After many requests to the original builders, I was becoming very frustrated at what was going on and decided to confront them and warn them.

They still had more houses to sell, and the last impossible, dangerous straw was that I found that I was falling asleep every night, and it turned out to be caused by the gas fire giving off carbon dioxide fumes. I said if my gas-fire were not correctly repaired within 48 hours, I would set my house up as an unofficial show-house and inform viewers of long-standing complaints about safety aspects that had occurred. This time it got sorted, and they found a six-inch piece of wood blocking the chimney flue. Other members of the family and I could well have been actually suffocated because of the fire. Fortunately, this did not happen.

Regretfully, some years later, a sad incident occurred. After my friend's father had died, my wife and I found Philip Reid, living in an absolutely terrible state of neglect. He had just suffered a stroke. We quickly took him to our house where he could have a shower, and we could wash all his clothes and give him a good nutritious meal. We talked, and my wife agreed to go with him back to his house the following day, as he needed specialised help. She then also went the next day and cleaned the house for him. In the meantime, I complained to the health authorities about his council house and its condition.

He eventually came with us to our Anglican Church in Leicester and was very moved by the effects of the lovely service there, and found it comforting. He was then sent on a convalescent holiday and, believe it or not, wrote a short story about his stay with us and what had happened when we took him under our joint wings, as it were. He extolled on how much I, my wife and others had helped him. I think it did make all the difference to his life at that time, and everyone was delighted to hear this.

1982-83
My Part-time Post as Caravan Salesman

At about this time, I attended an interview for an additional part-time salesman job at the weekends with a local caravan company.

When I hadn't heard anything by the end of the second week, I telephoned and asked what was going on, and to my surprise, the manager said, 'As you are the first to show initiative, you can have the job!'

It took me six weeks before I could successfully sell my very first caravan. However, during the following six weeks, I was learning fast, the manager knew how to develop me, and I quickly improved. He had been educated at a public school and had acquired an air of confidence that excelled the various attributes of all other managers I have ever met. In fact, he eventually ended up as a director of the group of caravan companies they owned. I also negotiated a fuel allowance with him. He reluctantly agreed. However, once I got into my stride in successful selling, I sold sometimes as many caravans as the full-time staff.

I eventually learned to take details of all the people I approached at the weekend who wanted a caravan and assured them that if and when what they were looking for came in, I would telephone them. When starting work each Saturday, I would check all the caravans that had been taken in during the week to see if they were suitable for my listed customers who had already discussed the details of precisely what they were looking for.

If any were suitable and matched the specifications that the customer had stipulated, I would telephone the customer concerned stressing the urgency, if they were really interested, to come and view them that weekend.

Because I had achieved this level of selling and had the potential, the manager then suggested to me to use some of my holiday from East Midlands Gas (Emgas) so I could attend the prestigious caravan show at Earls Court in London. All my expenses were paid. At night, he and I went out to sample the evening dinners at various famous restaurants. He was teetotal, and I was not bothered to have an alcoholic drink because I wanted to be absolutely alert for my job. Therefore, we spent many an enjoyable evening together and got to know each other even better. Some evenings we discussed the day's business and what successes we had achieved during that particular day.

For twelve years, it was more of a holiday doing this work at the shows with my friend, the director of the company, and we enjoyed each other's companionship. We shared great interest in the challenge of the environment, as well as the many exciting and beautiful meals after a hard day on the floor selling. We sampled a variety of many specialist cuisines - Chinese, American, Mexican, Indian, Italian, Vietnamese, and high-class English fare from the most prestigious of restaurants. I well recall one customer I dealt with who had just acquired some considerable sum of money. She was interested in one particular caravan, which I then sold to her. When it came to the deposit, usually she would have only had to put down £300 as her deposit, but instead, she immediately gave me a cheque for the full amount of £3000. The director then showed it to the other salesmen as an incentive for them to see how a sale could be made. My friend, Jeremy, the MD, was overjoyed with me.

Over the years, my own wardrobe improved, as I was once told that if you want to be a manager, you have to dress like one. I well remember one individual, an existing director of a company in an elegant suit with a bow tie and a dashing red silk handkerchief that you could not fail to see protruding from the top pocket of his jacket. I did the same the following year as customers could use it to quickly identify you as the person to see when they returned to place an order.

At that time, I had an account with Austin Reed, where excellent advice was given to me, and the quality of the suits and other garments was superb. In fact, my best friend, Dave, eventually went there as well to get his suits made, as he was so impressed with how I was always turned out.

Part-time Canvasser for Cavity Wall Insulation

Colleagues at work had found a better way of making extra money in the evenings themselves. They were satisfied with the rich rewards gained from canvassing as a new job that they performed in the evenings. Eventually, they tempted me to do the same. We would all go canvassing at night to obtain names and addresses of people who wanted a quote for cavity wall insulation. We were becoming aware of the necessity to insulate homes to reduce the costs of fuel bills, and this would be a topical item that most families we called upon would want.

For each and every name and address, we received the sum of three pounds as a payment. At first, this was a nice little earner, until eventually the leads we were getting were not good enough. The company then changed the system, and paid a much larger commission, but only for an actual final sale. Ultimately, we all managed to improve our technique. We were able to persuade would-be customers, and were earning more money than before.

At this time, Tricia's demands for money were such that I suggested she come out with me at night and canvass, too, which she, initially reluctantly, did. I tried coaching her over a weekend what to say, and all that was necessary, and she eventually got the hang of it.

It was also interesting to note that caravan retailers at the shows were now employing more females to sell caravans for them, so I was following that trend. She eventually grew to like her part-time job.

Cavity wall insulation then became a necessity in the updated building regulations, and this helped considerably in convincing customers of the need for it to be installed in their homes.

Margaret Thatcher had allowed council house tenants the opportunity to buy their rented houses at a cost far lower than the real market value, and I considered that the council estates would be our bread and butter. This indeed proved to be the case, and very quickly we made a higher number of sales from those who had become private owners. They wanted to make sure their own house was up to date. It seemed far easier to convince them to buy the product, as well.

It amazed me that, when canvassing council estates, some tenants we came upon were unemployed and seemed worried to death about their own futures. Yet, if they were in listening mode, I would say things like, 'You have a car, what about thinking of driving as employment? You could be a taxi driver or delivery driver.'

Because people had done one job for such a long while, they could find that they had lost the ability to identify what strengths and skills they had developed over the years. Also, two part-time jobs are better than l nothing, and might possibly be easier to find than none.

We all have strengths and, in some cases, skills, and sometimes we have to think outside the box to survive.

I carried on working with my wife doing this part-time work for a few years, and it helped us to purchase what we needed for our current house and the children at that time. This was enough to satisfy my wife's needs and keep her happy. Also, the walking at night-time was good for both of us, and I am sure helped to keep us healthier, so there were hidden benefits in doing this work.

When I lost my driving licence through a reoccurrence of my disability, I had to rely on my young son, Andrew, or my wife to take me to work. It was such an imposition of their time, but they all readily helped me enormously. I am, of course, still grateful.

In fact, when I had to visit the other regional offices, my wife drove me to them so that I could carry out my duties. She did not get paid for her time in doing this, but we were married and had to help each other whenever it was necessary, and we certainly did.

The first time I lost my licence, through my epilepsy attacks, the legal proviso had been that I had to go for the subsequent three years without suffering a seizure. Fortunately for today's epileptics, it has now been changed to just one year. That three year wait, as you can imagine, was purgatory after you had passed your test and had been driving for a couple of years. Life didn't seem fair.

I had managed to save over a few years, and wanted to surprise Tricia, so took her to a garage to try out how she liked a Metro car. This was a relatively new car, as it was their demonstration model, and I wanted to see if Tricia liked it. She had a test drive and was delighted with it. It was smaller than her other car, so she felt it was ideal for her. After she had the test drive, I asked her if she would like one, and she said that she would.

So I asked her if it would be alright if I bought this particular one for her. She was flabbergasted at what I had said, and was also overwhelmed. Of all the cars she drove later, she talked very lovingly most about that particular one and cherished it. I think I got a kiss and a hug that day. My wife repeated this story to her friends many times, recalling her complete surprise at the present she had been given, my generosity and thoughtfulness, and how much she loved driving it.

Andrew, My Youngest Son

I am very proud of Andrew, as he has turned out to be a very hard working man and a loving husband, and an exemplary father to his two daughters. I am so delighted by his great achievements in being promoted to a relevant senior post in the company in which he has worked for many years. In this, he has excelled, and his latest job requires a great deal of selfless devotion and dedicated hard work on his part. He has risen through the ranks due entirely to his own efforts and abilities. Tricia and I always thought he had these tremendous potential abilities, and we have now been proved right.

He was eventually given a full-time job with East Midlands Gas (Emgas), and when he started off in the store's offices he became so conversant with the stock that fitters would frequently consult him for his much-needed and appreciated advice. His efforts quickly got him promoted through the ranks.

With his most recent promotion, there was a condition that he should study for a recognised qualification. I am pleased and proud to say that he eventually acquired the Chartered Institute of Purchasing and Supplies (Ch.I.P.S.) degree. I know his wife was very supportive in making him study and in assuring him he could do it, and she also organised their home to make sure that Andy had a room to himself to study in peace and quiet.

He achieved his aims, and he did this because she believed in him. I was so pleased when he received his final degree. In fact, I was over the moon and am very proud of my son. Tricia and I attended his degree presentation, and it was fantastic to see him go up and receive his certificate.

Afterwards, he had numerous photographs taken to mark the event, for which I had the privilege of paying, and indeed I was only too pleased to do this. Tricia and I were so proud of him, and delighted for Andrew, as we knew how hard he had worked and what he had finally achieved.

Some years later, it is also true that Andrew in an entirely different way raised money himself for charity. For various reasons, I am also very proud of his charitable and commendable efforts, especially in the task he took on of walking 100 kilometres in 24 hours to raise funds. Then there were several bike rides for numerous charities, which he undertook over difficult terrain.

1986
The Final Accolade - Higher Manager

In 1986, I finally achieved promotion to the higher manager's role of Assistant Gas Income Manager, which was a daunting experience. The jump from Senior Officer to Higher Manager was more like a tremendous leap. This took some time to adjust to and was a continuing revelation. You seem to drown before you could swim, but it was a fantastic experience, albeit a very trying one at times.

This was the year our company was sold to the public, which created a lot of work for everyone concerned. Staff needed briefing, and various details were sent to them with offerings of what they would receive and what else they could purchase. Also, a Sharesave scheme was introduced for all staff.

Dave, my best friend, had advised me to take out Sharesave options and, at his kindly insistence, we both did the maximum every year that we possibly could, and it paid off handsomely. I was so glad he made me do this since he always seemed to be a genius at saving and making money. Dave had premium bonds, ISA's, insurance policies, and shares, and also used a professional financial manager for his investments. He was an excellent, caring, supportive and highly skilled advisor and friend to me, and looked after my interests as though these were his own.

The reason he was like this was that his own father had died suddenly when Dave was only twelve years old. His father was in business and, for some unknown reason, became medically depressed, and tragically had committed suicide. His mother was a very astute lady and rescued everything she could so she could provide for her children. She never had much spare cash, so her children had to make it themselves, and they worked and saved throughout their lives.

1987-90
Our Charity Fund Raising

At British gas we started a charity fundraising project, ARMS (for multiple sclerosis sufferers) and Leukaemia Research, with others to follow. I ended up suggesting an auction be held, with me becoming the voluntary auctioneer. Amazing myself, I took to it so well, considering I was someone who had never previously experienced such a role. We encouraged staff to collect new or nearly new items that could be sold to the general public in an auction. It took months to collect 400 items for sale, and I am afraid my dear wife, Tricia, had to put up with them stored in our dining room and our garage. The whole idea was very well received by the staff.

People were very generous indeed in what they contributed, and employees had lots of ideas. This meant we had to find the best ways to advertise. Then, a suitable place was chosen to hold the auction and whatever else that would be needed to make it a success. The team had decided to provide hot bacon rolls and other such fare, plus coffees and teas to ensure bidders didn't leave the auction hall without buying something, and it worked very well. The delicious smell of grilled bacon and sausages, plus hot coffee, assured they had attracted plenty of customers.

The only problem was that I had never auctioned any artefacts before, so I needed some help. A very kind auctioneer came to reassure me and to watch me take the multiple bids from the audience. After about six items had been sold, he said to encourage me, 'You do not need me. Just carry on, Malcolm, as you are doing.'

So I did. I sold 400 lots, and with the takings of the refreshment sales, and we managed to make £2600 in all. We advertised the auction in a way which worked well. In advance, some of the younger girls from our firm dressed becomingly in top hats and tails. They were parading around Leicester city centre on the Saturday and passing out leaflets promoting the sale on Sunday, the next day, encouraging people to come and support us, and it worked!

The top hat and tails were kindly provided by a local company that I had persuaded to do free of charge. This was just one of the many companies I had to encourage to be generous and to vow to support us. We also had photos taken by the local daily newspaper, which added much to the publicity and invited the locals to come to participate.

Later, we presented cheques for £4000 and £2000 to MS and Leukaemia Research, which was well received.

The next year, I held and organised another auction at a different venue. Believe it or not, I received a snotty letter from Leicester City Council that I should have sought their permission officially because I was contravening some market act of theirs. I could not believe it and dumped it in the bin. However, we again made over £2000.

Tricia Referred to Private Consultant

Tricia, my wife, was taken ill with severe back pain, and this became very disabling to her. It went on for such a long while that I asked our doctor to come to examine her. He, for some reason, thought she had suffered a nervous breakdown, which seemed ridiculous as a suggestion or diagnosis. I asked for a referral to a private consultant to see what was wrong.

She went to a BUPA specialist and had been in such pain for over six weeks. The consultant was very thorough and admitted her to the hospital the next week for a single injection into her spine. She would have to lie still on her back for 24 hours, after which a steel corset would be needed for six months. This treatment resolved the problem, but she always had to be careful about her back after that and was not to lift heavy items.

1989
Planning Manager Secondment

On Monday, when I returned to work as Planning Manager, I had the pleasure of the head of finance coming to see me and congratulate us all on our charity efforts. I was not expecting this accolade but fully appreciated it. This, of course, was not only for my own efforts but also for the participation by all those members of staff who had given so much of their time and helped on Auction Day itself.

It wasn't long before my auctioneering ability was put further to the test. On this occasion, having had to sell for the company redundant furniture and other office equipment that was not any longer required. This was carried out during the hours of 4 and 6 pm. It used to be reasonably well attended. I think it was cheaper to use me than to have it collected by the auctioneers; it had never made very much when previously sold by them.

1990
25th Wedding Anniversary

We celebrated our 25th wedding anniversary at Walsingham Village, famous for being called 'England's Gateway to Heaven'. We had been there a few times over the years, and it held a lot of memories for us. This was at this time of the year a quiet place that brought a few moments of peace and joy to us. Our marriage was treasured, and by pulling together we had weathered many storms in our times. Our Christian faith gave us so much joy and happiness. We had booked a room in a cottage that allowed us to take our dog with us.

The trouble was, the beams were shallow and, being over six feet in height, I banged my head a couple of times, and that made it more memorable. However, the peace that we both found there and had experienced many times over the years was beautiful and uplifting. We went to Our Lady's Shrine at Walsingham, and while there saw a priest, who blessed our marriage and to whom, we were very grateful.

Coming home, we were asked to call in at my step-father's and my step-mother's house. Unknowingly to us, she had baked a cake and prepared a high tea for us, which rounded off the celebrations of our 25th wedding anniversary.

NHS Failure

It was so sad that much later on in life I was to learn that my Uncle Roy, who was best man at my wedding, had died from peritonitis after being misdiagnosed. When first ill, he had gone twice to his own doctor in one week and had only been given medication to calm the pain. As it turned out, my uncle had a fatal illness. It was not diagnosed, and his care was totally inappropriate and useless. By the end of the week, an emergency ambulance was called, but he had died as it could not reach him quickly enough. The irony of this disaster is that his own father had also died in his thirties of the exact same complication and left his mother with eleven children to bring up.

Raising My Own Profile

Years later, after I was promoted to higher manager level, I decided to encourage the use of a suggestion scheme more and to find out why staff were themselves generally not using it. After many sessions, it appeared that some employees did not think it was their job to suggest, while others thought suggestions about work should be put forward direct to the management, and they should not expect a reward themselves. Some of these attitudes really surprised me, but, we worked together with the suggestion scheme secretary, we managed to dispel a few myths.

I wanted to be different and improve team spirit, and make our staff innovative rather than reactive. I had used the suggestion scheme myself for years, and had created suitable innovations in this way.

I was appreciated for it, and wanted other staff to think this way to. This was because I wholeheartedly believed that the staff mostly knew what needed doing, but had not realised that they could put their ideas forward and have them assessed. I can remember some of the first suggestions that I put in were atrocious, but perseverance eventually brought its own reward.

Years earlier, my ultimate accolade was the Company Secretary wishing to see me and wanting to thank me personally. He said, 'I am signing reward cheques for a Malcolm Le-Hair, and I wanted to put a face to that name.' He applauded my efforts and wanted me to continue the excellent work. That reassured me I was doing the right thing. The thrill of that particular meeting and his recognition made me think that I should now promote it so that all staff should realise their own specific ideas would be welcomed. I am sure it dismissed a lot of myths employees already had, and you only have to look at the result now of British Gas.

With the secretary of the scheme, we gave presentations to all staff in gas accounts to increase the number of ideas. It was a tremendous success, and an increase of 760% was eventually achieved. Special presentations were made to some clerks, with a top prize of £200 and a £50 M&S voucher. Hopefully, since then, minds have been changed and generally management consider that to put a suggestion into the scheme is now looked upon more positively than it has ever been.

1991
Budget Payment Scheme

One of the major problems East Midlands Gas (Emgas) had was to ensure accounts were paid by our customers. It was, therefore, necessary to have a system put in place to make it easier for customers to spread the cost of gas over the year in monthly amounts.

The budget payment scheme was, fortunately, such a facility, but to succeed it needed better marketing, possibly in a more modern, appealing way.

I thought of finding a company that would donate and pay for a very desirable prize, such as a holiday at Disney World at Orlando in America for a family of four, and then I found one who agreed: Commercial Union.

We wanted the customers to join the gas payment plan and complete the Commercial Union request leaflet, and each name would then qualify for entry into the prize draw. East Midlands Gas (Emgas) agreed to put up vouchers for three more prizes of valuable appliances to be won to increase the general interest, and it turned out to be a great success. Our region was the first to launch a 'holiday of a lifetime' contest. This completion added thousands of more customers to the budget payment system.

Since we would be already sending gas accounts out to these customers, we would only have the administrative cost of inserting these in with the bill, which, in this case, was negligible.

We would insert a leaflet designed and printed by them, enclosed with their gas bills that would be dispatched for and during the following three months.

The leaflet was devised that would advertise the budget payment plan and also invite each applicant to ask to be sent a quote for insurance. The winner would then be drawn sometime after, at random, when all the leaflets sufficient for 13 weeks had been used.

Promotion by Staff

The next idea I had was to have an internal promotion scheme getting staff to sell the budget payment scheme to customers when they telephoned us or when we telephoned them. It was eventually agreed that £1000 would be given to Guide Dogs for The Blind for every 10,000 customer increase in the number of new budget payment customers. This promotion prompted the vital and excellent work of a leading valuable charity, so we were able to extensively help *Guide Dogs for The Blind*.

This would train and provide ownership of professionally trained guide dogs to blind sufferers. The training means two years of preparing the guide dog to become fully able to perform its complex guide-dog tasks and routines in protecting and looking after the blind person. Some of these tasks include guiding the blind person to walk in the street, the extreme importance of steering him or her across the road safely, and generally caring for its dedicated owner. To demonstrate these abilities to us, official dog walkers brought in a new puppy which was still being trained to show to the staff. Everyone was amazed at the versatility and caring for a person in need that these lovely animals show, and at the change which they can make to a blind person's whole way of life. The blind person's quality of living is enhanced so much that, eventually, the system has become world famous.

Also, employees were encouraged to name the sponsored guide dogs with a suitable link to the concept of the gas service; I think the very first East Midlands Gas (Emgas) guide dog was called 'Flame'. Our marketing of the scheme was to include staff also selling the plan, the leaflet where a holiday could be won, and this pushed the numbers up from 500,000 to 560,000. This was undoubtedly a fantastic result. We had presented the Guide Dogs for the Blind with cheques which would pay for the training of six guide dogs over the several years it takes to train them!

1991
Distant Relations Discovered and Reunited

One day, our telephone bureau at BG took a telephone call from a very talkative and satisfied customer. It was a certain Mr Arthur Le-Hair, thanking us for BG services provided, and when the telephonist accepted this particular call, she had commented that they had a gentleman – by name - a certain Malcolm Le-Hair, who was a manager at East Midlands Gas (Emgas). A male operator, who knew me, asked Arthur could he be a possible relation in view of the unusual surname. Of course, it was the unique surname that rang a loud, resounding bell with that telephonist. As I was out of the premises that particular day, he asked them to tell their Mr Le-Hair to call him as he would like to see if they were actually related. So, I was given Arthur's number to ring on my return. He turned out to be very charming indeed, and a caring friendly person, with, as we later found, a delightful wife. He said we two must be related. Then Arthur also complimented our company on the way brilliant they had attended to his gas fire.

Later, Arthur, invited Tricia and me to his 60th birthday celebration and a housewarming party at his beautiful house at Wymington. He wanted us to meet his, as he described her, a charming and even friendlier wife, Una.

Making friends with Arthur and Una raised the question in our minds, and especially in Tricia's, of genealogy, and Tricia became increasingly interested in this subject of our family history, relationships and ancestors. She started researching the Le-Hair family's extensive historical connections, and her own 'London' family name.

Following our meeting, Arthur and his family became firm family friends, as well as friendly relations. Our families were so closely connected arriving here centuries (sixteen hundreds onwards with the advent of the famous Hugenots of which they were part. This influx of emigees who were being persecuted occurred so many years before from France.)

We shared the same great-grandfather. It wasn't long before we were invited to both of their daughters' resplendent weddings. This brought such great happiness into our lives, and this marvellous closeness has stayed very precious to all of us.

Arthur many times has turned and looked to me as a brother. We have enjoyed many happy times together and continue to still visit each other often, and to care about each other's welfare.

Best Friend's Son Dies in Car Accident

On this particular day, we had gone to spend the day with these newfound relations, who lived in a lovely village, Wymington. My wife had taken a basket of strawberries from our garden and a bottle of wine for them. After enjoying the celebrations and being introduced to all the family, I made a welcome drink for us when we returned without realising the tragedy that had just happened. The next morning I got up, and decided to take some strawberries to my neighbours' house, as I wanted them to enjoy them too.

Sitting down to read my Sunday paper, I received the earth-shattering tragic telephone call from Dave, my long standing friend who told me about the absolute horror and total disaster that had just happened. I could not believe what he said! Wesley, his only son, had at only twelve years of age been killed the previous day in a terrifying car accident. The boy who was driving was seriously injured. His brother was also killed.

I was shocked to the very core, could hardly speak to my friend. Dave was too overcome with grief and emotion and could not carry on as he was speechless. He was devastated.

Dave and Glenys had been married, but were now living separated lives, and the boy, Wesley, had been up till then living with his mother. He had been their only child.

Also, the younger son of Glenys' new partner at that time was killed. This elder son had just passed his driving test and was presented with, I think, a Mini to drive. He decided to take his brother and Dave's and Glenys's son Wesley out, but all of them suffered this terrible accident. For the grieving parents of both boys, the pain for all was almost unendurable.

Some days earlier, I could remember having enjoyed celebrating with a load of friends at Dave's house and seeing his son balancing on an upstairs' window sill poised very dangerously and adventurously, and we had warned him. Yet another friend remembered him recklessly jumping over a certain spiked fence and being very fortunate he had not injured himself by landing on it, but sadly now he had been killed in this terrible car accident.

Wesley was one of the most handsome young men you could ever wish to see. He had fair slightly curly hair, and fantastic skin that bronzed as the summer lengthened. His blue eyes and cute face were well remembered by all who had ever met him. It was a very sad time for all of us. Mostly, he had the good looks of his mother and his father's natural joviality.

They were devastated, as they both thought the world of him. How could you ever forget? Words cannot express the feelings you have when such disasters like these strike you. Vivid memories of this terrible situation and sorrow caused to the parents are still indelibly imprinted on my own mind. David was my very best friend and Tricia and I felt for him deeply.

Still both in shock, Tricia and I could not believe it. As soon as it was possible, we went to see Wesley in his coffin, then knelt and prayed beside it for him shedding more tears beside his young body.

It was with the highest respect that I joined Dave and other male friends in bearing Wesley's coffin at his funeral. Finally, we carried it into the crematorium filled with sorrowing friends. Every single soul present was as shocked as we were at the suddenness of the loss. It was amazing how many people were gathered there. Scores present of people, all ages, who had come to support Dave and Glenys in their time of need. It was such an awful, unbelievable, desolate and sad time, which continued, of course, to be so for so very many years to come.

The Lord Works in Mysterious Ways

A miracle also coincided in that, on that particular night after the funeral, two people – a lady, called Flo Bull, who turned out to be a close, wonderfully supportive friend for life, and her religious and delightful friend, John Shirley, knocked on our front door. They had come to comfort us in the loss, told us they were from the local Baptist church. We did not really want to speak to anyone at this particular time and told them exactly why. They immediately said that they knew, and had been praying too for the whole family. So, of course, what could we do but invite them in? The following uplifting conversations could only be described as 'God being in the room with us all at that instant in time'.

Flo Bull knew that we had moved to our recent house at Whetstone, and I had encouraged Dave and his wife Glenys to come and live there near to us, and they had. Sadly, and unfortunately, Dave and his wife eventually divorced soon after this. Strangely enough, purchasing back his own previous home as it had come back onto the market. Their joint house in Whetstone had to be sold so that the divorce settlement could be finalised, and his wife amply provided for. However, I understand he had been very generous indeed to Glenys, and to their son.

By a strange coincidence, Dave's family had in fact sold their house in Croft village to Ron and Flo some many years before. John was initially worried about meeting our two collie dogs as he was unused to them, but he eventually realised they would prove to be affectionate, loving and not harm him. We all spoke together for what seemed like hours, admitting that we had stopped going to our former Anglian church, but reassuring them we had undoubtedly both retained our faith in God. However, during this period in time, our faith had been truly tested.

This time we talked about family, and I told them the burden on our shoulders of our worry for our much loved elder son, Richard. He had been missing from home for two whole devastating years. We had heard reports that he was back again living in Leicester, which was nearby. John, bless him, asked for details about Richard and said, quite boldly and reassuringly, 'I **will** find him for you.'

I found John to be a wonderful man, and being married to a caring, lovely lady called 'Beryl' of whom I am also very fond. They recently visited me and have supported me through several bouts of illnesses, to my great joy.

At the time, we were, as it was known then, 'lapsed' Christians, but not for long.

Looking for comfort at this time of deep sadness and reflection, we decided to go to their church, and the congregation welcomed us with open arms. Ron Bull, Flo's husband, was there to greet us with the most beautiful calm, reassuring smile and a firm, friendly handshake. He immediately told me that he had a ticket for me to listen to a guest speaker the following week at the men's society, and invited me to come along with him as his guest. How could I refuse such a request?

Tricia and I both agreed. What a pleasant and welcoming church it seemed! Refreshingly different from the Anglican Church that we had attended for the previous 25 years. Within weeks, our lives then took a different path. With choir practice, bible groups, house groups, church meetings and preparation for total baptism, we were immediately very much a part of the vibrant congregation. These particular two people today are some of my best friends. Flo Bull and her son, Martin, and John Shirley and his wife, Beryl, still visit me often, and we all share news over a friendly meal. The church regularly sends us their magazine every month and keeps in contact, which is very welcome. They all adored my wife and even reminisce about her as she made such a good impression on all whom she met.

We continued to make our regular journeys to visit Arthur, Una and family, and recognised the happiness it had brought to us. A few months later, I believe it was the Lord who led me to visit the area of Ringstead itself. This is on the way to Wymington. I had lived at Ringstead in my younger days as a child: it was where I was so unhappily fostered. This diversion took us to what is now a pretty village.

Reunited with My Father's Family

I enquired of an elderly couple there about whether they knew the Baileys, who had previously lived there. They answered that they had died but that their daughter still lived just round the corner at a bungalow called 'the Farm Bungalow'. This was to do with my father's family. After speaking to this elderly couple in the village, my cousin Rita, and her husband, Bill, welcomed us I am glad to say enthusiastically and warmly.

When Rita saw me, she flung her arms around me eagerly and shouted, 'Malcolm, we thought you were dead as we have tried hard to trace you without success!' It was such a joyous reunion! Within a short space of time, my cousin had arranged for a New Year party so we could meet her own immediate family and at the same time enjoy the beautiful meal which she cooked.

They filled me in with more details precious to me because I did not know these at all. These, about my mother and my own father, put more light on the reasons for their sad separation. Apparently, my father, who wanted to provide, had possibly ignored my mother's great feelings of insecurity, as she needed love and reassurance and constant company.

I was later fostered in the village in which, as it so happened, my father's relations lived, but they could not take me in to live with themselves at that particular time. Several reasons had prevented this. Firstly, their own mother was at the time seriously ill with severe delusions, dementia, and worse, and needed very close and constant care.

Rita told me that her mother was imagining every day that she was herself the 'Queen of England', and, while it was exhausting, looking after her, they could also recall the many laughs and joy they had with the mother at times when she was in her acting mode. Also, they had recently taken over the farm, which they had previously rented but were then buying. Two hundred head of cattle twice a day needed milking, and it was a very arduous working life. This was in addition to looking after their ill mother and 460 acres of land.

The mother had assumed a stance of being the Queen, and performed in a very autocratic, especially queenly manner. She had ordered them all around imperiously as though they were her real courtiers!

We continued to visit Arthur and Una of course, and also spent many a weekend at Ringstead, where my cousin Rita and Bill now owned this large farm. It was a very happy time. My wife enjoyed it, as I had purchased some expensive and lovely outfits for her and myself to wear for the forthcoming family weddings we were later invited to attend. I took her to Market Bosworth where elegant dress shops catered extensively (and expensively) for such functions. I bought high quality, beautiful outfits, which looked fantastic on my wife.

Looking a million dollars on the day, she was a very much more a beautiful woman at this particular time in her life. Over the years, she had really blossomed from a naïve young girl, and had greater inner confidence than she had ever possessed before.

In the space of a couple of years, we were invited to four superb weddings. It was a wonderful time for Tricia and for me which we enjoyed together as I rekindled my various rediscovered exciting family relations. This meant a great deal to me, as I had been, to a great extent, excluded in my childhood years by circumstances from ever attending such warm, family occasions, because of the split in the two families.

We spent many hours talking about our Le-hair family. They filled me in where there had been significant gaps. Rita and Bill told me they had both looked after my father when he had been ill, and I thanked them wholeheartedly for that. I certainly had not known this before, and it made such a difference to me to feel that he had such caring and love extended to him by them.

Some years later, I was pleased I had sold my home at Whetstone to Dave and Sue as I know they found it appealed to them so much, plus it had such a good sized garden. While I had improved this house that had formerly been mine, they also had then done much more. Sue still lives in and loves the house, and has done a lot to it to make it even better. I well recall their courting days with, on one occasion, some employees having an evening cruise down the river near Nottingham. Dave, and Sue had been part of the group, so I had taken a lovely photo of them. They were so much in love in those days, and it wasn't long before they decided to live together to enjoy each other's company in every moment. Sue and Dave found they were soon parents to be. They had a baby daughter, whom they called Elle.

They provided, as the years passed, the very best for their daughter, including a private education which brought, after her own individual extensive efforts, a university placement. Now, commendably, she has achieved an MSc degree. Regretfully, Dave, having died on the 11th July 2009, was not around to see her great success, and this was agonising for the family. He would have been so proud of her achievements. However, her mother now spoils her, understandably, and they get on well together. Elle enjoys the company of many friends and is a lovely daughter, of whom everyone is very fond and proud.

Over the years, I had accomplished the laborious task of successfully, simultaneously and voluntarily managing three jobs, one of which was my primary career. The unfortunate inevitable result was that this had taken its toll on me and affected my health. The LSD treatment had originally ruined my early life and sapped my strength, and I had to struggle so hard against all the odds to rebuild the rest of my working life. Despite the problems it caused me I did manage to win through and reach a senior position.

In my role as senior manager, presenting a project at work, for example, I would become very nervous indeed. Other managers may have had the wrong impression concerning my abilities, but I know that LSD has had this, long-lasting effect on my life, and I would warn any would-be users of the drug to cease from using it immediately. It is a very, very toxic drug, and also highly dangerous to take. In fact, it reacts differently with each individual, and therefore you cannot predict the full extent of the adverse effects it will have on you. This may be, perhaps either ruining your health, and possibly changing for the worse your whole personality.

The following information might emphasise these facts:

Dangerous Drugs That Affect One's Actions

It is strange but the biblical notes I have been reading lately describe the powerful emotions evoked when anyone has to address an audience. Public speaking is listed as our current population's actual number one fear, surpassing the fear of death itself (which is number five) and loneliness, which weighs in at number seven.

That means that, amazingly, most of us are actually less afraid of dying alone than of making fools of ourselves in front of other people. It is the fear of this unknown, the worry of forgetting everything you were going to say and your mind going temporarily blank, plus the risk of being out there in front of the audience alone. All of this combined is a very real, understandable human fear.

After this research, I am fortunately now confident and relieved that I am not alone in this regard and many others in my situation do feel the same as I do.

Having to work so hard day and night for so many years, I admit that my inner patience used to wear a bit thin with my sons, even with their problems and behaviour. I had flashbacks to the life-changing treatments I had suffered at the mental hospital all those years before, notwithstanding the epilepsy attacks which prostrated me and that I experienced as a consequence. The sedative effect of the particular drugs that I was forced to take were also a great problem as well as frighteningly powerful.

While everything in my life appeared to be well compared to many other people, the acute medical treatment that I suffered from the effects of the original unwanted, and unforgettable injections had been responsible for severe effects. These have been with me ever since the minute hospital-administered so-called cures and treatments were given to me at age 17. I would not want other people today, of any age, to ever suffer as I have done!

It is important to note. This is one of the reasons that I have written this book to warn others and hopefully prevent the terrible consequences for them! I would warn all readers who might be tempted to become would-be users of LSD to cease using it, as the effects it has on so very many people can be catastrophic. The psychedelic effects that the absorption of LSD has on one's brain are unbelievable too!

A Minor Disaster

A couple of weeks later, after coming home from work, and pulling up on the drive, I had forgotten to use the brake on my car and so had to then race back to try to stop it crashing into some wooden fencing. In doing this, I badly twisted my left foot, and I went to my doctor, who told me I had sprained it very badly.

The ankle swelled up, and I had then to wear a soft slipper as I could not get my shoes on. Despite this, I hobbled into work the next day and did my best. The foot seemed to swell more and more each day. After a week, I went back to the doctor and was told to rest the ankle when I got home and, if possible, as much as I could whilst at work. By the end of the second week, however, I went to our nurse at the office, who was immediately very concerned and telephoned my doctor. I was told to be at his surgery at 4 pm that same day. I hobbled in and, without being examined, I was told to go to the Leicester Royal Infirmary as I was to be admitted. Surprisingly, he had already prepared a letter for me to take with me into hospital. I went home and told my wife, who kindly agreed to drive me in, and as soon as I was there, the nursing staff and doctors appeared at my side. They all seemed to know what was wrong, or at least had already a good idea.

Heart tests, temperature and blood tests were quickly administered, and then they told me they were going to inject a dye into my bloodstream as they thought I had an actual blockage now in my leg. It was discovered to be a Deep Vein Thrombosis, commonly known as a DVT. They injected dye into the vein on the actual top of my foot and I felt every excruciating agony possible. I could have screamed but just about managed to control (I really do not know how I did this). Later scans were taken conirming their suspicions were absolutely correct. I was later admitted and put to bed with my leg raised up in the air. Afterwards the leg was monitored what seemed like every hour. I was given regular Heparin injections to thin my blood as an emergency.

However, I was pleased they had identified my particular problem. A couple of days later, three nurses came to my bed to inform me they were going to put my stockings on. They seemed to delight in doing this while laughing and joking with me, all in good fun. Following that, I had a few work colleagues visit then, which was pleasant and comforting. After a week I was discharged but put on drugs to thin my blood. I am still on these.

1991
Epileptic Seizures

I was given the job of Project Manager in charge of handheld terminals, and it was demanding, stressful work. I headed a team of staff who were very good at handling projects, and they supported me. Unfortunately, I suffered a few epileptic seizures doing this particular job as there was so much to worry about. Stress brought on attacks in my case. Meetings, visits and keeping up to date with how far we had all progressed with the project were all demanding. As usual, everything was wanted the next day or sooner. Everything was very technical and answers needed urgently. The invention of new hand-held terminals or mini computers would allow meter readers to input meter readings from the individual meters. These would then be downloaded at night so that a bill could be produced the very next day and sent to the customer. There were significant savings to be made from such a project. Most of the staff had already carried out this for a long while and knew what to do. However, I had to pick it up as the best I could.

There were times when I had an exhausting epileptic seizure while carrying out this job as it seemed to place an intolerable and disproportionate burden on me mentally. Talking and dealing with the technical staff was not easy either, since they knew what they were dealing with but I was non-technical in that particular sphere myself. However, l found I had a steep learning curve to achieve. I must try to cope with all this, but just about managed it.

Finally to get to the bottom of what triggered off my seizures, I, fortunately, did find some of the essential causes. These factors I recognised, and now I have my own stringent regime which I follow. I do not drink any alcohol ever. I set my tablets out for the week in a large, cleverly designed tablet organiser. Also, I try to get as much sleep as is necessary, and I pray to God and thank him for every day I am still alive and capable, fit, and for the very kind friends I have looking after me.

I did, however, manage finally to complete the executive summary and compose the report with its recommendations, cost analyses and all the other analytical detail they required. It could be signed off then, and the equipment ordered. I am pleased to say success then followed, after some initial setbacks.

1992-93
Debt Collection Manager

My last role at East Midlands Gas (Emgas) was that of The Debt Collection Manager, and what a tremendous challenge that proved to be! Not the job itself, but the staff under me. I had two lively union representatives within my section, and also teams that had some problems and needed a considerable amount of help. It was different because it was a standalone system that had its own computer, which was technically managed by an outside company if things ever did go wrong. My assistant knew the running of the system perfectly and did all the updates necessary, mostly over each weekend.

When I checked, I discovered that many staff had only been allocated to go on few, if any, courses. They needed to make up lost time and gain as many skills that would be necessary for their future development as possible. Privatisation had taken place in 1986, and, to me, it was apparent that our office would eventually be dispensed with, and therefore it was essential that all staff were as skilled as possible to cater for any future redundancies that they might suffer.

To assist in their individual training, I instituted one-to-one interviews with my staff where we could discuss their work and future opportunities. I needed to suggest to each person an area for their development individually, on which they were then required to concentrate.

I introduced the company to employing private debt collection companies to collect the money that was not forthcoming from its debtors, and where the individuals had been informed many times already of what they actually owed to British Gas.

East Midlands Gas (Emgas) staff employees were very highly trained and, most importantly gave opportunities for all staff a chance to succeed and if necessary, progress gas debts to court. In some instances they had to appear at court to present their case.

I made a point every Friday evening, before we all went home for the weekend, of personally going round, thanking every single member of my staff for their individual efforts. Not only was this the best attitude for a manager to take, the right thing to do, but it also created a harmonious team atmosphere. Members of my staff then felt that they could always approach me with any problems and receive real help.

1994
Redundancy, Selling Caravans and Tricia's Hobby

My enjoyable time selling caravans to delighted clients was eventually sadly brought to an end because I suffered yet another personal setback. My health had deteriorated and had become a serious issue again.

This was whilst I had to fight hard to recover from the DVT (Deep Vein Thrombosis) occurring in my legs and was also suffering at the same time from severe oedema (the severe swelling of the legs). Tricia did not want me to go out to work in case I found that the swelling worsened, dangerously. But I was reluctant not to go to the yearly caravan show itself as I had already booked time off to be able to work at this show. This company that I worked for part-time had been too good to me over so many years for me to let them down. I endured intense pain for the next agonising three days at the start of the caravan show.

The problem was so severe and excruciating because my actual job of selling, and advising clients on the caravans involved standing eight hours at least each day. This then aggravated the swelling of both legs, and the consequent pain was unbearable. By the third day, I had to reluctantly tell my friend, Jeremy, the MD, that I could not carry on. He could see the distress that I was in and viewed the severely dangerous swelling of my legs, and was very sympathetic. As he knew my total loyalty for the past ten years, he completely understood my situation. To make up the number of salespersons, he called in immediately one of his other staff members to take my place. So all was saved and an answer found by the thoughtful and caring nature of my boss. Jeremy cared for my welfare just as much as he cared for the success of his caravan sales company itself. At all times he was an incredibly high-minded person and totally admirable.

Later on, he came to and enjoyed our 35th wedding anniversary, and we stayed in touch for many years after that.

1993-94

However, the changes taking place at East Midlands Gas (Emgas) gave me the opportunity of taking the offered redundancy and to enjoy an early retirement. Owing to the rather fragile state of my health at this time and the fact that I did not want to move our family home to Birmingham or to any other office, I willingly accepted and welcomed this change of lifestyle. After choosing to take the redundancy settlement, Tricia and I visited the employment offices, where, after extensive, detailed investigations, the staff there suggested that I seek to apply for a disability benefit. After all, I had suffered the severe epilepsy attacks, also had osteoarthritis and thrombosis, plus polyneuropathy in my feet and fluid in my legs due to oedema. However, I refused to give up on life, so I just claimed and accepted the normal unemployment benefit for the remainder of the years left until my actual retirement. Now, I realise that it would have been so much more sensible for me to have claimed the disability benefit since this continues *after* a person has retired, provided that the disability itself still continues.

My motives were possibly at that time to obtain some suitable employment as and when it became necessary. I felt that I might well have needed to be able to find a job to add to my income if this did become necessary, but the Lord provided for me. I had, of course, always been our family's sole provider, and this had to continue still.

The thought of redundancy made me start looking carefully, scrutinising at all the household bills we received each month, and I made as sure as I possibly could that we were economical. Finally I managed to save about £30 per month for unforeseen expenses. Christmas presents were purchased by us in the sales, and other such necessary economies were made. I had a few investments in shares, and commitments to save for further shares. These were due to be deducted from my monthly pension. They were not expected to mature for a couple of years or more, and I did not want to have to cash those in either. The saving habit urged originally by my most helpful and knowledgeable friend, Dave, had made me fundamentally cautious with spending.

My past life had an effect on Tricia and me at this time. She told me that I now needed help and advice myself. I agreed with her, and I saw a psychotherapist, Dr Frost, who for seven years then counselled me and helped me considerably to put my haunting childhood experiences and associated harrowing memories finally to rest. There were some other problems which had stayed with me from childhood, and he detected those that I had suffered which also affected me over the years. He was very capable, and boosted my self confidence.

Around this time, it was made public that soldiers in our armed forces had also been, like me and my other contacts, experimented on using LSD and other even more dangerous substances. During one of my visits to see Dr Frost, the information he confirmed - as reported then in the media - was that over 4000 mental patients had been given LSD without their knowledge or consent. It was all experimental. Understandably, this was a revelation, and those who had suffered from its later effects were asked to register any claims they had against the NHS. The medical records, however, were missing. We were told these had been destroyed, but the one thing this LSD investigation did do was to resurrect distant, painful memories that were still deeply embedded and ingrained in one's mind.

The information below was recorded in 1967 and as such would have been available for reference by me, along with many others with similarly serious health implications for the sufferers. Notice the word 'illicitly' is used, inferring that the drug itself has question marks as to its purity. This is, I believe, the inbuilt defence mechanism that the medical profession resorts to so that they can discredit any adverse reactions to a drug that has been used. It emphasises the fact that after further treatments there were no reactions, but it fails to mention what the person who took it suffered afterwards from a year or so later.

Grand Mal Seizures Following Ingestion of LSD[25]

DUKE D. FISHER, M.D., AND J. THOMAS UNGERLEIDER, M.D., *Los Angeles*

VARIOUS UNTOWARD REACTIONS to lysergic acid diethylamide tartrate (LSD[25]) have been recorded in the psychiatric literature.[1,5] The authors[1] have themselves observed chronic psychiatric complications in patients following ingestion of the drug. In the case here reported the patient had no adverse psychiatric side effects from LSD but had two grand mal seizures after using the drug. So far as we could determine, there have been no previous reports in the literature of clinical seizures following LSD ingestion, although there have been several general allusions to the subject.[1,2,3,5,6]

Report of a Case

The patient was a 32-year-old Caucasian man, a graduate student in anthropology who worked as a night watchman for a film studio. He had ingested LSD for the first time approximately five months before he entered the UCLA Neurology Clinic for investigation of grand mal seizures. He said he believed he had taken 450 mcg on that first occasion, but since the LSD was illicitly obtained he could not be sure of the dosage. Approximately 30 minutes after ingesting the drug, the patient noticed hallucinations of color, feelings of unreality

From the Department of Psychiatry, UCLA Center for the Health Sciences.
Submitted 14 December 1966.
Reprint requests to: Department of Psychiatry, UCLA Center for the Health Sciences, 760 Westwood Plaza, Los Angeles 90024 (Dr. Fisher).

and preoccupation with detail. Approximately 50 minutes after ingestion, he had a grand mal seizure which included tonic and clonic movements, unconsciousness and urinary incontinence, all observed by the patient's LSD "sitter," a clinical psychologist. The patient recalled being confused and disoriented for approximately two hours after the seizure. The remainder of the LSD experience persisted for approximately 12 hours without further seizure activity. Afterward the patient noticed pain in the back, and x-ray films taken later in the emergency room of UCLA Center showed fractures of the fifth and seventh thoracic vertebrae.

The patient had four subsequent LSD sessions, using an undetermined amount of LSD, with no seizures. Approximately two months before he was observed in the Neurology Clinic, he took LSD for the sixth time and had another grand mal seizure in the presence of two friends. Concerned that he might have seizures without using LSD, he referred himself to the UCLA Neurology Clinic.

There was no history of previous seizure activity or of birth trauma, recent infectious disease or head injury. Nor was there family history of seizures. Except for the intermittent use of marijuana, the patient said he had not used drugs other than LSD.

Results of general physical and neurological examinations were entirely within normal limits. On examination of mental status the patient was noted to be quite anxious, without evidence of any psychotic material. There was no persistent LSD psychosis, severe depression, recurring hallucinations or delusions. The patient had identified with the "acid head culture" and was quite preoccupied with LSD, which he described as his religion.

An electroencephalogram was within normal limits. Lumbar puncture was performed; opening pressure was 160 mm of water and the fluid was clear and colorless. Closing pressure was 130 mm.

There was a case of a nurse who was also given LSD as hospital treatment, and she contacted me personally afterwards about this situation. She had developed epilepsy, but could not continue with her own particular claim and the case because of the cost involved, which she could not possibly afford.

Like her, I was told that I must have been already susceptible to epilepsy (which I could not believe).

I was also told that the LSD more than likely caused the first seizure, but not the further subsequent epileptic seizures which happened after we had been discharged. This statement is totally incorrect, but worse, also being in complete ignorance of the dangers of LSD and the brain damage it can cause. It is an assumption which bears no validity, and which doctors involved use to hide behind in a court of law.

I believe that LSD does cause brain damage, and when it does this it may manifest itself in many different ways for each individual. Epilepsy is the result in some cases. Such dangerous experiments were carried out on us, then innocent and helpless teenagers, in our early years. I was only 17 and was never ever asked for my permission to be given the LSD drug injections. Neither was my mother asked for her approval/permission on my behalf as she was then my sole next-of-kin responsible for me up to age 18.

With the LSD legal situation, I spent the next six years in litigation fighting a case that was forced to collapse simply because of judicial incompetence and because, I believe, the government did not want it to succeed. This was due to the considerable amount of compensation involved that they would have to finance. Most of the cases were legal aid supported, and the government apparently did not want to pay these fees either. However, in my particular individual case, I had suitable legal cover on my house insurance policy, which the insurers agreed to use to pay the solicitors' costs. Unfortunately, I had to ride, as it were, on the back of the other cases paid for with legal aid. I am sure that if I had then been assertive enough and chosen my own solicitor, the outcome might well have been very different indeed and much more remunerative in respect of our sufferings.

After seven years - yes, after seven years - the government pulled the plug on their support. The excuse made was that the professor who was a key witness when questioned by our solicitors would not be able to present the case in court also for the defence case. A letter was received by us from the solicitors saying that they would not pursue the situation as it would not now be supported by the government.

COMPENSATION

A finite, small sum of money had been given to be divided by the government amongst the forty plus litigants, and I would receive £2500 of that amount. Appallingly this was with the unfair condition that it was to be accepted by me within the stringent time limit of the actual next three days. If so, there was to be also a secrecy clause, we were not to divulge the terms of this settlement to anyone. The facts of the matter are that if it had indeed gone to the High Court, I believe they would have found in favour of us and it would have cost the authorities much, much more in damages and in legal fees for each claimant.

I was amazed at this as the case was due to be heard at the High Court and had been withdrawn and yet there was no redress for us. The amount I was awarded was for the permanent disability that at the time I had already suffered already for at least forty years. Also and just as important I now have suffered for sixty years, having to take powerful medication (20 to 30 tablets often) for all that time to keep me in a state of health, but still with the threat of severe seizures hanging over my head for the remainder of my life. Under the law, (because my claim had been paid for by my own insurance company), I asked what fee the solicitors had received, and was informed that it should have been £8730, but they had decided to, and then did reduce their fee to £5543.43. They received almost twice the amount I finally received!!

I would recommend all readers to ensure that they have legal cover included in their buildings and contents' insurance, as it will provide anything from £50,000 to £100,000 of cover should they ever need it. Some policies do fortunately include this as standard practice.

BMJ. 2002 Mar 2; 324(7336): 501.
PMCID: PMC1122436
PMID: 11872538
NHS settles the claim of patients treated with LSD
Clare Dyer, legal correspondent
Author information Copyright and License information Disclaimer

The NHS has agreed to pay a total of £195,000 ($279 000; €319000) in an out of court settlement to 43 former psychiatric patients who were treated with the hallucinogenic drug lysergide (LSD) between 1950 and 1970.

The patients were treated for illnesses including severe depression, schizophrenia, and postnatal depression at a few hospitals where the drug was thought at that time to be of therapeutic value. The main centre at which this treatment took place was Powick Hospital in Worcester.

The claims, which were funded by legal aid, have been settled for a fraction of the value put on them by the claimants' lawyers. David Harris of the personal injury law firm Alexander Harris, who acted for more than 90% of the claimants, said that the two main hurdles for claimants were the legal requirements to sue within specified time limits and the fact that the standard of care expected of doctors was lower 40 or 50 years ago than it is now.

The NHS Litigation Authority had also agreed to a fixed sum towards the claimants' legal costs. A very important statement was made by Mr Harris which said that the full costs were about £750,000 but that the firm would absorb their own loss and none of his clients would have any values subtracted from their damages to make up this shortfall. Very responsible attitude from Mr Harris.

'I know that some of the clients were very disappointed with what they got, but some have been delighted," he said. "We will take the hit ourselves, and every client who was involved in the settlement will receive all the damages they have been awarded.'

A spokesman for the authority said: 'The legal costs of proceeding to trial in these 43 cases alone could have exceeded £3m, with a trial continuing for around six months. No admissions of liability have ever been made, and the settlement was motivated by a desire on behalf of this authority to limit the continuing accrual of legal costs on both sides, which have become disproportionate to the damages involved.'

This was appallingly disproportionate and unfair, of course, and was suffered by every one of us, the claimants. Ever since suffering from this disability, as I said already, I have had to take at least 20 tablets every day, and in some instances, if I develop a cold or another health complaint, this could increase to over 30 pills a day. Also, I have suffered numerous falls and injuries in some episodes of epilepsy. Dangerous falls occur when you fall over unconscious following or during a seizure, and you often damage your head, badly bruising or cutting your face, your head, or your body.

I had spent the previous six years of the legal case itself informing the solicitors and providing them with the answers every time the defence asked a question. I was just so fed up with this case that it reminded me of that of an American soldier, who was officially reported to have been given LSD and had also developed epilepsy. Forced to take his case to the highest court in the USA, he did eventually receive compensation of eight million dollars!!!!

I argued the whole situation with the solicitors, informing them that a professor, who they had engaged in my case, had said that LSD had most probably started off my epilepsy. In reply, I was informed I must have actually had already a tendency to the condition. This is all supposition: the fact is that LSD does cause epilepsy. You only have to look on the internet to see the overwhelming proof.

There are also numerous instances on the internet in which LSD takers have themselves suffered severe seizures. It was bizarre that this information was only released after payments had been made to the litigants. Only this week, I myself found out this latest relevant information, and can add it to the other very important evidence:

It is interesting to know that whereas catalepsy is a sort of freezing, rigid type of paralysis, on the other hand epilepsy, although similar, has similarities in that the person loses control, falls to the ground invariably out of control and already unconscious.

More relevant information about LSD and its effects:

Medical Reports

J. Neurol. Neurosurg. Psychiat., 1953, **16**, 7.

THE EFFECTS OF METHEDRINE AND OF LYSERGIC ACID DIETHYLAMIDE ON MENTAL PROCESSES AND ON THE BLOOD ADRENALINE LEVEL

BY

D. W. LIDDELL and H. WEIL-MALHERBE

From Runwell Hospital, Wickford, Essex

The psychological effects of drugs and their applications in psychiatry are of theoretical as well as practical interest, but their study has rarely penetrated beyond a description of symptoms and little is known of their mechanisms of action. Since a method for the estimation of adrenergic amines in blood has recently been developed (Weil-Malherbe and Bone, 1952) we decided to study the changes of blood adrenaline levels during drug action and to correlate them with mental changes. In this communication we report on results obtained with d-N-methylamphetamine hydrochloride ("methedrine") and lysergic acid diethylamide (L.S.D.).

The application of methedrine in psychiatry has been investigated by Levine, Rinkel, and Greenblatt (1948), Delay (1949), Rudolf (1949), Hope, Callaway, and Sands (1951) and Hoch, Cattell, and Pennes (1952b). In schizophrenic patients the drug is claimed to produce an increase of accessibility, emotional discharge, and verbalization of repressed or delusional material. Delay (1949), on the other hand, states that catatonic features, if present, are accentuated.

The psychological effects of L.S.D. in normal and psychotic subjects were first described by Stoll (1947) and his results were subsequently confirmed by Condrau (1949), Becker (1949), and Fischer, Georgi, and Weber (1951). DeShon, Rinkel, and Solomon (1952) studied the effects of L.S.D. on normal subjects and Busch and Johnson (1950), Forrer and Goldner (1951), and Hoch and others (1952a) similarly investigated its effects on psychotics. De Giacomo (1951) drew attention to the capacity of L.S.D., given in large doses by mouth, of producing symptoms of catatonia in schizophrenic patients, an effect resembling the action of bulbocapnine. Others have commented on the analogy with the action of mescaline.

Though the various authors tended to stress different symptoms as the chief characteristic of L.S.D. action, all are agreed as to its potency, for as little as 10 µg. by mouth has been sufficient to produce results. Psychotic patients, however, seem to be less sensitive and to require larger doses. When L.S.D. is taken by mouth symptoms appear within half an hour, reach their maximum in about two and a half hours, and gradually pass off in the following four to five hours. Occasionally mild after-effects are noted over the next few days.

The subjective complaints after a dose of L.S.D. are chiefly of headache, malaise, giddiness, nausea, feeling cold, anorexia, and palpitations. Objectively the examination of the autonomic and central nervous system is equivocal. On the other hand, psychological changes are prominent. Thought and speech may exhibit retardation, acceleration, blocking, and hesitancy; the speech may be slurred. The effect is one of euphoria, but depression as well as apprehension and depersonalization may occur. Disturbances of perception are common, especially in the visual sphere, as manifested by distortion, wrong perspective, or incorrect estimation of distances; colour perception may be poor or faulty. These effects increase with larger doses and may result in hallucinations. In the behavourial field under-activity with lack of initiative is most frequently observed, but restlessness and even agitation is sometimes noted. Unmotivated smiling and forced laughing have been described.

Busch and Johnson (1950) have drawn attention to the possible use of L.S.D. as an aid to psychotherapy since they found that psychotic patients responded with an increased production and verbalization of psychopathological material.

EXPERIMENTAL

Previous investigators gave L.S.D. by mouth. We, too, have used this route of administration in preliminary experiments, but later the drug was given by intravenous injection. This procedure, being independent of the individual variations in intestinal absorption, had the advantage of producing a more standardized and less protracted time curve of effects; moreover the comparison with the effects of methedrine, which was also administered by intravenous injection, was facilitated. Forrer and Goldner (1951) found that L.S.D., when taken by mouth, is not toxic up to doses of 6 μg./kg. It was felt therefore that the intravenous injection would not involve undue risks. Initially small doses in the order of 25 μg. in 10 ml. of normal saline were used, but since these proved safe, the dose was eventually stepped up to 60 μg. dissolved in 5 ml. of normal saline. A stock solution of 1 mg. in 5 ml. saline was prepared and stored in the frozen state for not more than one week. It was further diluted immediately before use. Methedrine was employed in doses of 40 to 60 mg.

The subjects were investigated in the forenoon after an overnight fast. They were under constant observation in a quiet room and their psychological and neurological symptoms were noted. They were encouraged to lie down, but this was not insisted upon and they were allowed to move freely if they wished. Blood samples were withdrawn from the cubital veins before the injection and at five, 10, 20, 30, 40, 60, and 90 minutes after the injection. In three patients who were examined after oral administration of 40 μg. L.S.D. blood samples were withdrawn before ingestion and 0·5, 1, 1·5, 2, 2·5, 3, and 3·5 hours after ingestion. Blood sugar was estimated in duplicate on 0·2 ml. samples of whole blood by the method of Nelson (1944) after $Ba(OH)_2$-$ZnSO_4$ deproteinization. Adrenaline was determined on a sample of plasma according to Weil-Malherbe and Bone (1952).

Ten cases were investigated after the intravenous injection of L.S.D. and 11 after the injection of methedrine. Further patients who had been similarly treated are not included because of differing dosage or incomplete investigation. The two groups consist of an approximately equal number of male and female patients varying in age from 22 to 61 years. Four cases received both drugs in separate experiments. The diagnostic composition of the two groups is shown in Table 1.

TABLE 1
SURVEY OF CASES INVESTIGATED

Diagnosis	Number of Cases	
	L.S.D.	Methedrine
Depression	3	0
Paranoid schizophrenia	2	2
Other forms of schizophrenia	4	4
Anxiety hysteria	0	2
Psychopathic states	1	2

RESULTS

Symptomatology

L.S.D.—The intravenous injection of L.S.D. produced a train of events occurring at a relatively constant time interval. After five minutes a flushing of the face was observed in five patients and seven patients appeared more relaxed and at ease. Some spontaneously commented on this with remarks such as, " I feel I can concentrate better ", " I look at you relaxed ". Talkative patients became calmer.

After 10 minutes mental symptoms became noticeable, chiefly in the sphere of thinking, speaking, and behaviour. While depressed patients became more retarded in both movement and speech, cataleptic phenomena were noted in some non-paranoid schizophrenics. Blocking, incoherence, perseveration, echolalia, poor production of material occurred in all six schizophrenics in various combinations, and in one of them the pupils became unequal and eccentric but reacted to light and convergence. After 15 to 20 minutes changes in mood and affect appeared. The mood fluctuated between euphoria, excitement, and depression. In the euphoric phase the subject may laugh happily, make erotic advances, propose marriage, and behave flippantly. The swingover to depression may take place rapidly and may be associated with crying, expressions of guilt, and occasionally the onset of abreaction; this may be followed, equally abruptly, by a swing of mood in the other direction. It is during this period that repressed material or new delusional thought contents may be produced. The emotions are appropriate to the thought content. These rapid mood swings were observed in all schizophrenic and psychopathic cases and persisted for two to three hours. Depressive patients, however, showed a steadily enhancing gloom and an accentuation of ideas of unworthiness and of mental retardation.

Changes in autonomic functions were observed in five cases after about 30 to 40 minutes. They consisted in subjective and objective shivering associated with goose-flesh and piloerection on the forearms in the case of men.

In six of the cases a change in the mental picture occurred after about 40 minutes. Apprehension and tenseness increased, sometimes progressing to agitation. Others showed an increase of mannerisms and grimaces. Only two schizophrenic patients gave at this time evidence of visual and auditory hallucinations. They appeared frightened and were completely inaccessible. This relatively rare occurrence of hallucinations is in striking contrast to the experience of most other observers who gave the drug by mouth. Four other patients became increasingly restless and agitated and one retarded depressive woman screamed

Citation

Perera, K. M. H., Ferraro, A., & Pinto, M. R. M. (1995). Catatonia LSD induced? Australian and New Zealand Journal of Psychiatry, 29(2), 324-327.

http://dx.doi.org/10.3109/00048679509075930

Abstract
Australian & New Zealand Journal of Psychiatry
The Royal Australian and New Zealand College of Psychiatrists
5.084

Impact Factor - Catatonia LSD Induced?
K. M. H. Perera, MBBS, PhD, MD2, A. Ferraro, MBBS, M. R. M. Pinto, MBBS, MD, PhD, MRCP, DPM, MRCPsych
First Published June 1, 1995 Case Report
https://doi.org/10.1080/00048679509075930
Article information

Abstract
'Discusses catatonia developed 2 days after the ingestion of LSD in a 21-yr-old female. The S presented initially with an acute atypical psychosis with affective lability, paranoia, verbigeration, and echolalia. Her clinical state deteriorated and stereotypy, catalepsy, negativism, posturing, immobility, and stupor became evident. Full blown catatonia was preceded by the use of neuroleptic drug treatment. The psychosis was precipitated by the use of LSD.

Database Record (c) 2016 APA, all rights reserved)'

What is a catatonic seizure?
The acute catatonic syndrome is a condition that can be caused by a variety of metabolic, neurological,

psychiatric, and toxic conditions, including neuroleptic malignant syndrome. Epileptic seizures in patients with the acute catatonic syndrome.

My conclusion: LSD was clearly to blame.

For my own seven years of litigation, the London solicitors who took up my case seemed to have numerous staffing changes, and it seemed that every six months or so there was a freshly employed new solicitor who would be allocated to be on my case and used for it. Each one was entirely new to the case, and would have to read, learn and digest what action had been taken and what else was then needed to be carried out. Upon reflection, this was very unsatisfactory as I would have thought continuity of staff in such a case would be essential in dealing with such a serious and complex case. Also, why did it take six to seven years for the professor, who formerly was a pivotal witness for the claimants, to be found - in their eyes only, of course – subsequently to be considered unreliable as a witness?

I believe many people who had suffered in the hospital, without their willing participation, were denied justice as well because we were at the time classified as mental patients or ex-mental patients, so their evidence was illegally consequently discredited because of that fact. After this, I was befriended by so many of the other ex-patients, who would telephone periodically and ask me for information on what progress we were all supposed to be making. In some cases, they called in to discuss their own personal financial situations. There were at least four thousand patients who had been given LSD in this particular situation, but only forty-six were included in the final legal claim. Many were too frightened that they would not be able to claim because they did not qualify for legal aid and they were informed they would have to pay their own legal expenses if the case was lost and withdrawn. Such expenses could run into thousands.

About 400 were in the first batch, and the aggressive questioning from the authorities frightened many who still suffered from their own very severe mental problems. As a result, they quickly dropped out. There was nothing to force the authorities to identify and inform all the patients who were involved. Information was very poorly distributed. It was advertised in the papers and other media, and it was just left up to the patients to notify their own solicitors. But most of them were not able to look after themselves with simple every-day essential tasks and needs, let alone be aware of the fact that they would be losing these important awards.

The problem with this was that a lot of these patients had long-term mental health problems and were, for a time, detained in the hospital so could not, or would not, have even known if they had been experimented upon, or exactly what to do next. A terrible position for anyone suffering in this way to find themselves involved in!

This situation and that of other litigants who sue the NHS should be reformed similarly to some other countries, like Australia, who have a 'no blame' culture. This would save a fortune in legal fees, and I believe could bring about a fairer and more efficient way of dealing with such incidents.

I have always had a strong sense of justice and fairness, especially for people less fortunate than myself. In this case, it appears totally unfair that the medical profession seemed to know more, and actually revealed less to the solicitors, for some as yet unknown reason. I am beginning to suspect the medical profession of being more than a little economical, even being not forthcoming, with the truth. This is not only to protect themselves, but also to preserve the NHS. We all agree that the NHS is a marvellous asset to everyone and there would not be many of us alive if it were not for their utter dedication. We want that to continue always to be the case, of course.

Outstanding Medical Claims

NHS Resolution, formerly known as the NHS Litigation Authority, estimates that the total liability for medical negligence cases it is already dealing with currently could be as much as £56.1 billion!

With such money, the suffering involved, and protracted delays, it would appear to be an opportune time now to consider a 'no blame' culture, in which compensation would and could be provided much earlier, and legal costs also minimised. It would also provide an opportunity for errors to be openly admitted so that procedures could be amended to save any repetition of this type of total unfairness to innocent sufferers.

Mine is not the only instance where a family have suffered through the NHS. You will come across other cases in which clearly something better should have been done. When the service is excellent, I think there is nothing to compare with it, but when things go wrong, it seems the NHS is on the defensive stance.

We all make mistakes in life, and it is far better to own up and to admit it. It saves money, it saves time, and it saves litigation costs. It saves months, if not years, of stress for those affected, and most of all gives them the opportunity to address the balance.

I do feel, however, that some members of my family and I have not at times received the best of treatment and care required. Unfortunately, they were not like me and did not sue the NHS for compensation. I am sure in those instances they would have been offered settlements.

Nevertheless, like many other incidents in my life, I had to put it all behind me. It was another difficult and very disappointing time to add to all the other events that my family and I have had to suffer. During this time, my health always suffered markedly, and I was eventually given the opportunity of taking redundancy and my firm's pension. Knowing the company was going through privatisation and was to vacate its Leicester head office, I jumped at the chance. It was a golden opportunity. I had spent, with others, 25 years trying to integrate the industry, and in about 25 months' time it was virtually going to be torn apart, being very upsetting for a lot of the people who worked there at East Midlands Gas (Emgas).

1994
After Redundancy

After redundancy, I continued to live at Whetstone but then Tricia felt that she wanted to move, and we eventually decided to change counties, and move out of Leicestershire to a pretty village, West Walton, in Norfolk. There, we would be able to live and, for a while, attend the Baptist Church at Wisbech which was at that time our nearest Baptist church.

Our object, which we achieved, was to grow in our faith, as we had at our church at Whetstone, but there were more than enough very gifted volunteers were more than able to meet the demands of that particular local church. We wanted a change, and possibly a challenge, and we indeed received all that and more.

1995
30th Wedding Anniversary

Being now retired for over a year, and not having had many wedding celebrations in our past lives, I decided to hold a big one and spend some of my redundancy money for our thirtieth anniversary. Choosing Leicester University for this special occasion as it was a beautiful location, and artistic invitations were sent out to everyone as I wanted everything to be just right. Enjoyably, we all sat down to a banquet to celebrate the event.

Inviting about a hundred and fifty people in all, we made sure everyone was included. Anna, my cousin, daughter of Arthur Le Hair and Una, was also there. She was by then a famous, talented concert pianist, and she played for us that evening. Most of my old friends were from work, and many of our relations were also there. It was a fantastic celebration, as Tricia's mother was also able to enjoy the evening, together with her brothers and sisters. I had also invited a couple of friends (caravan managers from my part-time job), who really enjoyed themselves, and I was pleased to renew their friendship. One of the managers had a disabled son, whom he, as a caring father, was initially going to leave behind at home, but I quickly replied that he would be welcome too. The boy had the time of his life dancing at the disco, and his father was overjoyed that we had invited him and couldn't thank me enough. They were grateful as they very rarely got the chance to all go out together to an event. We also had two ministers, one from our present church and one from our former church. Relations from my father's family, most of whom had farms and had made their wealth through sheer hard work, came to the event and celebrated our anniversary with us.

There was a disco after everyone had had their photos taken and also eaten the delicious three-course dinner. Drinks were on the house, and later at night, we had arranged for a buffet to be also provided for those still hungry. We were absolutely delighted to see that everyone enjoyed themselves and had a good time.

1996
Death of Tricia's Mother

Tricia's mother had been ill on and off many times over some years. She had COPD and other illnesses. She, bless her, refused to eat properly, but she was 80 years old and had a mind of her own. Unfortunately, she was taken ill in April and admitted to Hospital on the 9th in the evening. She was evidently not well at all, but we had been there in that situation so many times before, previously, that we were used to this and she had then recovered each time. Unfortunately, no sooner had we arrived home than we had a telephone call to say she had just passed away peacefully. I was very sorry for Tricia that we had not realised the end for her mother had been so near, but, upon reflection, she had expressed a very meaningful 'thank you' for us looking after her in her later years before we actually left the hospital. I should have recognised her feeling of impending death, or sensed its nearness at that moment.

Tricia's mother had been to our church a few times, and it was so kind of them then to celebrate her life with her funeral being held on its premises. Tricia had found this so reassuring, and I was glad for her. It may have been the fact of the worry that we were planning to move house that could have expedited her mother's death, but I sincerely hope not. In fact, had she been alive when we moved, I am sure she would have spent a lot of her time again with us as she had always done.

Suddenly, on top of other serious problems, I had issues arising with my feet and had to go to Addenbrooke's hospital to have tests. It was established that I had developed a strange numbness, which had got worse on both feet, and it turned out to be polyneuropathy. It seemed they could prescribe some more tablets, but that was the last thing I wanted to take. After all, I already had been prescribed at least 10 pills for epilepsy, and suitable other tablets for other ailments. This increased to 20 pills, and has carried on for so many years, which is a great strain, of course, on one's body. The tablets are active and some of them exceedingly, worryingly dangerous. It is essential to carry out a rigorous regime, so you do not miss even one single dose. The consequences are dire and so dangerous if you do miss a dose, and even can be deadly dangerous!

On a more cheerful note, I had developed a certain skill. Over the years I bought and sold houses, improved them, and made significant profits. Ultimately, this enabled me to move to a much more desirable home. From an original terraced house, I had moved the family to a semi-detached, then to a detached one, progressing then to a bigger detached, and finally to a very much larger detached.

1996

For our House in Norfolk this property, Mulberry House, I had made up my mind for the improvements to be extensive, and included the addition of a double garage, a copious study, utility room, and two new bathrooms. In three of the bedrooms I added fitted wardrobes to the largest bedrooms.

In August 1996, we completed the purchase of this house – already a much larger and much more palatial one than we had ever possessed. We found this particularly lovely mock Georgian style modern home that I felt had not yet been designed and finished off to its full potential. I determined to change this!

We had moved to a lovely village, West Walton in Norfolk. Our nearest town, the historic Georgian Wisbech, was only a convenient couple of miles away. With its long curving drive stretching from the road to the front door, I could see great potential in this spacious house.

I started to turn our somewhat exteriorly 'ugly duckling' of a house into a simply beautiful, elegant

Georgian style swan. This, in our hands, became the Georgian style residence one dreams about.

The first task was to sort out the land boundary, which had been very badly initially diagnosed and whose actual boundaries remained in dispute. After one whole year of getting absolutely nowhere, I telephoned my solicitor and surveyor and arranged to hold a meeting with my two nearest neighbours. After much arguing and wrangling, we eventually all agreed on a specific solution of redrawing the whole boundary lines themselves. I decided that I would pay for a fence to be erected to delineate firmly this line. The neighbours were delighted to agree, and I paid for all of it for everyone's benefit!

After that, I arranged for the single garage to be demolished, and then I had plans prepared for the erection of a double garage with an integral capacious utility room, plus a study connected at the back of it. After knocking the original garage and a garden wall down, I then started reclaiming the bricks myself and cleaning them up as this would save considerably on cost and there would be sufficient to build the front elevation. It would essentially match with the brickwork, so the front would then be unbroken, smooth and totally harmonious. To this day, the whole of the brick façade of the double garage matches splendidly the house itself, so that all the bricks look precisely the same forming a harmonious matching exterior.

The one thing you find in The Fens is that people were and are still very resourceful, and if they couldn't do it themselves, they would find somebody very skilled who could. Many of them self-build their own houses as this can be so much cheaper. In fact, one person whom I met has now produced four homes and sold them while still serving as a policeman. He contracted work out to specialists, and when you build your own, you can claim all the VAT back in addition to making a substantial profit from building your own place, and then selling it.

It took a little while before I could start building, as I had to wait for planning permission and then source more of new bricks to match the house. After numerous visits to brick merchants, I eventually found these literally, as it were, 'on my doorstep'. The first step was footings, which had to be dug specifically to the required depth to ensure stability. I had contacted two companies and received quotes, but one of the other contractors I had engaged gave me a much better price, and, since his work was of a high standard, he was finally awarded the job.

It was not long before all was in place and building work started. It was soon completed, including the roof. Windows were fitted to the rear utility room and study. This really improved the whole property and put it into a different class of building.

After studying how the house then looked, as a final finishing perfect entrance, I then decided to find a porch from a highly specialised glass fibre merchant who could build actual copies of Georgian columns that included a porch with roof to match. After many searches on the internet, I found one located in the south of England. I contacted the company, placed an order, and it was to prove to be a very successful addition indeed to the house. Importantly, this porch would make it look resplendent as you drove up and approached it. The swan had emerged in all its glory! This made the house highly desirable both for people to wish to live in and also to drive up the long gravelled driveway leading to the porch. Friends still gasp with admiration when they view the photographs.

We then possessed a double garage and required an automatic door for it, so that in the bad weather you could just drive in without getting wet or cold. The quote I received was very competitive and I quickly agreed and snatched the supplier's hand off. When the company delivered the porch and its attractive columns, they looked fantastic, and I could then visualise it all coming together. I was fortunate that some of the tradesmen I had already employed informed someone they knew to come and do the job of fitting the porch.

Peace, quiet and tranquillity reigned. The house finally looked an absolute picture, and Tricia and I adored it, and so did our friends who visited, and stayed periodically with us.

That was, however, until our peace was eventually dramatically tragically broken, you could also say shattered, with an incident that was a terrible shock. It happened out of the blue. Entirely unexpectedly, we suddenly had persons moving in next door to us and they were what seemed to be 'problem neighbours.' The serious consequences are described in more depth later on in the following pages. They were only solvable eventually by us moving from this - originally - our dream home.

However, back to the joy of creating a lovely, beautiful and colourful garden too for Mulberry House. This was professionally redesigned, and I was then introduced to a wholesale company. They, at a reduced cost, provided plants, shrubs and trees of every description, and even filled my hanging baskets to overflowing with fresh, glorious colour. I bought a garden house especially as a treat for Tricia to use, and she spent many a happy hour relaxing in it, her favourite pastime being her homework on the new hobby she had acquired of researching the family's history.

I became more involved in the garden, which I had never bothered about before except for cutting the grass.

In the summer we would travel to Hunstanton or Old Hunstanton. My wife loved the sea there and especially the beach. In our younger days, we would both swim at Old Hunstanton, where it was very safe to bathe, and enjoy a long day together, and sometimes the Lord would reveal a beautiful sunset for us and others to admire for hours at a time. This is a superb west facing beach.

The storm that was on the horizon, however, was that due to the price of property at that time in Norfolk being so low, the house next door to our Mulberry Houses in West Walton was sold to a family. A family that brought with it its own serious problems. These turned out, to be almost fatal and created for us and the neighbours very upsetting instances. However, I applauded the fact that they were trying to improve their property, but their move into it and their alarmingly hostile presence proved to have its own dramatic adverse effect for those of us who lived nearby.

Due to its affordable sale price, this property had attracted people who would not usually have been able to purchase it. Disaster followed. The road, with its peace and tranquillity, had already drawn three doctors and business-people, and they lived peacefully and quietly there. It had become possibly the best road in the village of West Walton.

We spent a couple of years sorting the house out, redesigning and improving it as explained, living in there in comfort and security. After the bathroom and en-suites were replaced, the spacious kitchen redesigned, and quality wallpaper purchased, we became aware of a specialist shop where the owner was excellent at helping us choose precisely the outstandingly suitable patterned wallpaper.

In the end, all these renovations became quite an expensive project, but an enjoyable one. However, we carried on and what we finally achieved enhanced the house to a high standard. Sometimes the specialist concerned would bring wallpapers and come to the house advising us as to what would be the most appropriate and tasteful patterns to use. By the time I had finished, it was a truly magnificent house. It satisfied my original longing for a majestic yet attractive Georgian mansion, and was spacious enough for anyone and for all of my family to live in when they visited us.

Below is my own final photo of Mulberry House. This is what it looked like after I had finished my considerable alterations and planned improvements to it.

However, many new unexpected problems then arose, and I had to deal with them very firmly. More of this particular enthralling story in a few pages' time.

Wisbech Baptist Church

Firstly, however, we were reluctantly accepted at our new Baptist church in Wisbech, but I think they were wary of us initially because of the questions we would ask and the livelier worship that we were used to and expected to happen. Letters of approval had been sent by our previous minister, recommending Tricia and me to the other new church members. However, the elders of the new church still persisted in interviewing (almost interrogating) us, which was strange, off-putting to an extent, and unnecessary. We did not want to belong to a church that was old-fashioned in its worship, because the church that we were leaving had shown us so many benefits, and we wanted to have the same at our next chosen church.

Tricia found the services very dull and the singing even worse. They seemed to use a limited number of hymns and choruses that were very staid and not at all uplifting. The sermons were even more boring; at times it was enlightening to listen to of course, but it was more of a lesson designed for young children.

After some weeks helping in the youth club, we were encouraged to undertake the whole running of it as the present person running it wanted and needed a break. It was usually held on a Friday evening, and my wife and I decided to take it on and see if we could do some good. The young people who attended were mostly, however, somewhat out of control, and it was hard work trying to help and educate them. Unfortunately, most of them were rebels, and they had no interest in religion. They wanted to play football and table tennis, and have drinks, chocolate, and other such sweets.

Some wanted to smoke, and it was a hard job for my wife to stop them as they were mostly young girls.

To help us raise funds so that we could take the children out, I sold sweets, biscuits, crisps and drinks, hoping that I would be able to make a profit for the benefit of the church and its funds. I will always remember one little boy who looked so sad and downhearted who asked me what he could get for ten pence. Taking pity on him, thinking that this was all he had, I offered him something far above ten pence, to which he replied, 'Then I will have a pound's worth!' I found we apparently had some crafty kids, and I decided that I had to watch my step with them in the future, although it was, of course, laughable.

One night, I asked the children to sit in a circle and discuss how we should try to resolve or should look at personal problems. I am afraid that I was shocked at what I heard in reply from the children. One child had only been told just that week that her brother was not her brother. Another said that she had seen her father out holding another woman. Many of the others had problems of a less severe nature, but they all consulted each other as a form of therapy. This was very uplifting, and it was good that we were all open with each other and that they had found our efforts so helpful.

Our own Alpha Course

We made friends with another Christian couple, Brian and Elizabeth Baker, who lived in the same village, and very soon we were having meals at one another's houses. Our Christian aspirations took precedence, and it was not long before the four of us had agreed to do an Alpha Course at our home.

The Alpha course is an evangelistic course which seeks to introduce the basics of the Christian faith through a series of talks and discussions. It is described by its organisers as "an opportunity to explore the meaning of life". Alpha courses are being run in churches, homes, workplaces, prisons, universities and a wide variety of other locations. The course began in Britain and is being run around the world by various Christian denominations. Between us, we knew others would be interested, and gathered together about ten people to dinner each week. In those days, I could source sufficient food of good quality to satisfy our hungry guests, and we all enjoyed the course itself, with Brian taking the lead. It was tiring for Tricia and me, but it was gratifying.

We had played football with a young man who just lived for it, and when we gave the youth club up, he wrote us a letter about two pages long, thanking us for helping to run the club. It was very thoughtful of him and at the same time rewarding to us.

Later, my wife did much more work on her study of genealogy and became quite active researching past and present relatives on the internet. It was beautiful to see the number of people she had already befriended and the thoughtful comments and memories they had of her when so sadly she later died. They remembered the Christian work she had done in reassuring people and witnessing her own personal faith and experiences to those in need. I never realised the full extent of what she had done on the internet, and after reading the beautiful words said about her, I was very proud of the work she had done helping others in distress, and, of course, very proud that she was my wife. When she was on her laptop, she seemed to be lifted into another world, tracing family history and making contact with numerous people.

Many times after we had moved to our lovely Mulberry House in West Walton, she was able to visit Norwich council offices, where she obtained a plethora of information about her own family. To me, researching genealogy was boring, so she would go on her own sometimes, and spend the day there, making more contacts that could help her in the future. Sometimes we would go at three in the afternoon and get there in just over half an hour if the road was clear. These spontaneous visits made her day.

Tricia got on well with Elizabeth, our newfound Christian friend, and they both decided to study at a religious course held at Peterborough, and while I was preoccupied with the house renovations, Tricia was doing her best to improve her Christian knowledge. This pleased both of us, and I was so delighted she had made a good friend and found something so worthwhile to do. Considering that Tricia did not, at that time, use the internet, but did all her studying and writing from what she had read, she succeeded well, and I was proud of her.

1999
Tricia and her Genealogy Interest

After finishing her religious course, Tricia started researching her mother's own family name of 'London', finding that they had connections with Great Yarmouth. This interest carried on until just before she died. She was besotted with finding out as much information as possible concerning her own mother's family, and this interest carried on for fifteen years. In fact, at times it seemed the only topic of conversation, and she just could not help introducing the subject if anyone came to visit us, and even when we went to church.

In addition to altering my house, I myself took up another interest. Our doctor's practice decided to ask for volunteers amongst all their patients who would be willing to set up a patient participation group. A meeting was held, and all interested parties were invited to attend. About ten of us turned up, and the doctors came and explained to us details of what we could get involved in. The meeting decided that it would be good to have a Patient Care Group (now known as PCG) and a committee was formed to discuss issues concerning our particular doctors' practice. Funds were to be raised through various ideas put forward so that we could hopefully get others involved. We held trendy quiz nights, car boot sales with cake stalls were arranged and proved a success when held in the surgery car park, and visits to other local doctors' surgeries were organised for those that had already established PCGs.

After its creation, some issues were discussed, and it was considered that we should carry out a survey on patients, who came to the surgery as to what they thought of the service, then evaluate the performance of the staff and hopefully suggest any improvements they thought could be beneficial. Although a meeting was only held once on a particular day each month, or possibly sometimes extended to every six weeks, there still was a lot of work to do within that time frame. I was eventually asked to be the chairman. This was a post that I really didn't want, but I could see that it would need some expertise in getting the whole concept successfully off the ground. The patient survey was excellent and gave some indication only of a hint of some minor problems. Most of the participants, if not all, were very satisfied with the service that they had received. Quiz nights produced a large number of people eager to put their knowledge to the test, and

I understand that these still continue to be held. A car boot with a cake stall was a very welcome money earner in the beginning. You only have to look now at their web page to see the additional equipment that the PCG has purchased for the surgery. I am glad it is a continuing success.

When I wrote a suitable term of reference for the group to use, I stipulated that a chairman, when appointed, should only serve for three years. After that, a new person should be selected. I think this was best as it allowed a fresh brain to see if the team could improve on what had already been achieved, and provided an opportunity for the inclusion of new ideas.

2000-2002
Feuding Neighbours Appear

Living at Mulberry House sadly eventually turned out not to be always idyllic. One winter's evening, I can remember every moment so well, hearing a loud noise which I thought was my wife banging something. I shouted to her to see if everything was alright with her. She replied that the bang came from outside our house. So, thinking there could have been a car accident, I went into the front and saw a man, holding a shotgun, standing and deliberately shooting at each of the windows until the glass fell out in the next door bungalow! To say that this was a shock would be a total understatement of how we felt. In this quiet, select, peaceful haven of village life, we were suddenly facing actual damaging gunfire. When the man with the gun finally noticed me, he jumped swiftly into his car, (which had no number plates on it) and speedily drove away.

People in the street then hurried out; police were soon on the scene, but were themselves reluctant to get involved at first. It appeared that the police knew of this particular family concerned, and I also believe that the family who had caused the damage were part of a two-family feud. Previous to this - whilst the bungalow was being actually built - they had lived in a caravan, and that had been set on fire on one occasion, everyone presumed deliberately, and it had to be replaced.

There were other incidents with our new neighbours, and individuals related to them, who it seemed were part of a local ongoing feud, as the police had informed us. Fights occurred then at a local garage with the two families concerned fighting each other, this time with machetes! As can be imagined, this was quite upsetting, especially in such a peaceful spot. Returning home from church one Sunday morning, we were to find police with dogs at nearly every house. Obviously, everyone was wondering what the hell was going on. The cops, we felt, must have considered that some further disturbance was just about to happen, but it in the end it did not, and peace was finally restored. One of the neighbouring families sold their bungalow and moved away, and the trouble was lessened for a time.

We decided that we deserved and needed a holiday that particular year, and wanted to make sure it was a good one. Secretly, I had always wanted to try a cruise, but had to encourage Tricia to want the same. Strangely, we were shopping in Westgate in Wisbech and, as I had some shares in Thompson's, I noticed a cruise offer advertised. It was one week cruising the Mediterranean and one week residing at a 4-star hotel. It looked fantastic, and it was a reasonable price. My cousin, Rita, used to go on cruises, sometimes three a year, herself and kindly recommended one for us. On the spur of the moment, we booked this one and realised we had a few weeks to sort all that was necessary, and then had the time of our lives.

We refreshed our wardrobes with the best clothes we could afford. I had purchased dresses for my wife previously from Harrods and Debenhams in their sales and from other sources. The beauty of a cruise is that people dress up specially at night for evening banquets held on board cruise ships, and also, in other of the ship's dining restaurants. Almost everyone, dresses smartly for the sumptuous dinners provided. All seem to be able to converse amiably with each other as though they are old friends. It is an atmosphere of pleasant comrade-ship. Often, as though you have found long-lost friends, it was as though we were all the same and had known each other for years!

The best part of a cruise is that you wake up every morning visiting a different port, or a new country. It was a fantastic holiday and at an excellent price. The food was as good as the best of five-star hotels could possibly provide, and the week that we had on land following this at a five star hotel was excellent too. I think Trish and I satisfied each other's separate demands with it being a mix of the cruise and a hotel stay.

2000
Dear Friend Ron Bull (OBE) Dies

Another disaster was that our dear friend Ron, who was Flo's much-loved husband, had been taken ill with a recent heart attack and was suffering a great deal. Flo came on the phone to us so upset and asking for us to pray for him, which we did, and we expected him to recover, but he sadly deteriorated and died on the 31st July 2000. It was a sad time for those left behind, and especially for Flo herself, his charming, ever-devoted wife.

In the short time I had known them, they had both become wonderful friends to us, and I have missed him dearly. I can well remember five years previously suffering some bouts of depression myself, and he had that time telephoned my wife that afternoon to tell us to be ready as he was going to take us to the Bull Hotel at Stamford (a famous five star.) He arrived with Flo in his Mercedes and quickly drove us all there. Out of thoughtfulness for me, he deliberately chose a very scenic route through the Leicestershire countryside and it increased my tranquil level immensely. It was a lovely evening, with plenty of light-hearted and uplifting conversation and a very enjoyable meal. We all revelled in each other's company so much, and, when you don't have this later on in your life, you realise just what you have missed. He really did cheer me up at that particular time, and the trip out for a companionable evening made me feel so refreshed and reinvigorated afterwards.

When we moved house, he and his wife loved to visit us to see how we were both getting on, and obviously to have a meal with us.

Persevering for some years with our neighbours and the terribly stressful lifestyle they caused, we reluctantly put the house up for sale through some local estate agents since we had decided to move to a newly built home, only six months old, at a village situated between March and Wisbech called Guyhirn. This new house, 'Gallery Hall', was impressive inside, whereas the previous Mulberry House, which we sold, had been far more impressive from the outside.

2002
My Stepfather Dies

Regretfully, on the 3rd December 2002, my stepfather died, and again I believe he was failed by his own doctor, who had sent a letter requesting an appointment for him to see a specialist when he should have been sent urgently and immediately to the hospital A&E as an emergency case. After a short holiday when he came to see me, he could hardly get out of the car. Within the next few days, he attended the hospital and was admitted immediately. They discovered that he had cancer of the lung, and he stayed in the hospital for only a couple of weeks before he came home to die. Because of the discomfort he was in, he slept in an armchair for a few days until they could bring a hospital bed for him. The day they brought that bed in was the night he died.

Incredibly, within a matter of a few days, more or less instantly my stepmother had everything else transferred into her name. She amazingly informed me that she did not want my children to be present at the funeral. I had to tell her they would be there, as they had every right to be there. Then I emphasised that he had been their own caring grandfather much longer than she had been married to him. After the funeral, she gave me his gold ring, which unfortunately I lost only a month ago. I was told later that even the solicitor suggested that she should not be so impatient in her demands in having everything transferred into her name as he, her husband, wasn't even cremated yet. It seemed as though she had had nearly everything else already carefully and previously assigned to her name. I later asked for a copy will and was told by the authorities he had left no will and no estate.

I did my best at the funeral to describe my stepfather kindly, and the relationship we had, and it was warmly received. In fact, another gentleman congratulated me on how honest and sincere I was about him, and said he wished his stepson had the same kindly relationship with himself.

My stepfather, soon after my mother died, met this lady who quickly became his new wife. When they got married, he seemed to somehow afterwards to have cut off all ties with us, and it was my sons who eventually wanted to see their grandfather again and regain that former relationship back that they once had all enjoyed together. Through my step-parents visiting us, in time, my wife and I brought them to believe in Jesus, and they then both took an active part in the church they went to. My stepfather had been a non-believer at one time, but became the sacristan carrying the cross that went before the religious processions at church. My stepmother took charge of some social functions, cooking and preparing the food, with the help of other people.

After living a few years at our well-loved Mulberry House, the house that had been sold next to us had encouraged undesirable people to purchase it. Later, this meant we would eventually be forced to put our own house up for sale. Having placed it with a wide range of estate agents, none of whom could produce a buyer, the housing market being, in fact, dead at that time and this carried on for months. I was continually being asked to reduce the price, which I flatly refused to do.

One Sunday after church, the Lord encouraged and inspired me to go to Spalding, and I walked into the first estate agents we came across. After discussing details with them of my home, which had five bedrooms, a master bedroom with ensuite, all fitted wardrobes, two lounges, utility, study, and so on, these Spalding agents quickly agreed to market our house. The reason I had gone there was the market in London itself was moving upwards, and Spalding had a railway station and attracted a lot of would-be buyers from the London area with plenty of money. We quickly found that one of the staff lived at Wisbech but worked at their offices in Spalding. He then visited us the next day and took all necessary details, measurements and photographs. In fact, he said that he thought the house was absolutely beautiful, and I had to admit, the extensive work we had done on the house meant it was indeed now a real bargain. My wife loved this house, and we had put a lot of our time, effort and money in sorting it out, but it was time to move on.

Strangely enough, it worked, and within a few weeks the first couple they brought to view did purchase our home. The Lord works in mysterious ways. When viewing potential properties to buy, we always had two or three houses in reserve that we had considered as desirable, and we quickly sorted out which one we wanted. Exchanges of contracts took place very rapidly, and it wasn't long before we had exchanged and settled in our new mansion.

Our previous house would have looked excellent value to most Londoners; in fact, the persons who bought it said that it would cost more than double where they came from in London.

Although I had estate agents' signs up, I refused to tell our neighbours until I had finally sold my own house. In fact, I waited until we would be moving out the very next day. I wanted it to be a shock to everyone, and it was. We had needed a change, and this, the next very spacious house, had the benefit of larger rooms, a very extensive garden with great potential, and more possibilities for further development. Also, a parish councillor lived just four doors away whom I was sure would maintain the well-being of the area.

This next house we purchased was called 'Gallery Hall', at Guyhirn, and it was in 2004 when we moved in, and it had much more luxurious accommodation, larger rooms, and a fabulous staircase and type of minstrels' gallery onto which the bedrooms led. The master bedroom was 24 feet long and had a dressing room and an ensuite. The house itself was very well-built, but needed redesigning. This appealed to us, and, knowing what improvements we had achieved before in West Walton with our Georgian House, we felt that this would be ideal.

Since buying my first house, I had enjoyed getting contractors to do the work for me, and wanted to turn this external ugly duckling into a stunning swan just like my previous house. I saw a lot of potential in this particular one. It was impressive already, and it certainly had many beautiful features. These comprised the open tread, butterfly design, solid mahogany wooden staircase and gallery first-floor landing surrounding three-quarters of this. The entrance hall, when you first entered the house, took your breath away. It had not long been built. In fact, it had been built by the owner's family. It was much larger than our previous one, and I made it even bigger still after Tricia and I moved in. When I had finished with it, there were five double bedrooms, three ensuites, two lounges, a very spacious dining room, a shower room and toilet, kitchen and a utility room. There was an enormous deck outside in the garden. This took up the width of the house, and had a depth of fifteen feet by at least 50 plus feet wide. There were wooden steps leading to the garden and an integral double garage at the front of the house.

I redesigned the whole house by turning the massive double garage into another large lounge and dining room and moving the oil-fired boiler, which was in the garage, to the kitchen, and built another new double garage on that side of the house. We then had two lounges, a separate dining room/study, a kitchen, a utility room and a shower room downstairs.

Upstairs, we converted a dressing room in the master bedroom to another ensuite for the guests, which was conveniently next door. Then the main bathroom was what is known as a 'Jack and Jill', which also served as an ensuite for the third bedroom. With the conversion completed, we moved our dining room suite into the large lounge formed by converting our double garage. The existing dining room was converted to an office, primarily for my personal use.

The family that I purchased the house from had just built four large homes previously for themselves as they already owned the land and put it to good use. The only thing they did not do was the design of the garden. This was simply massive, and because there was a spare piece of ground to the side of the house, I had made it a condition that I could purchase that as well, and they agreed.

One of the most important aspects of the property was this size of the garden. I had found a well-known local garden designer, Claire Simpson, who came and prepared some plans for me and she attached them with suggested planting plans. She had started her career and completed a three-year course at Askham Bryan Horticultural College in York, with the middle year divided between Leicester University Botanic Garden and Brighton Parks Department. Following this, she spent a year at Chelsea Physic Garden, studying garden design. She set up a business in London with Sarah Knox and spent several years designing and building both large and small gardens in London, including roof gardens. It was during this time that she met and married Mark Simpson. She was a lovely and helpful woman who was a director of the famous Elgoods breweries and gardens. Sad to say, I noted with deep regret that she died only just this year from a short illness, still relatively a young woman.

In my enthusiasm, I had to spend thousands on the garden, as 'Gallery Hall' was at least two feet high in weeds when we purchased it. The land had not been turned over for years, and had become compacted, and we eventually had to hire a massive, heavy-duty machine to turn the land over. The soil was so bad that I could not see or find a single worm wriggling in it. Eventually, to help improve the quality of the soil, I had regular cartloads of compost from the nearby mushroom farm delivered, and spread it out to help nourish and break up the soil. That only cost about ten pounds for a tractor load, and it helped break down the soil so that it was much easier to dig. On reflection, I should have had a tractor plough it first. However, it was amusing, as occasionally we had a few mushrooms poke their heads above the lawn just to remind us of what we had put on it to nourish the soil.

When it was completed, the garden had five circular lawns, fragrant borders, and delicately designed paving stones. Some years later, I was professionally advised having been bowled over by its beauty, that I enter it in the Gardens in Bloom. I didn't at that time, and now wish that I had. Believe it or not, I had not taken any interest in gardening before. I managed to source most of my plants and shrubs wholesale or the final bill would have cost a lot more. It made the final touch to this lovely house and put it into another league altogether. I was very proud of it, and Tricia spent many a happy hour enjoying sitting in her new garden house I bought for her, reading in peace in the sunshine, which she loved so much. To prove all this, I have put a photo of our garden below for you to see.

As I grew older, I began to find the garden much harder going, as it suffered from persistent weeds. They were here, there and everywhere, and it took a lot of effort to keep on top of them. I used to spend two days each week weeding as the garden was so big. Tricia suggested that I buy mulch, which I was reluctant to do but eventually did, and she was proved to be right. It kept the weeds down and made it easier. I think that alone initially cost £500 and at least another hundred pounds every year to keep the garden soil covered as much as possible with this wonderful, successful mulch.

I had designed it in accord with the garden designer plan so that there were, in all, five lawns, each oine edged with paving bricks. This enabled one to use the garden sit-on mower and trim right up to the edge of the grass. I could never actually myself edge a lawn, and this method was so much easier.

Tricia then suffered one of her severe spells of extreme tiredness. I was worried about her and rang her doctor. I had put her to bed. The doctor, however, suggested that I bring her to the surgery that same day before 5 pm and he would examine her. I did as asked, and he took a blood sample and sent it off for testing. The test results were not what he thought as Tricia had now developed rheumatoid arthritis. He arranged for her to see a specialist so that the most suitable medication could be prescribed. She found the housework more and more difficult to complete to her satisfaction, and we then engaged a cleaner as there was still a tremendous amount of cleaning to do in such a large house. This helped considerably, and Tricia soldiered on for a few years until the effort of even small amounts of housework started to affect her much more severely, and it was then that we started seriously looking for a suitable bungalow to move to. We needed one that had less work, avoided the dangers of stairs, was spacious and comfortable for both her and me.

We always had thought that 'Gallery Hall' would be our last house and, if necessary, we could later use the dining room/study itself as a downstairs bedroom, since we had a shower room already on the ground floor. However, the garden and the cleaning of the house became too much for us, and, although we employed a cleaner, we later reluctantly had to agree to sell it and purchase a bungalow. The area was also becoming quite busy with traffic passing, and soon after we had sold our house, there were a lot more houses built.

Illnesses to Fight Through

After one winter, in which through illness and the cold the weeds had taken over again, I had to employ a gardener to help me. The first morning I suppose I rushed too energetic to do the gardening. By the time I had finished working that particular day I suffered a heart attack and had to be taken by emergency ambulance to Peterborough. I was then transferred the next day to Papworth hospital, which specialises in chest and heart problems.

However, after having the first stent fitted at Papworth, I felt very hot, and was put in a room that had a working overhead fan above me. Exhausted, I then fell asleep. After suddenly waking up at about 3 am, feeling so freezing cold that I rang the bell, the concerned nurses came rushing in with blankets and had the fan switched off. During my time in that particular room, I believe I had also developed a bad cough. After the first stent was implanted, I was discharged, but within 24 hours after coming home, I was rushed back to Peterborough hospital again.

When I was admitted to Peterborough Hospital for the second time I started coughing up blood. The consultant, who sent me back a few days later, had referred to this matter in his notes, and asked them to deal with my chest problem as well. I reluctantly had a further two stents fitted and was returned to the ward, but the cough that I had was beginning to get worse, and I was still coughing up blood.

Papworth Hospital Again

My situation deteriorated, and soon after having a further two stents fitted I awoke to find myself covered in sweat. I told my wife I felt seriously ill and that I was on the way out. She said to my younger son, Andrew, who came over to see me, also knew I was not well. He had told the nurses, but nothing was immediately done. Suddenly, at three in the morning, I had lost so much sweat that I became dehydrated. The bed was wet through. I asked the sister in charge to get me a doctor as I needed help. It made me feel ill just to look at a glass of water standing next to me. A terrible feeling of fear of water, known medically as 'aqua phobia', came over me.

Within minutes, a doctor was there examining me and drips were being inserted into my arm, and I was being pumped with antibiotics and rehydrated. I was never told at that particular time, but I believe I had contracted a severe case of pneumonia. Fortunately, I was then monitored very closely by the hospital over the following year. They monitored me with chest x-rays and examinations for twelve months. I also had a camera inserted to view my lungs. As a result of this and my heart attack, I had lost two stone in weight and was very weak indeed. I was given oxygen whenever I needed it. They also provided me with a salt inhaler and nebuliser, which miraculously eased the soreness in my chest. This was administered through the nebuliser which relieves one's breathing and also heals the lungs rather brilliantly and effectively. Eventually, I was discharged after three weeks.

Following this serious incident, I was monitored, for a year, a variety of tests were carried out before I was eventually given the all-clear. After this, I was then encouraged by my doctor to go to a particular keep fit class at the Hudson Centre at Wisbech designed for heart attack patients in recovery, and needing Cardiac Care exercises, and I can enthusiastically report that it did me a world of good. When I asked the nurses where the so-called overweight people were who, I believed, were much more subject to heart attacks. She replied that those were the ones that didn't make it! The only reason I asked this was that I had noticed most, if not all the patients, attending the course were relatively slim or of average build! The considerable weight I had lost had done me good, and I felt the benefit of the operation as I could now walk with a walking stick.

While living in Guyhirn, we were blessed with pavements there. I used to walk at least a mile nearly every day to keep me fit, in addition to doing the considerable amount of hard and vigorous gardening that was required. After trying our best to get involved and bring beneficial change to the church at Wisbech, as it was sorely needed, we finally decided to give up our membership and joined a house church at Emneth. We then befriended a new couple who had taken over the church at Tydd St Mary. This couple did their best, but the congregation was very hard to please somehow, and selfish interests came well to the fore. Eventually, the kindly couple found they had to give in their notice at this particular church, and both returned to Wales. Unfortunately, we later learned that they had finally become divorced from each other. I think the strain of what they had suffered was too much for them. Another problem was that our minister and his wife could not have children and this was a great disappointment to his wife as she had suffered an ectopic pregnancy. Ministers and their wives, of course, do suffer like the rest of us from health and personal problems.

Situations such as this, in which such complaints are about ministers or church members, should always be brought to the notice of everyone in the congregation so that everyone who wants to help can pray for them. The chance at church meetings of resolving issues should be examined, too, then the necessary action in solving problems should be taken or decisions made as to what needs to be done. Procedure had been ignored by a church member contacting the head office directly and, of all things, making a complaint. This then had been the cause of this final outcome. On this, the church was divided, and half of us decided to move to the Baptist church at Long Sutton. I had hoped that this problem could have been dealt with in a much more understanding, kind and indeed a more Christian manner. This outcome for us was for the best, it transpired. The new church at Long Sutton proved to bring us all a really vibrant breath of fresh air, and we worshipped at it for a couple of years. This saw our oldest members from the former church, Fred and Flo, in their late seventies being baptised, and Fred eventually became a deacon at that church. I know they were so happy at the new church that he was then appointed an elder himself. He was also the benevolent figure of Father Christmas for the whole village and loved every minute. With his wife, they raised funds for the church by cooking dinner midweek for those in the village who needed or wanted a hot meal. The only necessary qualification for an invite to this meal was the individual's own particular needs, so many could come. It was very successful.

We were contacted by church friends who attended the Emneth House church who wanted to set up a church and youth club at Rings End. This was only one mile from where we were then living in our lovely Gallery Hall, so we readily agreed to help. After a couple of meetings we got a youth club going, and Tricia thoroughly enjoyed it. Sadly, though, it was not to last long, since the minister who ran the Elm House church did not want, for some reason of his own devising, a Sunday morning service held there. As soon as that was suggested, he cancelled all that we had set up and told every single person to actually leave the church. Evidently this was more important to him -

that services were held inside his church house where he himself lived, for some strange reason of his own.

March Evangelical Fellowship

It was 2005, and I had had enough of such nonsense, and I suggested to Tricia that we would transfer to March Evangelical Church and support that instead. We had been there a few times already and always enjoyed services and meeting the congregation. We still belonged there, even when my wife was so ill. I always went there to worship on most Sundays when we possibly could.

Another unfortunate and damaging event then occurred. The decking that we had already at our house, and which had been placed there by a previous owner, became very slippery and so treacherous, when wet especially, and even more so in the winter months. Tricia succumbed first with a broken foot that needed a plaster cast on it for a few weeks. A wheelchair was borrowed from church so that it was easier to move her around, and eventually she recovered. I think it was a year later when I also fell down on the same decking in the December, and in this instance, I actually broke my leg badly. They tried to set it by giving me gas to put me out, but, in the end, had to operate and put in a six-inch plate to support the severe break in my right leg. I was unlucky in that the problem here was that a significant number of elderly people were at that particular time being admitted to the same hospital with broken hips, and they needed more urgent treatment at that specific time than I did. After six days, the other patients were asking staff why I was not being treated as quickly, and I was then, after waiting patiently for six days, operated upon during Christmas Eve itself.

Because of all the tablets I had to take, the anaesthetist had great difficulty in choosing what to give me to knock me out safely. Finally, he decided that an injection that numbed my lower half would be better. He said to me, 'You will be awake while we do it, but you will not feel a thing.'

When I arrived in the operating theatre, the surgeon asked me kindly, 'What music do you like, Malcolm?'

I replied, 'Opera, please,' to which he responded comically and said, 'I am sorry Malcolm, but you will have to have rock and roll instead!' He speedily placed the earphones on my ears. Everything went well, and I was returned back to the ward on Christmas Eve. It wasn't long before I heard the singing of carols as a choir walked slowly and gracefully through the ward. Listening to their singing was absolutely delightful. All the patients felt so much better and happier as they heard the carols ringing out through the entire hospital, commemorating the wonderful time of Our Saviour Christ's miraculous birth.

The worst part of that stay in hospital was the Christmas dinner on the day itself, which I had been so looking forward to. I feared it had been sabotaged, perhaps accidentally, with too much salt. I just could not eat any of it. Tricia, who had kindly joined me, on the other hand, was already tucking heartily into my Christmas pudding, so I had to make do with a packet of plain biscuits for my Christmas lunch!

2006-2010
Ivy, My Dear Friend: A Cockney Through and Through

During one of our Sunday church services, something quite beautiful happened.

It was there that I met a lady who was to become so precious and dear to me and a great, caring friend, Ivy. At the time I met her, she was in her nineties and very soon voluntarily adopted me as though I was her very own special son. An extremely kind, loving person who herself had a an only son who had walked out on her and his father when in his twenties. He never bothered to contact her again for the remainder of her life.

She had a sister in America and had visited there seventeen times and loved every minute of her trips. They, of course, also loved her so much too. Ivy's husband had died several years before. She had experienced having to stand on her own two feet, a thing she had never had to do before. Previously, her husband had taken charge of everything.

A kind neighbour called Jean had then, when they moved to March, befriended her and intoduced her to the MEF church. Jean and Dennis Jordan ran this friendly, caring church and Ivy then found another new happier life and made lots of friends as we all knew she would.

Such a lovable and comical person, it was a joy to be in her company. When it came to Christmas time, I was only too pleased to invite her and Jean Ross, this next door neighbour, to Christmas dinner and tea. Later they both told us how they loved coming to 'The Palace', as Ivy would often lovingly call our house.

I spent many an hour with her when she was ill, and also when she was taken into hospital, and later when in a local nursing home. She suffered many health problems stemming from the past that still caused her trouble. Because of her age and the fact that she had lived there for a good few years, she knew and got on so well with many of the doctors, who also visited her when she was ill. Obviously, she was such a character that they all remembered her well.

Eventually, Ivy spent a few days with her own son, but regrettably this did not work out, and although she had left him money in her will, he sent it to back to the executor, Ivy's brother, when eventually Ivy died. I think she thought she had done all she could to make friends again with her son, but he was very hard about what had happened in his earlier life. It was as though he had never forgiven either of his parents for past differences that had been created, causing such a very deep rift between them and himself.

Sometimes, I was with Ivy until 10 pm at night, waiting for doctors or nurses to come to help her. We grew very close to each as Christian friends, and I loved to have her to dinner as she always was such good company. She enjoyed her food, and was very grateful for us asking her. One of the things noticeable about Ivy was the fact that she always said a very sincere 'thank you' to those who kindly helped her, and meant it, and of course she was a truly lovable cockney.

Sadly, Ivy Huggett died on the 12th October 2010, and was so loved by our church members and many friends that she deserved the beautiful send-off that was organised for her. Always a very loving person to Tricia and to me, and we thought the world of her.

2010
Holiday

We did manage to get a week away at Great Yarmouth where Tricia could follow up possible local leads concerning her family history, besides indulging in her beloved sunbathing on the beach. I wanted to have a week that was something different, however, and so we went to a boutique hotel this time. It had been noted in, I believe, the Sunday Times, but to me, it seemed to us not much different than a standard guest house.

In fact, the holiday was terrific, and the food was excellent. Tricia was also increasingly interested in finding out as much as she could about her distant family connections, in particular on her mother's side. We decided that we would go to Great Yarmouth and try to find the addresses she had picked up from her investigations.

The CofE church at Great Yarmouth is one of the largest and prominent Anglican churches in the country. Tricia spent some time trying to find her related family tombstones, but couldn't. In the end, we decided to have a picnic and chose all that we wanted to eat at the M&S food store and took our feast to the park.

2011
Richard

I had, over the many years, been very worried about my elder son Richard, and although he had been to various medical experts throughout his life, they all said the same basic thing - that he was suffering behavioural problems. I never accepted this as a final analysis, myself, however, and, after watching a documentary about a disabled person, I became of the opinion that Richard had similar issues to this particular description of mental illness. His behaviour then came to a head, and I approached a medical charity named 'CLASS' (Cambridge Lifespan Autism Spectrum Service) and completed an assessment of him. After an interview lasting three hours, he was diagnosed officially as suffering from Asperger's Syndrome.

Why hadn't this been diagnosed before after all these years? It would have saved so much pain for Tricia and me. When a person suffers like this, his family also do, and it has an effect on them all. I had listened to so many so-called experts over the years and been conditioned to accept that what they said was correct. My son had been failed by the educational system and medical authorities, and had suffered severely because he was not diagnosed correctly for forty years. This has saved the country thousands because he could not claim the relevant allowance for being disabled until it was finally and accurately diagnosed. However, during those forty years of misdiagnosis, he also suffered because his behaviour led him to despair, and to sadly demonstrate his own feelings periodically of anger and frustration with other people, or situations that arose. Because the medical profession could find nothing wrong except behavioural problems, I had treated him as a healthy normal child.

When he left school and because he had a caring attitude, I had first advised Richard to go into a job in mental health care, and he became a mental health orderly. But when they wanted him to become a mental health nurse and go to training, he instantly disappeared. This lasted for two years, literally without contacting us. We presumed, of course, that he could not face the responsibility that this particular type of job would have inevitably brought to him.

Richard's disappearance caused his mother and me so much worry, and I can remember her searching through newspapers desperate, believing he had been killed somehow. One day, Tricia imagined, whilst in her car, that she thought she saw him getting on a bus and felt almost convinced that it really was our prodigal son. Still convinced, she followed the bus in her car until she realised, with complete dismay, that she had been totally mistaken. It was not her well-loved missing son after all.

When she read stories of bodies being found in rivers, his long, painful disappearance continuously played on her mind. It really was worrying. He went missing for two whole years in all without a word sent to us, and eventually, you just had to learn to live with it. But, of course, this was part of his disability in suffering from Asperger's Syndrome. When he returned at long last two years later, I then suggested he tried volunteering for the army. On this occasion I was thinking that it would help him to bring stability and discipline into his life. But, again after six months, he was discharged since he had dyspraxia and couldn't even put the parts of his rifle together. His commanding officer said to me that he had too kind a nature to become a soldier anyway.

Richard still suffers from a variety of disabilities that make him hard to understand, but he has great compassion for those in need, and disabled people generally. He is always trying to help someone else that he feels, or observes needing assistance, if he can. Unfortunately, his illness or disability affects the way he interprets other people's body language sometimes, so he cannot understand unfortunately if they are not interested in him, and his short-term memory for people he has met is poor.

Dear Richard has been such a worry, as he cannot cope with any sort of regular job. Also, like many others, he drank too much, which caused him additional problems. However, he did eventually, I am glad to say, give so much help at an important time in our lives. He helped me nurse his mother, Tricia, who by then was terminally ill with cancer, and whom he loved dearly. I shall always be grateful for that particular valued support. He now works hard and tries to sell magazines for a certain famous charity he believes in. Well known, The 'Big Issue' magazine each week sold by Richard. He has done so for seven years on and off. He makes a few pounds just to cover his expenses in travelling. He has helped me, and stays on weekends when he is able and does his best both in the garden and cooking nourishing meals for me. I am so grateful for the many jobs he now competently does in the garden, and, of course, for his charity work, 'The Big Issue'.

Richard's most significant problem, as with many others who have the same disability, is the depression he suffers from. There is also his periodic reluctance to accept taking prescription medication that he knows might possibly have adverse effects later on him, which he is not prepared to tolerate.

He is also prone on occasion to totally unkind and unfair ridicule from some members of society who think he is fit enough to do a regular job and, of course, the truth is that he is incapacitated and therefore unable, but certainly not unwilling, to help those in need. My garden here is evidence to show how much he, gallantly, cuts my lawns and waters the plants for me. He is always offering, kindly, to help Bettina, a family friend, too with her own exhausting jobs in her home and garden, which she thoroughly appreciates.

Richard has put a great deal of effort into helping his own friends in their various times of need. He occasionally helps to clean their houses for them. Many local ladies who are unable to do specific difficult tasks are indeed very grateful to Richard, and also some disabled friends of his are also eternally grateful for his friendship and freely given help. I am, and always will be, very appreciative and proud of both of my lovely, kind sons.

One of the main issues that this particular disability of Richard's highlights is the fact that there are over 250,000 people classed as missing in this country, and amongst those, I am sure many parents are grieving and worrying like my Tricia and I did. Also, this situation must contribute to a tremendous amount of sadness, depression and other deep sorrow. This is especially for those who are hurt in this way, as my wife and I have regularly done. Our suffering is the worry of his safety due to our son's heart-breaking periodic absences from us during which we cannot contact him.

2012-2013
A Winter of Illness and Suffering

Following this, the winter cold had brought us both seriously bad coughs. We were suffering so much that our many friends at church started regularly coming to help us. As soon as they knew we were not well, Dee came down in a taxi with a casserole to last us two to three days, along with many other essentials which she had cooked for us. Dee only gets three hours' sleep a night and had made up this casserole so she could bring it in the taxi. Dee used to stay a few days and talk to Tricia and help us both. That year was one of the hardest winters we had ever endured, especially with our respective serious health problems.

Tricia had no resistance to germs and viruses because of rheumatoid arthritis, which affects adversely your immune system. We were so very dependent on friends and also on Richard in helping us. Doctor Biggs was persistent in helping us and issuing all the medication we both needed. Colds also affected Tricia as she suffered from COPD (Chronic Obstructive

Pulmonary Disease), and her chest quickly became infected, which was very weakening. She had to fight hard to throw the chest problems off once she had caught them.

A church friend, Bettina, had heard of our plight and one Sunday morning arrived with a basketful of food that she had cooked for us that was delicious and didn't require much re-heating, so that we had plenty to eat without going out shopping for food or even ordering it to be delivered in the cold weather. In fact, we wouldn't have been able to leave the house as we were both so ill, could not drive, and needed all the help necessary to recover our strength. She came four or five times a week, checking on us to see if there was anything she could do, and grew attached to us. It became as though we were members of her own little family and she was one of ours. She and Tricia emailed each other every day. Bettina did it to give Tricia the feeling of being in touch with ongoing church events, and what was generally happening. Tricia benefitted from being kept in touch and up to date with all the local news and events. Bettina also encouraged members of the church to contact Tricia either by phone calls or emails, which pleased my wife very much.

Emails from other church friends, especially from Adrian Cranstoun, a humorous, and very kindly character. He is much loved by all who meet him, and always thrilled Tricia the most. She told Bettina that his witty emails, almost every day, to Tricia made her smile and she looked forward to them so much. Often making her laugh out loud, he was and is always so kind, and such a good man that Tricia felt his special kindness emanating from his emails to her!

Through this outstanding Christian love and caring, that others felt for us, we eventually began to feel better and slowly recovered. Having made such friends, they then became regular visitors to our house, and our deep friendships grew. In fact, Bettina's husband, John, was very supportive too himself. He worried about us and at times visited us, getting on exceptionally well with Tricia. He has carried this friendship on by helping me during recent illnesses; his hospital visits were very welcome to me, and he recently gave me a massive, most expensive jar of Manuka honey (from New Zealand) to ensure my continued recovery following my serious operation.

2014
Holiday at Potters and Warners

After this episode, Tricia wanted to arrange a holiday for us in the summer of 2014, and I agreed. We decided to try Warner Leisure near Great Yarmouth, as we had heard favourable reports about it.

On the day of our departure, the only problem was that I had in my haste forgotten to pack a spare pair of my trousers, and it was necessary for me to go to M&S in Lowestoft so that I could purchase some more. I had kept them hanging in the wardrobe as I didn't want them to get creased.

While we were in Lowestoft, I can remember (how could I ever forget) the sight of my wife talking to a young man she had seen and counselled in Lowestoft town centre about God's love. Then he began to off-load the worries he had about his own father to her. She stood there with her comforting arms around him and started praying aloud about the Lord coming to help. People stood, stared and then walked off. Tricia never batted an eyelid nor did she, bless her, become worried; she advised the man what to do about his father and reassured him, as he was himself a believer, to hold onto his faith and trust the Lord.

Tricia had been on a Christian course a few years before and had studied diligently. She definitely knew more about God and Christianity than the average Christian. We said prayers every morning and grace before every meal; we tried our best to follow our faith, and we definitely helped others through their trials, tribulations, and illnesses. One of us, if not both, always attended church on Sundays.

The weather had been kind, and we enjoyed our picnic, and then I decided to investigate the local war memorial in the Park. Fortunately, there I did find the location of three of her relations, all named 'London', listed as having been killed in action. She was pleased I had discovered them for her, but was now armed with more detail to investigate regarding these ancestors when she returned home. After walking around, Tricia suddenly became very tired, and we decided to return to our holiday hotel and enjoy its many comforts.

While we were there, we thought we could also visit the Potters holiday hotel close by, where indoor bowling contests are held regularly. It was undoubtedly a massive complex when compared with Warners. The reports we received from guests encouraged us to think about staying there the following year. It was only a few hundred yards from where we were then staying, and it had a lot more going on, as we had found out, so we said we would stay there for a break on the next opportunity we found.

2015

Tricia had suffered for many years from a variety of illnesses: epilepsy, chronic obstructive pulmonary disease, rheumatoid arthritis, asthma, and irritable bowel syndrome. All of she bore with great courage. However, on the 26 January 2015, she had a drug interaction with her Doxycycline (for bacterial infections) and Prednisone after suffering terrible chest problems, and she went to the doctor's, but it steadily got worse. She was now, unbeknown to herself and me, suffering from the onset of lung cancer, which was later found to be a terminal condition.

One night, I had to call the emergency ambulance, and she was rushed into Peterborough hospital, where it was established that she had suffered a seizure. This was a reaction to the Doxycycline tablets she was then taking as prescribed. With the help of the staff, she recovered and came back home on the 30th January, but was still suffering with significant pain in her chest. Her doctor thought that this was due to her coughing and that she had strained herself. Some days later, she visited a local hospital at Doddington. They had already taken x-rays of her chest only some weeks earlier, and she asked them to kindly check again, but they refused. She then went back to her doctor, who again inferred that it must be that she had strained herself while coughing. At home for a few days she survived only on paracetamol until she could stand it no longer and asked me to take her to A&E at Peterborough hospital.

Now I knew my wife was seriously ill by the way she asked me, and had no qualms about taking her there at once. Upon entering, a sister in charge saw she was in great difficulties and immediately ushered her into her own private room, where she could see something was seriously. The sister picked up the phone and demanded a bed be prepared urgently, and, within a matter of minutes, Tricia's heart rate and body temperature were being monitored, her chest was x-rayed, and her blood pressure was measured. A doctor came and talked to her, and he was very kind. He seemed to know already that there was something seriously wrong. He tapped so gently all around her breastbone when he examined her to establish what was causing her the severe pain. Afterwards, he sat with the radiographer discussing the results, and then came to her to tell Tricia there was something wrong with her chest, and that a CT scan would also be required. He wanted her to stay the night, but she refused. He allowed her to go home on the condition that she attended the ambulatory care clinic the very next morning, which she agreed to do.

The next morning we attended this, tests were done, and a CT scan was arranged. It seemed like forever waiting until late in the afternoon for the results. In fact, because of the long delay, I had sensed something was wrong, and enquired at reception. When we were called in finally to see the doctor, my worst fears were confirmed. He told us gently the devastating news that Tricia had lung cancer, which had also spread to a lymph node. Tricia had tried on many occasions to give up but could not beat the deep depression she suffered which smoking seemed to relieve in a big way. This necessitated hospital care on at least four occasions. She had also tried hypnosis, herbal tablets, electric cigarettes. But nothing seemed to help, and, in the end, I found I had tried every possible cure and was forced to just let her smoke. I did not want to upset her or put any more pressures on her, for fear that she would suffer the same dangerous deep depression as she had in the past. It was strange because my wife had been very ill with coughs and colds before, and, in a moment of frustration, I had told her, 'You cannot keep putting the children and me through this. It happens every year, and it is not fair on them or me.'

Strangely enough, my wife had packed up smoking only two weeks before it was finally confirmed she had, in fact, contracted lung cancer and that it was terminal. Before that, she had said no one in her family had suffered cancer, but I reminded her that her aunt had died of it some years before. I said at the time, 'Do not invite the devil in,' but regretted I said that ever since.

It was what I feared and had feared for many years. I had begged my wife to pack up her habit, but, whenever she tried, she became so deeply depressed. It is right now that smokers are given every assistance to help them to stop smoking. The authorities have at last realised not only how difficult it is for some, but they also recognise the deep depression that people can suffer when they attempt to stop smoking altogether.

It was in February 2015 that Tricia was finally diagnosed with cancer of the lung at Peterborough hospital. I broke down. She asked the doctor if we could go to Costa's in the foyer of the hospital for a coffee, to which he replied, 'Yes, but please return.'

I was so upset, but Tricia seemed to know in advance what the result would be. Ever since we had got married, and she started suffering bronchitis, I had begged her to pack up smoking. We sat down in the coffee shop, and I went to get two cappuccinos. A black lady came over to my wife saying that she wanted to pray for her. My wife had told her what had just happened, and the diagnosis she had received, and the woman then prayed aloud in the coffee shop for my dear wife. Driving home from the hospital, Tricia asked if we could call in and we could then see an elderly lady friend of hers, called Patricia

Cartwright, who had been ill for months. She lived in Whittlesey. I do not know why she picked this person as the first to tell, but when informed of her cancer, Patricia broke down and started crying. However, she was so pleased that we had come to see her and felt privileged to know she was the first person Tricia had wanted to visit.

After leaving and driving home, Tricia coughed up some blood, which at first was alarming but happens with this illness, particularly as her cancer was located in the lower lobes of the lungs.

I recalled that for some years around 1976, when we had been married for ten years, there had been a TV programme on smoking and problems that people had in giving it up. It was on *Nationwide* with Cliff Michelmore. After viewing this, Tricia wrote to him about smoking and her difficulty in giving up, and it was arranged that she would be taken by car to Nottingham studio where she would then take part in a follow-up programme. She was asked the vital question, 'What goes wrong when you try to pack up smoking?'

Tricia quickly replied, 'Everything goes black.' She explained clearly that a deep depression took over and she could not cope with the immense effort of removing smoking completely from her life. Tricia had, on many occasions, tried to give up, but could not beat this severe depression she suffered as a consequence whenever she tried. This necessitated her being given hospital care on at least four occasions. I had to accept, for her and our whole family's safety, that she was utterly unable to give up this terrible addiction. Then forced, reluctantly and after much reflection, to give up my own extensive efforts to stop her, I decided that I had to just let her smoke.

In fact, when we had only been married about ten years in 1975, a doctor came to attend to her because she had developed a nasty bout of bronchitis, and suggested she should pack up at that time. I laughed, and he quickly retorted that I should too, and thus set an example for her. I agreed, and he prescribed some tablets for me and said, 'I want to see you every two weeks.' I did as he said, and within weeks, with a massive effort, I had shaken off the habit. I was in my thirties at the time, and had read that if you quit by then, your lungs can repair themselves. That doctor was, I later found, to be the then chairman of ASH - the leading anti-smoking charity. Later in his medical career, he was ostracised by the BMA for claiming the cause of death in a patient as being due to smoking. Yet he had succeeded in my giving up some 40 years ago. Strange how the facts and beliefs about smoking have changed over the last few years. Thank God that they have!

Many times, Tricia witnessed to people about her faith while in the hospital, in coffee shops, at church and on the internet. Throughout our lives together, Tricia testified even to the doctors that examined her. She was so bold, confident and assured, and rarely judged other people. Whenever we moved, Tricia would ask the new doctors if they believed in God, and all of our doctors did, so that pleased her and reassured her. Their answers would be met with a loud 'Praise the Lord' from her. Becoming a Christian had apparently changed her from the shy, timid and quiet young lady I had first met to the relatively confident, caring, fiesty and essentially God-fearing woman she had now, in her mature years, become.

These appointments came very quickly, and we were one of many undergoing these and other tests. A biopsy of this cancer to determine precisely what type it was then was found to be necessary and carried out, and the results were as I feared. Tricia was suffering from small cell lung cancer, which is cancer in its most virulent form. She had been given only two to four months to live at that time. I was devasted, but my wife was so strong. There were so many people who it appeared had severe health problems waiting to be seen. All of them were suffering in some way. and I could not help but think that it was all so sad and depressing.

We eventually got home, tired and exhausted. It wasn't long before we both went to bed. I couldn't sleep very well, as you would expect, and kept breaking down. A hundred and one things were racing through my mind as to what I was going to do. In the morning, before we got up, I made us both a cup of tea, and we sat talking. I said to her, 'We will make every day yours. You tell me what you want to do, and we will do it,' to which she gratefully agreed. When you are told such devastating news, you walk around in a daze, not concentrating, and find it difficult to take in every single tiny thing that is happening. You start doing a job, and then a thought comes to mind as to how you are going to live eventually without the love of your life. Then you think of your wife and wonder how she is going to cope with the knowledge of her imminent death. You then have to pull yourself together and think of your wife and all the things you can do to make her happy for however many precious days she has left.

I had arranged to pick up my son, Richard, as we had not yet told him about the diagnosis my wife had received. I was so sad and downhearted, but had to shake myself out of it for the sake of all my family and friends, and especially for Richard, as I knew just how very fond of his mother he had always been. When we arrived home, my wife told him. Because of his disability, Asperger's Syndrome, he would have some difficulty in realising its full implications. He surprised us and said he already had thought that his mother had probably developed something severe because of how ill she had lately been.

2015
Golden Wedding Anniversary Celebrations

After exhaustive tests at Papworth, finally in February 2015, Tricia was given 2-4 months to live. At the time, I was arranging a celebration for our actual forthcoming 50th wedding anniversary to be held in the following August, initially at the local village hall. Sadly, I had to cancel it being held in this hall. I was just lost as to what to do at that moment because, should the timing forecast of her death be correct, my wife could not possibly make our 50th wedding anniversary.

Addenbrookes Hospital

Although three doctor examinations, three x-rays, and CT scans had been done, it was only confirmed by an MRI scan taken at Addenbrookes that the latest additional pain in her chest was a broken breastbone. The doctor concerned with this diagnosis could now understand the excruciating pain that she complained of, and had suffered from during the previous two months. Furthermore, after making a complaint to my doctor, no one could explain how her breastbone had been broken in the first place.

The first thing Tricia wanted to do was to splash out and spend some money on some new clothes, and also find a beautiful outfit that she could use on her golden wedding anniversary day. I couldn't help but agree with all that she asked, as I loved her so much. Tricia did make it to our anniversary, and wore the particular special outfit and looked beautiful, and, true to her wishes, was later buried in it.

At first, Tricia wanted to be buried with her relations at Leicester, but our friend, Dee, finally convinced her that as our son, Richard, who had never married, lived in March, so it would be better if she was buried there. He would be able to visit his mother's grave easily and find it a source of comfort to him. After considering this suggestion carefully, Tricia then wished to be buried there. She knew he would and could tend her grave. Richard was very close to his mother, and that would be some comfort for him later, after I had gone, and this son would be on his own. This action has been right, as when Richard gets depressed, he goes to visit and take flowers to her grave. What delighted all of us was he found and bought for her a beautiful cross, carved with an ivory-like white material gravestone, and it helps him with his grief. This is stood against the beautiful headstone I had chosen with gold lettering and a kneeling guardian angel, also in gold.

Tricia then agreed with Dee and saw the sense in all this, and quite boldly said she wanted to order a grave situated just opposite our present church in March. She also went to visit the undertakers with me to discuss details of what she actually needed and had chosen, and what it would cost. She said that she was going to be buried and, under no circumstances, wanted anything else, to which I agreed. Tricia wrote out the hymns and passages from the bible that she wanted for her funeral service and gave them to our minister, Dennis Jordan, with her exact instructions. I was a believer in cremation myself. I think I was turned against burial after seeing my mother go to the cemetery every week, whatever the weather, to visit my first stepfather's grave. My mother's own wish when she died was to be cremated.

Unfortunately, over the next few weeks, we did not have much time, as I decided to make plans for our golden wedding anniversary celebration. I said that, if for some reason she didn't make it, the meal would go ahead anyway and the day would be a great celebration of her life, which she agreed was indeed a lovely and uplifting idea, so that was what we finally planned and did!

2015
Our Holiday with Richard

We had already booked a few days' holiday at Potters and this time, we took our son Richard. Tricia needed a wheelchair because she soon became tired if she had to walk far. Richard wisely said, 'You will require me to push the wheelchair as it would be too much for you, Dad.' However, we had already agreed to take him on holiday there with us as a reward for all the help he had given us, and he was looking forward to the hotel's food, which we had previously raved about to him, extolling its virtues and high standard.

Unfortunately, the food that particular year turned out so very disappointingly terrible, so much so that I made a complaint about it. I know we only stayed a few days, but this we knew. It would be the last holiday that Tricia would ever have now and the first one in years for Richard. It was so very upsetting. Both Tricia and I were so sorry, more for Richard than for the two of us. We had, on previous visits, been interested in the nightlife. In fact, we did not go to any on that visit, as we were all in bed by 9 pm as we were tired out. I think the fresh air had got to us, but we were at least united for our very last chance to be together as a family unit on holiday with Tricia.

Our Anniversary on the 21st August 2015

Our family and friends all agreed that we needed to keep Tricia positive and that every day would be hers until she could not even want to go out. We had to keep looking forward so that she lived as long as possible. After reaching specific goals before the run-up to our anniversary, we set July 9th (my birthday) as one of these interim goals. We then said her next goal was 21st August, our actual wedding anniversary. After that memorable occasion, the next celebration would be Tricia's birthday on 17th December, and so on. Everything would be done to help her reach our 50th wedding anniversary in August 2015, but, hopefully, of course, she would survive to later dates.

As time passed by, and we reached the beginning of July, I could see that there had been fortunately little, if any, deterioration in my wife's health. It seemed as though she would easily still be alive and able to enjoy a well-organised party, so I had to start looking at what I could do to celebrate our actual 50th wedding anniversary. I talked things over with her and finally arranged for us to plan a hog roast and a buffet in our garden at our lovely bungalow where we then lived in the countryside. Relations and a considerable number of people were invited to this, our anniversary elebration, along with our many friends from our previous church at Leicester and our current one at March. I estimated that about one hundred and fifty guests would attend and catered accordingly for them. I decided that my wife had every intention of living up to the date of our anniversary and even longer still.

Tricia was so confident; she had already lived five months after her hospital diagnosis, and the way she was going would probably survive longer so she could also reach Christmas. Her health had remained relatively unchanged, and she was not seeming to be getting any worse, and I thanked the Lord and her doctors for this.

To save deciding at church which members should be invited, absolutely everyone was to be included, and all that was asked was that 'No presents, only your presence' would be required. The Lord had been good to us, and we didn't want people going to unnecessary expense. We just wanted them to celebrate with us and share our special day. Fortunately, on the day of our celebration, not a drop of rain had fallen. Richard Hinchcliffe, my dear Christian friend, and others were there the night before, organising the putting up of the marquees and setting out the tables. He had also downloaded music carefully chosen by him from our favourites that could be played through his extra powerful speakers linked to his computer to provide, as it did, a great background of beautiful music for the whole of that memorable day. I do not know how I could have managed without him, in particular!

The arrangements I had made at such short notice were coming together well, and all looked forward to our golden wedding anniversary celebrations. It was the hottest day of the year, and guests came from far and wide. Tricia sat outside in the front garden with her friend Dee, welcoming the guests. She was entirely in her element and loved every minute of that day. She had previously gone to Wisbech and chosen what she wanted me to buy her to wear on the day, and a few touches of her Chanel No 5 perfume completed her appearance and this was her favourite one.

I circulated amongst the guests, thanking them for coming, and was pleased that my sons and Andrew's family, Sarah, Laureen and Kellie, were so kindly helping out. Sarah, my daughter in law, and Andrew, my younger son, operated the bar and served drinks. Richard waited on those who needed help and directed people where to park their cars. It was a beautiful day, with so many church friends from Whetstone also present, along with those from our beautiful church in March, and, of course, our other friends and relations. Friends and family had worked hard the night before getting tables and chairs off-loaded and then set out in the garden. Two marquees were erected so that guests had some cover if it should rain, and tables were dressed. Richard Hinchcliffe had his computer with music that he knew Tricia and I enjoyed, which he played pleasantly in the background. The atmosphere was one of happiness, and Tricia looked so well.

The Hog Roast Company was there early in the morning, and they had their own stall and staff, who quickly got things on the go. The hog had been partly roasted already, and, when served, was excellent. Drinks were available, and my granddaughters and Sarah and Andrew attended to all those in need.

As I described, there were many people from our Whetstone church at Leicester who came, and, of course, our relations and our own friends. It was a very joyous occasion, and I am sure that they all had a good day. Renewing friendships with old acquaintances was very uplifting to both Tricia and to me. Sue, my best friend's wife, whose husband Dave had died suddenly some years previously, came early with Claire, who had worked with me at East Midlands Gas. They dressed the tables to make it a more festive occasion for all of us. It was lovely to meet them again, as Tricia and I had a fond affection for both of them. I noticed that Tricia spent some time reminiscing about the old days when all worked hard together so harmoniously for many years at the company.

I was so glad that everything turned out alright. Admittedly, my wife was tired out by the end of the day, and I had to help her later on after the guests had gone. I got her safely and happily to bed. It had been a beautiful day, and we both thanked God for all that He had provided, and especially for the fifty years of marriage with its many ups and downs. But that is married life. The one thing was that there was a deep love that we both had for each other that had helped us through all the difficulties we experienced and made the good times even better. That particular day was one of those good times.

Before the final guests went, it was fortunate that they kindly helped to stack the tables and chairs away in the garage so they could quickly be loaded when the lorry came to collect them up later that week. Glassware and crockery had already been dealt with, and I had ordered high-quality disposable plates and dishes and cutlery that could all be put in the refuse bin and disposed of later on.

I must give thanks here to Richard Hinchliffe, my very dear friend, for his excellent help in organising marquees and beautiful, uplifting and memorable background music for the event, and also for all the additional support he offered to make it a wonderful, memorable celebration for all who attended. I was also so thankful for the computer expertise that he always gave to Tricia and to me over many years. Richard has always been a true friend indeed. He is also now constantly on my mind due to a great deal of problems, and stress that he is now dealing with.

It was, in fact, a hard few days preparing everything necessary, but what mattered most was that Tricia was so happy with what had been organised. She loved greeting and meeting friends old and new, and especially her relations, as she liked to talk about her extended family.

Chemotherapy

The doctor, who saw my wife at Peterborough hospital, had explained the intricacies of chemotherapy to her, but he knew or seemed to know that my wife would have a reaction. However, he had indeed made it very clear before the procedure took place that I was not to leave her on her own at any time. After arriving home, my wife had not seemed well, and this feeling got worse. We had been told that she must drink more water, as otherwise she would become dehydrated. My son Richard and I tried our hardest to increase her water intake, and continued to keep her body hydrated, and this also helped the dryness in her mouth as we both continued to do the very best we could for her.

Emergency

Eventually, Tricia had a massive seizure while sitting on the toilet. I had to hold her head supported, so she did not hurt herself, and then hold her and allow the seizure to take its course. An emergency ambulance was called and rushed her to the hospital, where she received treatment for a week. She was put into an induced coma. By the end of the week, she had recovered and came home again, which was precisely what she told us she wanted! Back in the comfort, security and peace of her own home, she recovered, much to my relief. This was the result of just one single chemotherapy treatment. I later learned these reactions are common with chemotherapy, but at what a cost to the individual receiving it, and to the health service!

About a couple of weeks later, an appointment arrived for her to attend chemotherapy treatment, so she went in to see the doctor, and he said, 'We will recommence chemotherapy treatment.' But Tricia refused to have any more treatment, and quickly replied that God would look after her. She also added, 'You may cure my cancer, but that stuff will kill my brain.' It is interesting to note here that my wife lived for another 18 months longer without that treatment. She had looked on the internet and found information that few doctors would agree to have chemotherapy treatment for themselves in particular circumstances, and would make the same decisions that she had just made. Going through the pain of seeing my wife having seizures, after going so many years without them, brought back all the memories about when we had first been married.

Then, a day of fasting and prayer was organised at our church by her friend, Angela, (dear Angie) who was training to be a nurse. In this instance, once Tricia had been diagnosed, it was heartwarming to see how many people turned up, so I treated them all to a meal at a restaurant at the end of that day. Every opportunity was taken to ensure my prayers for her were successful. In the end, a few people were left who had fasted on that particular day while they were praying for her to be relieved of her pain. I took all of them and treated them later to an evening dinner. So, Tricia, bless her, was able to obtain the blessing of being with us much longer due to God's blessings, and to enjoy every day left of her life after that prayer weekend devoted to Tricia.

It was wonderful some time later to know that Angie had achieved an honours degree for nursing and was pictured on the front of a nursing magazine in her university attire, in an article all about the NHS.

2015
Strain, Illness and the Final Months

The strain of looking after my dear Tricia was, at times, very hard, mostly towards the evening, when I began to feel myself utterly drained, lifeless and tired. Sometimes, I would feel exhausted during the day, but a ten-minute power nap would help me restore my energy levels. I am still anaemic now, and have a low-active thyroid, but with the excellent help of loving and caring friends around me, I am beginning to see improvement in my health.

Towards the end of her life, Tricia found that she did not need food as much, so her diet was therefore enhanced with consuming nourishing protein drinks. To maintain her fluid levels, we substituted ice lollies of fruit juice, which she liked and which were made of water. Within the last months of her life, Tricia was admitted to hospital with a very early and severe infection that seemed to take hold of her within only one hour. Everything was normal, and we were sitting in the kitchen having our afternoon tea when Tricia began to feel cold but started at the same time perspiring and shaking a little. This became quite frightening. We put her to bed, and then, although perspiring still, she was now cold, and began to seem to be in distress. An emergency doctor came sometime later, examined her and said that she had to be admitted, and an emergency ambulance took her there in a very short time with the siren sounding.

We later learned that she had developed sepsis, which is a highly dangerous infection. She was treated with antibiotics and a drip and discharged six days later. I realised afterwards from studying the internet how fatal this particular infection can be. Thousands of people die each year of sepsis, and in our local A&E reception at Peterborough hospital there are large placards now containing warnings and a lot of information about detecting sepsis early by the presence of a rash, or paleness of the patient's face. It can at times be hard to distinguish, but new teaching has taken place to an alert all medical staff of just how dangerous it is.

Tricia was very strong in spirit, but needed human contact. At one point, she was admitted to the marvellous and uplifting Sue Ryder Hospice at Peterborough, but after only two days spent there, she could not stand it as she was so lonely there. Sleeping and living in one room was never for her. At first, I could not understand this, but she replied, 'There are other people far more in need of this bed than me. This was very self-sacrificing of her, as she did not want to prevent anyone else from benefitting from the available hospice room. Tricia did not want to deny anyone who apparently needed it more than herself. She had been admitted for pain management, but I think her pain was also heartache for her home, her family and the beloved computer friends she had made on the internet and whom she emailed regularly almost daily.

NHS

When a doctor suggested that Tricia should withdraw from Primidone and change to another drug, I had to remind him that you cannot do this sort of change to drug intake immediately, as the Primidone changes its composition to a barbiturate, and with its rapid withdrawal the danger is that it will bring on seizures. I know that because when they reduced my own phenobarbitone dosage in my prescription, it brought back the occurrences of my seizures. I read about this on the internet, and it confirmed my suspicions. At the time, I was unaware of this particular reaction. That is why I am now ultra-cautious in what medication is prescribed for me, and how and when this is withdrawn. Bravely, Tricia stopped taking morphine soon after she was first prescribed it, and continued to refuse such pain relievers, except for paracetamol and her anti-convulsant medication. She was prevented from taking Primidone tablets, which she had taken for 50+ years, and moved to a liquid anticonvulsant, the name of which I have forgotten. However, I do know the amateur dramatics we used to have when Tricia had to take it, but it smelled and tasted horrible. It was hard work, but she eventually got used to it. When she took her medicine, I had to have a small wine glass full of fruit juice ready and waiting for her to drink to mask the horrible taste.

Tricia was admitted to hospital on emergency six times during the period January 26th 2015 to 13th March 2016, mostly for epileptic seizures and twice for sepsis infections. In March 2015, during one of her admissions, doctors found an AAA (abdominal aortic aneurysm) that was 4.7 cm in length. I was told that if it grows to 5.0cm, it is then considered hazardous, and the patient has to have an operation. If it should burst, then death is quick. I have an AAA also, and have to have it checked every year to see if it has got any bigger; at present, mine is only 3.75 cm.

The aorta is the main blood vessel that supplies blood to the body. Sometimes, the wall of the aorta in the abdomen can become weak and stretch to form a very dangerous aneurysm. When this happens, there is a risk that the aorta may split or tear (rupture). A ruptured AAA can lead to severe blood loss that will need immediate emergency treatment. Not every AAA will rupture, but if it does, the chances of getting to the hospital and surviving surgery is very poor, sadly to say.

NHS

Tricia was also on the two following drugs, which appear to be the most dangerous drug combination it is possible to have. Methotrexate is a chemotherapy drug and used by many rheumatologists and other practitioners to treat rheumatoid arthritis, along with prednisone a steroid! This is a deadly combination, especially when used long term.

Tricia died on the 28th September 2016, with her first Marie Curie nurse, myself, and my elder son, Richard, by her side at the very end. Strangely, my wife had been very difficult the night before, but when the Marie Curie nurse came, my wife knew she was dying and told the nurse just that fact. Being very gentle and sympathetic to my wife, this kind nurse sat next to her all night. After being advised myself by this same nurse to snatch a short sleep because we were all so shattered, she then promised me if there were any deterioration in Tricia's condition she would call me immediately.

Later this kind Marie Curie nurse then called us to be with her for the last precious hours of Tricia's life. It was so sad sitting beside her, watching her slowly die and not being able to do anything to stop the process. At times like this, you think how helpless you are, and there is nothing you can do but hold her hand, kiss her and tell her how much you love her and have loved her.

I thank God that I was able to nurse my Tricia with help and carry out all her wishes. I only hope that I can be as strong as she was and that my faith will never fail when it is my turn to meet my Beloved Saviour. I have nothing but praise for all the Marie Curie nurses who came at night and left in the morning, and who spent so very many hours looking after my wife. Kindness itself, and thoughtfulness, they were and tenderly compassionate, despite how exhausted they must have felt. Their nursing at night gave us the essential chance to recharge our batteries so that we could carry out Tricia's wishes during the day, and always be there for her. Care workers who came during the day helped to sustain us so we could meet Tricia's other regular needs.

My young son, Andrew, could not be with us, as my daughter in law at that time needed to have a gallbladder removal operation herself, but my son Richard was here that day she died. We celebrate and remember Tricia on the 28th September, which was the day she died. My sons, Bettina and I all have a meal together, and then usually go to visit the grave. We lay flowers and say prayers, and we do this again on her birthday, 17th December. Often, we read out one of the lovely poems that are suitable for such occasions.

Below is one of the poems Bettina read out as part of the official tribute to Tricia at her funeral, and this is inserted below. Everyone was moved to listen to this and remarked on how apt it was when we all spoke together at the end of the service.

Malcolm Le-Hair and Bettina Croft

'Don't grieve for me, for now, I'm free,
I'm following paths God made for me
I took His hand, I heard him call,
Then turned, and bade farewell to all

I could not stay another day
To laugh, to love, to sing, to play.
Tasks left undone must stay that way
I found my peace… at close of play

And, if my parting left a void,
Then fill it with remembered joy
A friendship shared a laugh, a kiss.
Ah! Yes, these things I too will miss.
Be not burdened… deep with sorrow
I wish you sunshine of tomorrow
My life's been full, I've savoured much,
Good friends, good times,
A loved one's touch.
Perhaps my time seemed all too brief,
Don't lengthen it on now with grief
Lift up your hearts and share with me,
God wants me now… He set me free.

The Final Farewell

I arranged for all her close friends and family to meet at our home and be taken by funeral cars to follow the hearse from our bungalow. I think there were four funeral cars with friends in theirs also following. She had the most beautiful of oak coffins, and the best attention from the undertakers. This was to the extent that the head director getting out of the hearse and personally stopping the traffic at the notorious roundabout at the end of Whittlesey Road, March near us. This was so the funeral cars could all be kept together. I thought of all the times that Tricia remarked about that roundabout and some of the near misses we had endured and now, sadly, when she had died, it was they who had to stop for her.

    I recalled that Tricia had grown from a timid, shy, mollycoddled individual into a confident, outspoken, caring, beautiful, loving person. Through us both pulling together, we had shown to others how successful our marriage had been, and had discounted all the fears that others had held and felt for us. We had made a fabulous twosome. Like most, if not all, marriages, we had our ups and downs, but had weathered the storms and grew stronger in our love for each other, which had strengthened our union. We both had an intense love for each other. Our faith in God and Jesus Christ sustained us and taught us that there was also so much to look forward to in our future lives with Him.

Tricia's funeral service took place at our Christian Centre in March, and she is buried across the road from there at Eastwood Cemetery. The large congregation gave her a lovely send-off. Bettina kindly read out a tribute she composed for me, after much consultation and agreement with me. Originally, she arranged it for me to speak myself, but I was not feeling able to do so, and was so grateful for her elegant and timely delivery.

My wife had chosen the hymns she wanted at her funeral, and also the scripture readings. Her friends said a few words, with dear Bettina and Flo Bull recalling for the congregation many happy memories in the tributes they gave to her. Bettina had been preparing this far-reaching, embracing tribute to cover all the many aspects of Tricia's life. We had both gone over this with extensive additions and amendments to make sure it was exactly what I wanted. Bettina then ensured everyone who had helped was to be mentioned, and finally carefully presented our agreed version to the whole congregation. Most people listening there on that day said how impressive a life it had been, and that they enjoyed Bettina's reading the eulogy to Tricia out to everyone. She had only done this because she reasoned, rightly, that I would not be able to stand up on the day and read out the words. She was right. I was indeed be too upset to do so.

In advance, Tricia had also picked her grave plot and arranged details of her own burial with caring local undertakers. People remembered her many times getting up and proclaiming her faith out loud to all in the church services. Her closest friends described beautiful memories they had of her in some of the most eloquent words, and, in one particular instance, a description of a jovial occurrence whilst on holiday. Afterwards, there was a sumptuous buffet at MEF (March Evangelical Fellowship), where many recalled their personal experiences of her Christian and very loving life to others.

Tricia's faith was firm and unquestionable, and, through that, she gave strength to others. You only have to see some of the lovely comments people put on her Facebook page. In fact, I have picked a few out of the many posted for you to see below what people thought of her.

From New Zealand:

1. Anita Hargreaves and Patricia Hargreaves
I will miss you deeply. We will never meet in this life,

but we will in the new life. It was a blessing to have known you, my dearest cousin. I will always remember you. With all my love and thoughts with Tricia's family. God bless. Patricia (Auckland, New Zealand)

2. Kevin Southon
- Off to say a final goodbye to a dear friend shortly and thought of these lyrics.
- Farewell my dear friend Tricia Le-hair
- Always you will be part of me
- And I will forever feel your strength
- When I need it most.
- You're gone now, gone but not forgotten.
- I can't say this to your face
- But I know you hear.

3. Mindy Hinchcliffe (Richard Hinchliffe's wife)
IN LOVING MEMORY OF Tricia Le-hair...Those special memories of her will always bring a smile to me. Her life was a blessing, her memory a treasure. What an incredibly cheerful, strong lady she was. Praying that God grants peace to her friends and family.

From America:

4. Jonathan Dinsmore
About 21 yrs ago I met your mum and dad while touring England and Scotland with my college choir (Bethel Singers). I wrote a few letters at first but, for so long nothing, until just recently I've shared a few tiny

messages every few weeks or so on Facebook. I was afraid for so long to try, figuring she'd forgotten all about me or whatever--but "whatever" never mattered with this angel we all are proud to know. She is always so forgiving...the definition of love and kindness, wrapped in a humble smile. Cancer took my mum too ten yrs back, and today she welcomes your mum to God's side with a big, big hug...not because of ever having known her, but because of the grace, your mum has shown me and so many others! Bless you, Rich, and bless you, Malcolm.

Tears come to my eyes reading some of the lovely comments made about my wife. I know she wanted to die at home, and at times it was hard going, but I am glad we nursed her every day, even though my own health suffered severely and I am only now, after more than three years, just beginning to recover some of my strength. I never truly realised the power her faith had on others. Marvellous, too, was the advice she gave to others, including to friends she made worldwide, and I discovered later that via the internet she had also befriended so many people.

I have lovely friends who have been so kind and understanding to me. Yes, I have been through a lot in my life, but it has helped me to develop love and compassion for others. I try to exercise that as much as I can in helping others. It is a beautiful feeling to know that you are assisting people who really need you and that they appreciate it.

During the last three years, my dear friend Bettina has been there supporting me and in helping me to overcome my loss. It is through her love, skills, expertise and encouragement that I have been able to write this book now. Hopefully, you will find it exciting, rewarding, encouraging and uplifting, and will find in it some real help in your own lives. No matter what trials you may have to face - ill health, disability, or other serious problems - I hope you will find one, if not many, parts of my story an inspiration. Most of all, I hope this book helps you to adopt a positive attitude to whatever life has dealt you and, when in need, think, if necessary, outside the box to overcome those problems.

It would not be right for me to ignore the fact that I am a Christian and that the good Lord has had the most positive influence on my life. In fact, He has provided all that I have needed and more. I could not have worked as hard as I did if The Lord hadn't been there; I could not have born the sorrows throughout my life if He wasn't holding me up. I would not be where I am today without His guidance throughout my life. I would not have the friends that I now have if it weren't for Him leading me. It takes time and patience and faith to know the wonders that the Lord can do in your life, and believing in Him is the first and most important. If you do not know Him, then find Him for yourself, believe in Him and see what He does for you find out what you can do for Him, as you will be amply rewarded and blessed.

Many of us have at one time in our life come to face great trials and disasters, but, with caring friends and supporting families, for those of us fortunate enough to have them, we will positively rise above these and survive! However, most importantly, I hope you have found my book a good read.

Epilogue

I would not want to end this story on a sad event like a funeral, however important and memorable. Therefore, I consider it worthwhile to describe events leading up to my own considerable hospital drama, which occurred just before Christmas. I was admitted as an emergency patient with what I later learned was acute pancreatitis. The events over the next 17 days when I was in the hospital were an absolute nightmare, apart from the fact that I had an angel, my friend Bettina, by my side visiting daily, and doctors and nurses who could not do enough for me.

Latent health problems continued to be discovered, adding to the complexity of my illness.

I do not ever want to bore you, with details, but again I was in hospital for 17 days of agony, and by some miracle I have survived thanks to a wonderful surgeon and staff at Peterborough hospital.

Looking back on it now, I am pleased and grateful to be alive, and can only be thankful for my Christian faith, and trust that all my treasured friends and the medical experts did everything they could. At one time during my illness, I asked the Lord to take me home, as the pain became so intense that if I had possessed a gun I would have shot myself.

The Challenge and Another Miracle

I was placed under the care of a specialist in this area of medicine, and I was admitted with acute pancreatis and this resulted in no food nor drink being administered for at least seven days. Ms Ong was my consultant a very talented surgeon and took immediate charge of my care.

Nil by Mouth! I was put on a drip and given just a sip of water to take with my tablets.

Because I was being sick and bringing up bile that particular afternoon, I was prepared for endoscopy, as they wanted to see my insides and what was going on.

The very next day I was given a stomach pump by a number of junior doctors that withdrew countless large syringes of black material which was later confirmed as blood.

I had somehow also suffered the build-up of too much warfarin in my system. This necessitated a Vitamin-K antidote being drip fed into me, which left me with a thundering headache for two days.

Having this internal bleeding and the overdose of warfarin that had built up I asked the doctors to take me off warfarin immediately and to find one of the more recent drugs to suit me, and, bless them, they did! I had been reluctantly taking warfarin for over 30 years, and this had reduced my quality of life. It had limited the choice of foods I could eat and also warfarin was contra-indicative to many of the drugs I had to take for my other ailments.

Within the first seven days of being in the hospital, another severe problem was diagnosed. I later learned that I had contracted hospital acquired pneumonia.

I was placed on oxygen for most of the time I was in the hospital. However, Pneumonia had caused fluid on my lungs to build up, which then affected my heart. This also caused difficulty in breathing. I had previously suffered a heart attack and had three stents implanted.

I remember It was about this time that a situation occurred which I never expected. The despair and pain caused me to ask the Lord to take me to Him one night.

However, the Good Lord obviously still had other things for me left to do in my Christian Life life, and I gradually began to recover to some extent, little by little, from the multiplicity of health problems which I was suffering.

I was administered oxygen and pain killers more or less continually while I was there; sometimes they gave the painkillers intravenously. I never slept properly for the whole time I was hospitalised. I hated the nights since I tossed and turned, and I was always awake from midnight until 6 am when morning came, during that time I was being sick.

Most of this was bile from the liver. Retching made my stomach just as painful. During that the time I had pneumonia, I suffered from cold, and then my body would shake and shiver severely. I was, at times, given morphine and morphine substitutes to reduce the pain and to help relieve the agony. After seven days without food and water and living on drips into my arm to keep me going, I was then allowed to eat a tiny amount of some bland food, but I realised then I had very little appetite.

Also, I was prescribed some strong antibiotics to cure the pneumonia. Some days later, the antibiotics eventually caused diarrhoea. This meant I then had to be moved to a room on my own without other patients to ensure I could not pass any infection on to them.

During my stay in hospital I had numerous blood tests, xrays CT scans MRI scans Cardiography and Ultra sound examinations and received first class treatment and care.

All this time,in my life the one thing that the Lord did provide was an angel: my dear friend, Bettina, who sat beside me for all the 17 days in the hospital.

She felt for me so much, and nothing was too much trouble for her. She held my hand willing me, praying for me, to get better. She was a breath of fresh air, and the kindest person one could ever wish to meet.

I always wanted to lose weight, and during my stay in hospital I lost a stone and have kept the weight off (fortunately). After being discharged Bettina and her husband looked after me for the following four weeks, making sure I had someone there by my side every moment, day and night. I was so weak, and had to recover from these serious illnesses I had suffered. It took two months for me to feel almost recovered. As I suffered from gallstones, I now had to have a very simple, bland diet, which I am getting used to, although I do miss my fish and chips, but all fried food is absolutely forbidden.

One of the senior anaesthetists wanted to see me. He was most pleased after examining me and the various test results, and was happy to have found that it was not as bad as he had actually feared, He later told my surgeon, who was herself delighted for the operation to go ahead. The senior anaesthetist reassured me that my consultant was one of the most careful, talented and best surgeons in this field. On the 28th February 2019, I had a vital consultation to see my brilliant consultant, who was now pleased with my progress and the recovery in my health and vitality that I had made. She said there was still, however, the existing severe problem of the gall bladder. This was still full up with gall stones, and in genuine and imminent danger of becoming inflamed again. It needed to be removed as soon as possible, as it would be dangerous having such an operation in an emergency since I was on blood thinners which, if not managed, presented complications.

I am so delighted to tell you all that I am at last free of the horrendous bag of gall stones, and the pain in my bladder itself. I now am recovering under the expert care of my dear friend, Bettina, once again.

God has been my Deliverer, my Healer and remains my Hope in times of Trouble, my Saviour, and my Friend. I hope he is and will be yours also.

www.ingramcontent.com/pod-product-compliance
Lightning Source LLC
Chambersburg PA
CBHW071115080526
44587CB00013B/1349